JORGE
LOUSADA

Praise for *The New Emerging-Market Multinationals*

"A brilliant analysis of how the multinationals from emerging markets are succeeding globally. It is conceptually solid and a joy to read!"

—Jagdish N. Sheth, Charles H. Kellstadt
Professor of Marketing, Goizueta Business School,
Emory University, and author of *Chindia Rising*

"Research-based valuable insights into emerging-market companies becoming formidable global players by moving beyond being low-cost operators to business model innovators and brand builders. Packed with lessons for global companies and aspirants all over the world!"

—Vindi Banga, Partner, Clayton, Dubillier & Rice, and
former President, Foods, Home & Personal Care, Unilever

"This book offers an insightful and impressive analysis and understanding of the business dynamics of the past decade. Readers from EMNCs will learn how to expand their businesses globally and how to build and sustain premium brands to compete against incumbent TMNCs. Readers from TMNCs will understand EMNCs' capabilities and strategies, helping them to penetrate and compete in these booming markets."

—Michael Ahn, President and CEO North America, LG
Electronics Company Limited (2004–2009), and Senior Advisor

THE
NEW
EMERGING
MARKET
MULTINATIONALS

THE
NEW
EMERGING
MARKET
MULTINATIONALS

FOUR STRATEGIES FOR
DISRUPTING MARKETS
AND BUILDING BRANDS

AMITAVA CHATTOPADHYAY AND RAJEEV BATRA
WITH AYSEGUL OZSOMER

New York   Chicago   San Francisco   Lisbon   London
Madrid   Mexico City   Milan   New Delhi   San Juan
Seoul   Singapore   Sydney   Toronto

The *McGraw·Hill* Companies

1 2 3 4 5 6 7 8 9 10   DOC/DOC   1 8 7 6 5 4 3 2

ISBN 978-0-07-178289-0
MHID 0-07-178289-3

e-ISBN 978-0-07-178290-6
e-MHID 0-07-178290-7

This publication is designed to provide accurate and authoritative information in regard to the subject matter covered. It is sold with the understanding that neither the authors nor the publisher is engaged in rendering legal, accounting, securities trading, or other professional services. If legal advice or other expert assistance is required, the services of a competent professional person should be sought.
—*From a Declaration of Principles Jointly Adopted by a Committee of the American Bar Association and a Committee of Publishers and Associations*

McGraw-Hill books are available at special quantity discounts to use as premiums and sales promotions, or for use in corporate training programs. To contact a representative please e-mail us at bulksales@mcgraw-hill.com.

For more information, visit www.emncstrategies.com.

To all those we learned from,
most of all our parents, spouses, and children.

Contents

Acknowledgments

Writing this book was a long but rewarding journey. It brought us into contact with many innovative companies and incredibly smart and dedicated executives. Thus, our first debt of gratitude goes to all the executives from the 39 companies we talked to, who shared their vision, knowledge, and insights freely with us. Their names appear at the end of this note, organized by company. Of those we talked to, we owe special thanks to Michael Ahn, Mauricio Bellora, Mehmed Evyap, Gautam Nagwekar, Nakul Gupta, Tarik Hadi, Rajesh Jejurikar, Arun Nanda, Hüsamettin Onanç, Eunju Park, Jessie Paul, Vijay S. Subramaniam, and Tom Thomas, for going out of their way to support the project by spending many hours talking to us, as well as for putting us in touch with other key informants for this book.

Getting access to companies is not an easy task. Several colleagues and friends helped us reach out to companies where we did not have contacts and obtain secondary data that we did not have access to. For such help and for other assistance, we would like to thank Rama Bijapurkar, Esteban Brenes, Viveca Chan, Sumanto Chattopadhyay, Rohit Deshpande, Deepak Dheer, Wally Hopp, Pannapachr Ithiopassagul, Ken Lieberthal, Rakesh Mathur, Bharat Patel, Hart Posen, Monica Sacristan, C. K. Sharma, Haizhong Wang, Brian Wu, Arthur Yeung, and Penpoonsuke Zreekum.

We would also like to thank Professors Sendil Ethiraj, Anil Gupta, and Jose Santos, who read portions of an initial version of the manuscript and suggested how to structure our ideas. Special thanks go to Professor Fang Wan, who read an entire initial version of the manuscript and suggested many improvements, including pushing us to think more about how to present our ideas visually. Professor Prashant Kale cowrote our acquisitions chapter (Chapter 3) with us, and Professor Michael Levy of Babson helped us with the distribution content, available as a web appendix to Chapter 5 on the book's website. And we owe thanks to those who read a pre-publication draft of the book and offered observations on it.

Thanks are also due for research assistance to Tanu Aggarwal, Liliane Junqueira, Ayesha Kohli, Malavika Lakireddy, Sai Krishna Nanduri, Peren Özturan, Adithya Pattabhiramaiah, Luciana Pereira, Vidhya Prakash, and Hamidah Salim, who helped over the years with the background research on the companies we talked to. Our agent Herb Schaffner guided us ably through the proposal and publication process, our editor at McGraw-Hill, Knox Huston, gave us valuable suggestions to make the manuscript more focused and readable, and Janice Race supported us with a superb job in copyediting the manuscript. We would also like to gratefully acknowledge partial financial support for this project from INSEAD R&D, the Ross School of Business, and the Williamson Davidson Institute at the University of Michigan.

Naturally, writing this book was an enormous investment in time, time that might otherwise have been spent with our families. We would thus like to thank our spouses, Mahima, Priscilla, and Insan, for their support throughout the process.

Finally, for the record, the first two authors contributed equally to the book, and the authorship order was randomly determined through a coin toss.

LIST OF INTERVIEWEES

Apollo Tyres (India)	Mr. Avik Chattopadhyay
Aramex (Jordan)	Mr. Fadi Ghandour
Arçelik (Turkey)	Mr. Hasan Subaşi
Asia Pacific Breweries (Singapore)	Mr. Edmond Neo
Asian Paints (India)	Mr. Tom Thomas
Bajaj Auto (India)	Mr. Rakesh Sharma
Chigo Group (China)	Mr. Peter Liao
Dabur (India)	Mr. Sunil Duggal
Dilmah (Sri Lanka)	Mr. Merrill J. Fernando
	Mr. Dilhan Fernando
Evyap (Turkey)	Mr. Mustafa Arin
	Mr. Mehmed Evyap
	Mr. Serdar Sarıgül
Godrej (India)	Mr. Hoshedar K. Press
Grupo Britt N.V. (Costa Rica)	Mr. Pablo Vargas
Grupo Modelo (Mexico)	Mr. Daniel Gómez
Haier (China)	Mr. Michael Jemal
HTC (Taiwan)	Mr. John Wang
Indian Hotels Company Limited (India)	Mr. Ajoy Misra
Infosys Limited (India)	Mr. Srinivas Uppaluri
Jim Thompson (Thailand)	Mr. Eric Booth
Lenovo (China)	Mr. Deepak Advani
	Mr. Reid Walker
LG Electronics (South Korea)	Mr. Michael Ahn
	Mr. Shin B. Moon
	Mr. Chang Min Ma
	Ms. Eunju Park
Mahindra Group (India)	Mr. Rajesh Jejurikar
	Mr. Gautam Nagwekar
	Mr. Arun Nanda

Mahindra Group (India)	Mr. Pravin Shah
	Mr. S. P. Shukla
Marico (India)	Mr. Vijay S. Subramaniam
Mavi (Turkey)	Mr. Ersin Akarlilar
Midea (China)	Mr. Leling Zhang
Mitac (Taiwan)	Mr. Chris Wu
Mobile TeleSystems OJSC, (Russia)	Ms. Cynthia Gordon
NaturaCosméticos S.A. (Brazil) ✓	Mr. Mauricio Bellora
Pollo Campero (Guatemala)	Mr. Roberto Denigiri
Ranbaxy Laboratories (India)	Mr. Sanjeev Dani
Savola Foods (Saudi Arabia)	Mr. Tarik Hadi
Tata Global Beverages (India)	Mr. Percy Siganporia
Tata Motors (India)	Mr. Ravi Kant
Temsa (Turkey)	Mr. Mehmet Buldurgan
Titan Industries (India)	Mr. Bhaskar Bhat
Turkish Airlines (THY), (Turkey)	Mr. Temel Kotil
Ulker (Turkey)	Mr. Cafer Findikoğlu
Vara Food and Drink Co. (Thailand)	Mr. Tedsak Kiatsukasem
Vitra (Turkey)	Mr. Hüsamettin Onanç
Wipro (India)	Ms. Jessie Paul
	Ms. Priti Rajora

Introduction and Overview

In the past decade, a new breed of challenger businesses and brands has burst upon the world stage, and in many categories—such as appliances, automobiles, consumer electronics, mobile phones, computers, personal-care products, telecommunications equipment, and beer—has built up significant new *branded businesses* with a *broad international footprint*. Consider Taiwan's HTC, the company behind Sprint's 4G Evo and Google's Nexus. Since entering with its own HTC branded phones only a half dozen years ago, it has been on a tear, with sales of its state-of-the-art smartphones growing exponentially and with an estimated revenue in 2012 of more than NT$600 billion. In 2011, it became the world's third largest smartphone producer,[1] and it has launched new mobile phone models, such as the HTC Thunderbolt, which the media have dubbed one of the most "highly anticipated smartphones" to be announced at the 2011 Consumer Electronics Show in Las Vegas.

HTC is not alone. China's Haier has a global share exceeding 5 percent of the "white goods" (appliances like refrigerators, dishwashers, and washing machines) category, making it the fourth largest player in the category.[2] Huawei, also from China, derives the majority of its revenues from outside China and is today the number one challenger to Cisco. Turkey's Arçelik has 10 percent of the European appliance market, and Temsa, also from Turkey, has a similar share in the French commercial vehicle market. India's Wipro and Infosys have achieved higher profitability levels than their IT industry competitors EDS and Accenture.[3]

These new multinational corporations (MNCs)—with names such as Acer, Arçelik, Apollo Tyres, Bharti Airtel, Bimbo, Bright Food, Geely, HTC, Haier, Huawei, LG, Lenovo, Modelo, MTS, Natura, SAB-Miller, SAIC Motor Corp., Tata Motors, Tata Tea, Ulker, and Vitra—are not from the United States, Europe, or Japan, the "triad" nations from which large MNCs typically come. Rather, they are from countries such as China, India, Brazil, Russia, Turkey, South Africa, and Mexico, all relatively poor countries with per capita incomes of around US$10,000 or less, as compared with incomes of US$34,000 or more for the most developed (G7) countries.[4] These countries are known more for firms that produce inexpensive products of dubious quality or for firms that serve as contract manufacturing sources to the more dominant triad-based MNCs (the TMNCs), rather than for firms with world-class branded businesses that are viable competitors on the global stage. Today, however, the emerging market MNCs (EMNCs) listed above and others (e.g., Hyundai Motors and Samsung Electronics) are strong, profitable, branded players that have managed to wrest significant share away from much larger TMNCs—even though they started out small and disadvantaged, with very limited budgets, commodity products, and poor-quality perceptions.

BusinessWeek warned about such EMNCs in 2006 as the "emerging giants" ("be afraid, be very afraid").[5] Consulting firms BCG and McKinsey have written about the EMNCs increasing stature,[6] and GE chairman and CEO Jeffrey R. Immelt and his coauthors, in a 2009 article, acknowledged that "GE has tremendous respect for traditional rivals like Siemens, Philips, and Rolls-Royce. But it knows how to compete with them; they will never destroy GE. However, the emerging giants very well could" (p. 5).[7] Other recent books, both popular and academic, have begun to point out the significant threat posed by these emerging giants.[8]

We are left wondering, though, exactly *how* these relatively small, under-resourced EMNCs have managed to build sustainable and profitable branded global businesses, fighting and winning against much larger incumbent market leaders. How did these new MNCs from emerging markets (the EMNCs) dramatically transform themselves to fight and win against much larger incumbent market leaders? It usually takes enormous R&D and brand-building investments and deep organizational skills—resources they do not possess—to create a large, sustainable, and profitable branded global business. How then did these small, under-resourced, businesses go about "competing from below"? What can small, disadvantaged challenger businesses everywhere learn from their strategies and tactics?

We report in this book the findings from our in-depth study of 39 cases of such EMNCs, based on our personal interviews with their senior executives and our research into their challenges, strategies, tactics, and results. Some of these EMNCs have grown through headline-grabbing acquisitions—buying up (or gaining stakes in) storied brands like Godiva, Miller, MG cars, Tetley, Dunlop, Sara Lee, Starkist tuna, ThinkPad, Jaguar, Land Rover, and Volvo, to name a few. Such acquisitions are indeed important, and we will present their stories in this book. But much can also be learned from the experiences of HTC, Haier, Wipro, Natura, MTS, and the many others that have chosen instead to "build," rather than "buy," the brands with which they are growing their global businesses, and we will examine these too, in depth.

Such EMNCs face two key challenges: they need to build *global businesses,* and they need to build *global brands.*[9] Without a sustainable global business model, building a global brand is a waste of time and resources. On the other hand, a global business built on an unbranded commodity basis is not likely to be very profitable or sustainable long term. In building their new global branded businesses, these EMNCs have had much to overcome. Yes, they often have lower-cost labor and manufacturing facilities to take advantage of, and they often have the advantage of high economies of scale from large domestic market volumes. However, they usually do not have the deep pocketbooks (or easy-to-tap capital markets) of their TMNC competitors, work with less-developed managerial systems and knowledge bases, and typically face more skeptical consumers and customers when they proclaim the high objective quality of their products.

This book is about the stories and experiences of these EMNCs—the unique challenges they face and the clever "competing-from-below" strategies and tactics they have used to overcome those challenges. The 39 cases we present in this book, and the lessons we distill, are inspirations for and provide guidance to other aspiring EMNCs, and indeed under-resourced challenger firms from around the world, in developing their own business and brand-building strategies. They also help TMNCs understand and proactively respond to the new and difficult challenges that these EMNCs pose. We discuss these lessons in each chapter and consolidate them in our concluding one.

The EMNC Challengers We Study Here

The growth of EMNCs has been remarkable. In 2005, there were only 44 of them on Fortune's list of the top global 500 firms; in 2010, there were 113 such companies.[10] A look at this 2010 Fortune list makes clear that many of these are companies in businesses deriving in large part from national natural resource endowments such as oil and gas—Gazprom, Sinopec, Petrobras, Pemex—or domestic giants in the heavily regulated telecom or banking sectors, often being "state champion" companies. Such companies are *not* the subject of this book, for we seek to understand here the stories and lessons of those *without* such resource or regulatory advantages. The industries to which the firms we studied belong include foods and beverages, personal care, apparel, watches and jewelry, automotive, appliances, consumer electronics, building products, IT services, and consumer services. For company details, please visit www.emncstrategies.com.

Why Are These EMNCs Pursuing Global Growth?

Our interviews with EMNCs revealed four reasons for their initial international expansion efforts. For some companies, international expansion was due to a historic accident. For instance, the Y2K scare created international business opportunities for many Indian software companies. Other EMNCs seek the global market simply because they need more room to grow. For example, India's Mahindra Tractors, China's Lenovo, Saudi Arabia's Savola, Guatemala's Pollo Campero, and Costa Rica's Grupo Britt increased their global presence after they dominated their home-country markets. Some EMNCs look to global markets out of a need to lower their economic-cycle risks by diversifying across multiple economies, as did automotive manufacturers Temsa, Bajaj, Mahindra & Mahindra, and Tata Motors. Still others went international to learn about global standards to be able to fight encroaching TMNCs in their home markets. For instance, the Taj Group needed to portray itself as international in its home market to compete against the new global entrants, and Arçelik needed new design and technology capabilities to remain competitive against the TMNC appliance makers entering Turkey.

However, these opportunistic, growth, risk-reduction, and learning reasons are not the main reason for their recent global growth. The main reason for the recent global growth is simply that many of these *EMNCs have the ambition, vision, and confidence to want to become global giants themselves*. EMNCs that now have the confidence and ambition to become a global giant are aggressively building or buying the competencies in technology, innovation, design, and marketing that will ensure that they are treated with the same serious respect given today to incumbent TMNCs. While these EMNCs might earlier have been satisfied to bide their time as low-margin, high-volume suppliers of "private label" and "original equipment manufacturer" (OEM) goods to branded triad-based players, their skills and sights are now at much higher levels. They have learned about developed-country market needs through their supplier contracts. They have now acquired, licensed, or innovated the needed technological competencies. They have established the quality-control, management, and supply chain processes and routines needed to run global operations and now are eager and prepared for the next stage of the game.

Put differently, these firms have moved from purveying commodities to adding and capturing value with consumers through the appeal of their brands. While some EMNCs once merely leveraged "country-specific" advantages of lower-cost labor or cheaper natural resources, many now possess what strategy theorists call "firm-specific" competencies in technology, design, and quality—and marketing and branding—that mark them as strong, capable global players in their own right. These EMNCs are not content with the 3 to 8 percent gross margins that typically go to OEM and private label suppliers of electronics and appliances, such as Foxconn (Hon Hai), a manufacturer of Apple's iPods and iPhones. Instead, they want the 40 percent margins and deep customer pull and loyalty that Apple itself commands for its highly branded products.[11] Hankook tires from South Korea are rated among the top four in the United States in customer satisfaction—but need to be priced 20 to 25 percent below competitors like Goodyear to reach their 5 percent share of the U.S. passenger-tire replacement market.[12] To get the desired high prices and margins, these EMNCs now create high-quality and high-design products, using deep marketing insight into unmet consumer needs. They manufacture these products with low-cost labor and facilities, and they deploy the products with business models that allow the EMNCs to reinvest into low-cost R&D and innovate, not just copy. In this book, we will cover the complexities of this transformation of these newly aggressive EMNCs from low-cost, high-volume players to global branded businesses.

Building Global Businesses: Four Types of Strategies

In our research, we have identified four types of strategies these EMNCs use as they go about building their global businesses (see Figure I-1). (Naturally, these are conceptual distinctions, with a great deal of real-world overlap.) Two of the strategies are of the more traditional type, relying largely on country-specific advantages that have been understood and leveraged by EMNCs for decades. The other two strategies are new. It is these strategies that the newly confident and emboldened EMNCs are deploying as they build global branded businesses, strategies that rely on

Consumer Segments and International Expansion		
	Focus on Similar Emerging Markets (Speedy, Easy, Short Term)	*Focus on Dissimilar Developed Markets* (Slow, Difficult, Long Term)
S t r a t e g i c C o m p **Mechanistic Extension** – Leverage existing resources – Scale and cost as main competency – Relentless focus on cost cutting – Mastery over a narrow but extendable technology – Ability to identify similar customers	**Knowledge Leverager** – Mastery of narrow capability, e.g., making rugged and durable products – Ability to identify markets where they can win – Knowledge of poor customers – Manage businesses in volatile economies, with poor infrastructure and less transparent regime – E.g., Asian Paints, Aramex, Savola Foods	**Cost Leader** – Leverage local low-cost human resources – Relentless and continuous focus on cost, e.g., through scale – Develop and combine with firm-specific assets, e.g., process capability, to create novel process or business models – E.g., Chigo, Infosys, Mahindra Tractors, Midea, Temsa
e t e n c y B u i l d i n g **Dynamic Evolution** – Focused innovation – R&D capability acquisition – Customer insight generation capability – Competencies in leveraging customer insights – Flexible manufacturing capabilities	**Niche Customizer** – Lower-cost ability to customize – Self-owned, therefore more flexible manufacturing facilities – Lower-cost "frugal innovation" R&D abilities – E.g., Dabur, Marico, Mavi, Mitac	**Global Brand Builder** – **Focused Innovation Oriented** – Lower manufacturing costs (like the cost leaders) – Additional weapon of lower-cost home-based R&D – Higher investments in R&D, but at same time more focused – E.g., Haier, HTC, Lenovo, LG – **Acquisition Oriented** – Bring in the supply chains, technologies, brands, and distribution channels they currently lack – Add on to current strengths of large-volume production – Low-cost R&D and manufacturing – E.g., Apollo Tyres, Arçelik, Lenovo, Tata Motors, Tata Tea

FIGURE I-1 Four Strategy Groups

firm-specific advantages that take the EMNCs to the next level of global competitiveness and have them threatening the hegemony of the TMNCs.

The four strategies differ in their approaches to markets and competencies. The first difference is the market focus of the internationalization strategy. Some EMNCs primarily focus on similar emerging markets, where success is likely to be achieved more easily and quickly. Others, however, take the leap of focusing on less familiar and dissimilar developed markets, where success is less assured and will take longer to achieve.

The second difference is the degree to which the firms rely for their success on existing strategic competencies such as low-cost leadership. Some deploy these competencies to extend the firm, an approach we label *mechanistic expansion*. Others extend themselves through the deliberate development of new capabilities such as R&D, product design, brand management skills, and broader management processes and systems, an approach we label *dynamic evolution*.

The four types of strategies we identify, as a function of the consumer segments and markets targeted and the strategic competencies deployed, are as follows:

- **Cost Leaders** leverage existing low cost structures and large-scale volumes to extend their reach into developed markets.
- **Knowledge Leveragers** tap their existing resources and knowledge of home consumers and market to build branded businesses in other emerging markets.
- **Niche Customizers** combine their cost advantages in manufacturing with newly developed low-cost R&D capabilities to develop customized niche-segment branded offerings in other emerging markets.
- **Global Brand Builders** take their low-cost manufacturing and R&D capabilities to build branded businesses in developed markets through focused innovation that is targeted at specific products and segments. Additionally, they often develop the skills and resources they do not currently possess—such as distribution access, brands, international management capability, and the like—through selective acquisitions.

We discuss these four types of strategies in more detail next.

Cost Leaders

Turkey's Arçelik (Koc) owns more than 50 percent of Turkey's large appliance market, while India's Mahindra Tractors—because of its dominance of India's huge tractor market—is now the largest tractor manufacturer in the world in terms of units sold. EMNCs like these have created large-volume operations in their home countries by serving their large domestic markets and doing contract operations for overseas buyers, giving them huge economies of scale on top of the low manufacturing and assembly labor costs of their home countries. China's Midea and Chigo and Turkey's Temsa are other such examples, as is Indian pharmaceuticals stalwart Ranbaxy. These EMNCs also have mastered the frugal and lean business models necessary to flourish in their low-price home-country markets.

Clearly, these Cost Leader EMNCs have established competencies in creating low-cost products and services. They also focus relentlessly and continuously on driving down costs, often through innovations born of necessity. They use this cost structure to sell low-priced products in both developing and developed markets overseas, focusing on market segments that seek out such low-priced offerings. They thus "arbitrage" the well-known country-specific advantages of lower-cost human talent, cheaper natural resources, and large domestic volumes and scale that have been shown to be their typical sources of global competitive advantage.[13, 14]

Knowledge Leveragers

India's Mahindra & Mahindra and Tata Motors both market vehicles overseas that build on their deep knowledge of how to create tough, rugged vehicles that less affluent consumers seek and that perform, notwithstanding the bad roads and rudimentary service facilities that characterize emerging markets; and India's Asian Paints markets paints and coatings that offer a reliable and durable solution that consumers seek for the less-well-built homes that are typical of emerging markets. We call such EMNCs the *Knowledge Leveragers*. These EMNCs are applying to other emerging-market environments their home-grown knowledge of emerging-market conditions and the needs and limits of poor emerging-market consumers. They meet the needs of consumers in these markets for low-priced, functional, rugged, and durable product and service brands with a particular ethnic or regional character. Moreover, they can often manage in these markets more effectively, as they are more conversant with the poor infrastructure, economic volatility, and less-transparent political-regulatory regimes that these markets tend to have in common. Such EMNCs also seek to reduce complexity and the need for new knowledge by beginning with geographically proximate and culturally similar or "diaspora" consumers (consumers from the EMNC's home country who live in another country), who already know about their brands and competencies.

Given the growing importance of emerging markets collectively as a source of global market growth—Procter & Gamble estimates that two-thirds of its growth for years to come will be from emerging markets[15]—Knowledge Leveragers are tapping into a very significant competency to extend and grow branded businesses. Thus, although the Knowledge Leverager strategy may not be new, the dramatic change in the importance of emerging markets as a source of future growth makes this a much more significant strategy today, one that poses an important threat to TMNCs. Examples of this strategy in our company sample, in addition to Asian Paints, Mahindra & Mahindra, and Tata Motors, include Chinese appliance companies Chigo and Midea; Asia Pacific Breweries, Jim Thompson, and Varafoods of Southeast Asia; Savola Foods in Saudi Arabia; Café Britt and Pollo Campero in Central America; Aramex from Jordan; MTS from Russia; and Dabur, Marico, and Godrej from India.

"New-Wave" EMNC Business Strategies

The rise in size and prominence of EMNCs following the two business strategies described above seems natural and unremarkable, as they stem from the traditional emerging-market capabilities that these firms are expected to possess and use. But our research revealed that EMNCs offer growth and operations models of interest beyond their role as low-cost or resource-endowed competitors seeking to make a low-margin buck in the easiest and geographically closest way possible. We see many EMNCs developing significant new capabilities that are unique to the particular firm, going well beyond the "standard" capabilities being exploited by firms using the first two types of strategies.

Niche Customizers
Using its "3×3" philosophy, India's Godrej focuses only on hair color, soap, and household insecticides and primarily targets the markets of South Asia and Africa. Marico, another Indian player that deals in fast-moving consumer goods, focuses on prewash and post-wash hair care and targets South Asia, the Middle East, and North Africa; and Dabur focuses on roughly the same markets but targets consumers who seek natural herbal products. We call such EMNCs the *Niche Customizers*. This third type of strategy focuses on small, neglected, and special-needs segments primarily, but not exclusively, in developing markets. Thus we see Mahindra Tractors use its knowledge of small but rugged tractors to go after hobby farmers and golf course and lawn maintenance segments in the U.S. and Australian markets.

Niche Customizers take advantage of their cost structures to *adapt and customize*, given (1) their self-owned and, therefore, more flexible manufacturing facilities and (2) their own lower-cost "frugal innovation" R&D abilities, on a small geographic scale.[16] (These R&D cost advantages are elaborated on below, when we discuss the Global Brand Builders.) Since the Niche Customizers are from emerging markets and are focused on other emerging markets, like the Knowledge Leveragers, they too make use of their knowledge of poor customers, inexpensive products, and their ability to manage in this more volatile and uncertain emerging-market environment. This augmented strategy plays not only to EMNC knowledge, flexibility, manufacturing, and R&D strengths, but also to the weaknesses of their larger-sized TMNC rivals. These TMNCs, which stress ruthless standardization and the pursuit of large-scale economies and which often outsource much of their own manufacturing to EMNCs, reduce their own ability to modify and customize on the fly.

Another goal of such focusing by our EMNC Niche Customizers is to identify and take aim at segments that larger, stronger TMNCs either ignore or do not know much about. Marico's Vijay Subramaniam, CEO of the International Business Group, told us, "The larger multinationals . . . have brands which are reasonably strong but their primary focus lies elsewhere and their insight in these [areas targeted by Marico] is relatively small. [Our] segments would be just below their radar level." Saudi Arabia's Savola Foods CMO Tarik Hadi, added, "We do not compete with Unilever. That is the point. We usually compete only with local players . . . we are happy about that because we have something strong versus our competition. If it was against one of the big monsters, we would not have such a big edge." TMNCs that ignore these beachhead-building EMNC strategies do so at their peril: over time, these challengers will master these narrow segments and grow into bigger and broader threats.

Such niche customizing also means that the marketing and brand building by such EMNCs is characterized by authenticity and truth: they are building on skills they genuinely possess, which makes it easier for them to speak credibly and consistently to both external and internal audiences. "We sell an honest product at an honest price," says Mahindra & Mahindra executive director and group board member Arun Nanda, speaking about the company's superior delivery of functional, no-fuss vehicles.

Global Brand Builders

One of the exciting findings of our research is the new class of EMNCs we call Global Brand Builders. These firms build their own brands via focused innovation: a strategy of developing innovative technologies and products, but only in very narrow slices of the market. HTC has built up a branded reputation among knowledgeable "prosumer" consumers worldwide as the "quietly brilliant" smartphone company that leads in new and better Android and Windows-Mobile phone products. As another example, Brazil's Natura markets a cosmetics line that emphasizes biodiverse ingredients from the Amazon. The company has developed the ability to sustainably harvest plants traditionally used by the indigenous people from the Amazon forests, as well as identify and extract the active ingredients. It has successfully entered France with its skin-care and other cosmetic formulations, which take advantage of this capability. Others acquire and then build brands: Tata Tea with Tetley, Apollo Tyres with Dunlop, and Tata Motors with Daewoo Trucks, Jaguar, and Land Rover.

Focused Innovation. Global Brand Builders engage developed economies and markets on the basis of lower manufacturing costs *and* lower-cost home-based R&D (supplemented by licensing-in or overseas acquisitions of needed technical and design skills). According to one estimate, scientists and engineers in India earn less than 10 percent of what their peers in the United States or Europe earn.[17] We found several EMNCs in our research that aggressively took advantage of their ability to conduct such low-cost R&D, in addition to their lower-cost manufacturing competencies—HTC, Natura, Mahindra & Mahindra, and Wipro, for example.

While the R&D levels and outcomes of emerging-market multinationals are clearly not yet at the level of an IBM, L'Oréal, or Intel, they are still pretty sophisticated—and they are carefully deployed in market-impacting ways on a much larger geographic scale than that of the Niche Customizers. Just as Apple spends only about 3 percent of its sales on R&D, yet uses it in a coherent, targeted way for market-moving innovative products,[18] this new generation of EMNCs too carefully uses its low-cost R&D ability in just those areas where it makes the biggest difference to creating customer value. As an example, Natura's investments in R&D are relatively small compared with those of its main competitors; in 2009, it invested 3 percent of net income in R&D,

whereas most of its competitors spent more. Yet, notwithstanding this lower investment, Natura is able to produce a new product every three working days, which is an output level comparable to those of companies like 3M, and 65.7 percent of the company's 2010 billings originated from products that were launched over the previous two years.[19] This figure has remained consistently around 65 percent since at least 2004.[20]

These Global Brand Builders invest more in R&D than EMNCs typically do (Samsung Electronics, for example, invests 5.5 percent of its sales in R&D, a percentage almost as high as that of IBM)[21] and take advantage of the lower cost of R&D in their home markets and their own manufacturing skills. Such Global Brand Builders, by leveraging focused innovation, can then go to scale on a large number of new products and services that can compete with the offerings of larger-budget TMNCs. Consider these examples of such Global Brand Builders.

HTC, as discussed earlier, is now the world's third biggest smartphone manufacturer. It is now known for its innovations in leading-edge hardware design and easy-to-use user interfaces in this consumer electronics category. Once just a faceless "original design manufacturer" supplier of digital agendas (PDAs) and smartphones to Western multinationals such as HP/Compaq and Palm, with healthy but unspectacular margins, it now wants to be seen as the ease-of-use leader in the category. By 2010, it had achieved operating profit margins on par with that of RIM (BlackBerry), over 16 percent.[22]

Or consider Mahindra & Mahindra, which moved from being a manufacturing partner for Ford in India to developing—from scratch, it says—its own Scorpio sport utility vehicle (SUV), giving it the confidence that it could compete with global players in the SUV and pickup truck corners of the global automotive category. It is preparing to launch differentiated "clean diesel" and hybrid SUV models in Europe and the United States as this book is being written (2011). Mahindra & Mahindra claims the Scorpio was developed for $120 million, one-fourth of what it would cost in Detroit.[23] Similar local-development stories come from Turkey's Arçelik (Koc) Appliances, India's Tata Motors, China's Lenovo and Haier, and Turkey's Temsa, which all now possess and use significant product development and business model capabilities, evidenced, for instance, in Tata's Nano vehicles.

Next, look at the evolution of Wipro. Once thought of as just another Indian IT service shop, one of several for "body-shopping" and BPO contracts, it now has evolved into an R&D outsourcing partner; CMO Jessie Paul told us that Wipro owns more than 40 patents on chip design alone. It is now also a consultant on change management, emerging markets, quality implementation, product architecture, and other areas. It wants to be known for its "applied innovation," not merely for vast cadres of programmers.

Other brand-impacting innovations include those by LG in front-loading washing machines, Ranbaxy in drug-delivery systems, and Lenovo in notebook features. Tata Tea encourages its local units to create new, contemporary forms of ready-to-drink tea, and seeks now to also become a world leader in patented technologies to extract and process polyphenols with high antioxidant content to use in cosmetics and pharmacology as well as in beverages. Titan proudly markets its Edge brand watches, the slimmest in the world.

These EMNCs (and others we will describe in this book) have realized that their rapid, unexpected innovation not only creates superior differentiated products; it also garners media and influencer attention and plaudits—it builds the quality and leadership reputations that we believe are the foundation of truly superior global brands. HTC's CMO John Wang told us, "Our actions speak much louder than our words." (Just as it does for Apple.) We also see innovations in the tactical details of how these organizations build their brands. The brand-building stories later in this book will highlight the clever and entrepreneurial techniques the EMNCs use to build brand awareness and quality reputations. These stories of tactical innovation will show how the challenger EMNCs are, despite the odds and conventional wisdom, managing to build the strong brands and businesses the naysayers believed they could not. Innovation has become the foundation of their business as well as their brand building.

However, cognizant of their still-limited resources, these EMNCs focus tightly on innovation, aiming at particular slices of the relevant global product market, such as HTC's focus on smartphones with just Android or Windows-Mobile operating systems; Vitra's focus on bathroom interiors; Ranbaxy's focus on improved drug delivery and branded generics, but not new molecules; Mahindra & Mahindra's focus on SUVs and utility vehicles; and Natura's focus on identifying and extracting natural active ingredients from Brazilian flora traditionally used by the indigenous peoples of Brazil. If they carefully and strategically target their limited resources and efforts at product categories, market segments, and technologies where they have a shot at leadership, and if they spend small budgets in ways that quickly create tangible customer value, they have a chance to break out and win.

This strategic principle also applies to the more tactical aspects of brand building: limited media dollars get cluttered out if they are scattered around broadly; but if you use them in hypertargeted and creative low-budget ways, they can still create brand awareness and imagery among those who matter most to you.

Acquisition. Another group of Global Brand Builders consists of EMNCs that are also tackling developed markets worldwide, but that are using acquisitions to bring in the supply chains, technologies, brands, and distribution channels they currently lack. Examples include Apollo Tyres, Arçelik (the higher-end brands), Asian Paints, Lenovo, Mahindra & Mahindra, Mitac, Tata Motors, Tata Tea, and Vitra. Such acquisitions become easier and cheaper to acquire when EMNCs' domestic stock markets have high price/earnings ratios and their currencies are strong—as they both are in 2011, as this book is being written.

The acquisitions made by the emerging-market multinationals we studied were strategic. Acquisitions were used to overcome the weaknesses we reviewed earlier and complement their existing strengths of large-volume production and low-cost R&D and manufacturing, giving these EMNCs a more complete set of assets and competencies, which enabled them to tackle the more mature and less well-understood (by EMNCs) developed markets that they had chosen to target.

Many commentators have argued that EMNCs lack the skills to integrate and leverage acquisitions, particularly international acquisitions of often larger businesses from the triad nations. However, we will show later in this book that EMNCs do this no worse than their TMNC competitors (see Chapter 3), and indeed some seem to do better, applying a "soft touch" to the integration process.

What's New About the "New-Wave" Business Strategies: Global Brands

The new-wave strategies we have described are significant because they identify a new class of EMNCs effectively building brands on a significant regional or global scale (e.g., LG Electronics, Haier, HTC, Lenovo, MTS, Natura, Tata Tea, Vitra, Natura, Turkish Airlines, and Savola). Some earlier commentators have acknowledged these new EMNC successes in building or buying design, supply chain, technology, and distribution competencies. Often, such commentators assert that these new EMNCS, for all their newfound competencies, will still have difficulty establishing the needed skills in marketing and branding to build really profitable and sustainable global businesses. In particular, it has been claimed that while these companies may indeed eventually learn how to move up the value chain in technology and design, they are unlikely to ever have the resources and skills needed to build global brands to the same scale that TMNCs have. Writing in 2009, strategy scholars Louis Wells, Jr., and Alan Rugman concurred. Wells wrote, "Evidence suggests that [EMNCs] are still weak when it comes to developing brands," and Rugman said, "As yet there are no emerging economy multinational enterprises with pure brand-name marketing firm-specific assets."[24] In this book, we will demonstrate that this is apparently no longer true.

Why is such brand creation and ownership so important to the building of a sustainable global MNC business?

Why Do Brands Matter?

For any company, it is well recognized that building and owning strong brands is a key strategic competency; after all, strong brands allow companies to charge higher prices and garner higher margins; win above-normal market shares and retain them in the face of competitive attack via higher customer loyalty; build greater market power against distribution channels and other intermediary customers; grow revenues via brand extensions into contiguous product categories; attract and retain the best employees; and, as an outcome, build a more highly valued enterprise.

For the EMNCs we interviewed, the stakes are even more fundamental, given their brands' low initial awareness levels and negative country-of-origin imagery. A strong brand means more trust and confidence and more invited proposals for an IT supplier like Infosys or Wipro. For Ranbaxy, it brings the ability to market branded generic drugs rather than commodity generics, yielding higher margins that can be plowed back into R&D. And a strong brand allows the kind of market differentiation that increases customer demand and prevents a downward spiral into commoditization, as with Evyap foods, MTS telecom, and Tiger Beer.

The EMNCs we spoke with recognize well that businesses with strong brands are able to launch into a "virtuous cycle" of higher profits that businesses without strong brands cannot reach. With higher profits they can more easily create innovative and differentiated higher-priced products. To quote Hüsamettin Onanç of Turkey's Vitra: "Brands are very important. If you are not a brand, you cannot capture the value-added sufficiently. There are enough commodities in the world. At the moment you can buy similar products from China at half price. They are nice imitations. You can also buy them from Egypt. There are always people who make them cheaper than us. That's why it's a 100% must for us to be a brand."

Arçelik's Hasan Subaşi, former vice chairman and board member, draws similar conclusions about why and where branding matters most, based on very insightful segment-specific analysis: "There are three segments in the market [referring to the Western European appliance market]. First: the premium segment. This typically makes up 20% of the market, and branded goods are sold in *this* segment. Second, there is the mass market which is 50% of the whole market. Here, alongside a brand, the price becomes an important dimension. Finally, there is the economy segment. Generally, this makes up 30% of the market, and the prevailing dimension of the product is price. Nobody looks at the brand; the good which is cheaper sells more.

"If you go into the no-brand market at the entry level, as Arçelik did when entering the European market, even if you acquire the whole segment, you only reach 30% of the market. Not to mention that since it is the entry level, it is most open to competition. Tomorrow when a Chinese firm comes and offers a price $10 lower, your market share instantly drops. Entry level is the level with lowest *sustainability*.

"If you want to go after a sustainable market, you should enter the mass and premium markets. Brands are important in these segments and serve two functions. First, it provides access to a large market; if you don't have a brand then it means you are limited to 30% of the market (economy segment). Second, it determines your margins. While you are earning 12–15% in the premium segment, mass market brands earn 3–5%, and no-brands earn only 1–2% profit. That low! Therefore, *a brand first increases the volume and secondly improves the margins*. As long as you have a brand—if you have a strong brand—you have a sustainable business."

As we will discuss later in the chapter on brand strategy, while Arçelik entered the European appliance market from the economy segment, over time it chose to move upward into the mass (middle) segment with its own Beko brand and then into the premium segment with its acquired brands Arctic, Blomberg, Elektra Bregenz, Grundig, and others. Today it claims over 10 percent of this premium market. Arçelik is thus an EMNC that has displayed great strategic and tactical skill in winning in the "brand wars" in a highly developed, very competitive market. Arçelik is hardly the only EMNC to have done this.

Clearly, these new-wave strategies that focus on global brand building are very dangerous for TMNCs, as they strike at the heart of TMNC businesses, vying for the same most lucrative customers who bring the highest margins. Importantly, the new EMNC emphasis on R&D and technology is now getting added on to their earlier scale and cost advantages in manufacturing and labor, providing them with higher margins, compared with those of their TMNC counterparts. Used wisely, in a virtuous cycle, this double-barreled EMNC competency can in the longer run be devastating for the incumbent TMNCs.

Key Idea: Building Branded Businesses Through Focused Innovation

We are witnessing in 2011 the quantum leap to a qualitatively different type of EMNC: one that competes not only on low costs and high-volume manufacturing, as well as emerging-market knowledge and skills, but also on its ability to innovate and lead in tightly focused product-market spaces—and to use such innovation as the foundation for attention-getting, image-changing brand building. And this competing-from-below business strategy is worth considering by challenger businesses everywhere.

This new-wave strategy is in sync with, and benefits from, several important "disruptive" forces in today's global economy. The new marketing communications environment we see today is one in which the flow of consumer-to-consumer information via the Internet, blogging, and social networking favors those marketers with genuine innovation and value over those that simply have deeper pocketbooks. Tire-buying consumers in Europe who research and buy brands on the Internet can now as easily learn about tires made by Apollo Tyres as they can about tires made by Continental, Michelin, and Goodyear. The post-2007 economic shocks and slowdown in the mature economies of the West mean consumers there are more actively seeking superior-value offerings today, even from newer corporate or national sources.

Today's global flows of technology, knowledge, skills, and talent now also make it easier for companies in the "economic periphery" to build high-tech plants and lead informed marketing and branding efforts with the same caliber of people that run them for companies headquartered in the triad nations. LG Electronics, MTS, Ranbaxy, the Taj Group, and Tata Motors, for example, now have top managers who previously headed up West-based MNCs, and employ the same branding and design consultancies (such as Landor) that their West-based MNC competitors do. As Infosys's former global head of marketing, Srinivas Uppaluri, told us, "New models are disrupting the world." EMNCs seem to be aggressively taking advantage of these disruptions.

About This Book

This book is based on our own field research into the strategies and tactics used by 39 EMNCs for building their global businesses and brands. Our research began with interviews we conducted with their senior managers and executives. The Appendix at the back of this book provides a brief look at these companies and identifies the people we interviewed; we encourage you to skim this section now to gain familiarity with the background of the challenger firms we studied.

We supplemented those interviews with an extensive study of "secondary" published material (such as written cases and media articles), acknowledged in our endnotes. We also consulted with subject-area experts in specific areas, such as acquisitions, to tap their expertise for specifically identified supplementary materials in the book. (Professor Prashant Kale of Rice University, an expert on acquisitions by EMNCs, cowrote the acquisitions chapter with us.) By researching the histories and talking directly to the main protagonists of the 39 companies we discuss, we sought to answer three questions:

1. How are EMNCs building global branded businesses?
2. What can other aspiring EMNCs—and challenger businesses everywhere—learn from the ways in which EMNCs go about building strong global branded businesses, given the resource and country-of-origin challenges EMNCs face?
3. What can the TMNCs that are increasingly threatened by this new breed of EMNCs learn from this analysis, and thus what strategies can they proactively develop to respond to the new challenges?

To address these three questions, in the first section of the book we examine the strategic choices these EMNCs make and the competencies they acquire—in areas as diverse as market selection, products, and technology—as the basis for building their new global branded *businesses.* We next discuss how they are overcoming the challenges of *building a brand,* given their constraints and disadvantages, based on the insights from the firms we studied. Brand building on a *global scale* requires management capabilities that can deal with markets that are culturally, economically, politically, and geographically distant and diverse. This is the focus of the third section. We close with a final section that brings together the key lessons for other aspiring EMNCs and for challenger firms in general; this last section also identifies the increasing threat to TMNCs and the ways in which they might be addressed, and it provides a look at the future. What factors might accelerate or retard this potential onslaught by EMNCs in the global marketplace?

How You Can Use These Findings

If you are an EMNC like the ones in our book, these shared experiences and lessons can provide insight into the strategies and tactics that will help you to build these more-sustainable and more-profitable businesses and brands in global markets. The road to these strong businesses and brands is paved with challenges that need to be overcome: finding ways to build brand awareness, identity, and associations despite weak financial resources, and overcoming (usually) negative quality imagery stemming from countries of origin. Many EMNCs have struggled in their efforts to build sustainable branded businesses overseas—Titan watches in Europe, Acer in its notebook business in the United States in the 1990s, BenQ with its failed acquisition of Siemens Mobile, and LG with its Zenith acquisition (although LG did and continues to make money from Zenith's patents). This book's analysis of both the business-building and brand-building strategies and tactics used by the EMNCs that we have studied here should be valuable to you. (For every company we talk about in these pages, a dozen more are waiting in the wings.) And our findings also should provide useful policy directions to governments and trade organizations in the emerging-market countries seeking to enhance the global competitiveness of companies from their countries.

If you are a company in the "developed triad" that already is, or will soon be, competing with these new EMNCs (or sometimes partnering with them), the stories and strategies we tell might suggest new ways to disrupt and fight them. If you know the strategic intent and business models of your new EMNC competitors, and their competitive strengths and weaknesses in depth, it can only help you fend off their attempts to carve out larger and more profitable customer segments from you. We point out such lessons in each chapter and consolidate them in our concluding one.

If you are simply a small challenger business, going up against much better-endowed, larger market leaders, the many detailed cases we provide of low-budget competitors managing to compete and win ought to provide you a game-plan on how your resource limitations can be side-stepped. While some of the ideas and lessons we offer doubtless already exist in other strategy texts, you will find here multiple real-life illustrations that bring these "competing from below" principles vividly to life, inspiring and guiding you to succeed.

For those who simply want to better understand the strategies and tactics needed to build strong global businesses and brands, these case histories and examples provide fresh instances of the many creative pathways through which these can be built. At some abstract academic level, the strategies and tactics we report here may perhaps not be seen as new. But their specific implementation by companies so challenged in their resources and starting positions—but not in their determination and imagination—is extremely interesting and inspiring. We learned much from their stories, and we hope you will too.

Some Common Strengths and Weaknesses of EMNCs

- **Strengths.** EMNCs typically have the skills and the size to be able to manufacture high-quality products at a relatively low per-unit cost. Many of the companies have learned to design and manufacture high-quality products by serving as offshore suppliers to OEMs and trade buyers overseas. Their large-volume, cost-reducing economies of scale come from their work in their large domestic markets and in their service as contract manufacturing for overseas OEMs, trade buyers, and relabelers. They use their own manufacturing facilities, and so they need not outsource production. Their labor costs are often lower that TMNCs' costs, and occasionally R&D (technical and engineering) costs are also lower. These tangible cost advantages are often combined with a mindset that always seeks frugal, "good-enough," low-cost ways of doing business. With their relatively low-cost facilities and R&D costs, EMNCs can more easily afford to create customized products for particular market segments than the TMNCs, which typically focus on globally standardized products in order to gain cost competitiveness.

Apart from their cost structures, these EMNCs also naturally possess a good understanding of how to serve the needs of consumers and customers in developing-market environments like their own—which often (but not always) means knowing how to make low-priced, functional, rugged, and durable products. Such low-priced products are of interest not only to consumers in other developing countries, but also to a small but growing group of consumers in the developed world—a trend that may outlive the current recession. They also know how to conduct business in tough business environments— those with poor infrastructure, volatile economies, and non-transparent government—similar to their home markets.

- **Weaknesses.** While these EMNCs have access to cheaper R&D human talent, they are usually not yet at the high technical level and scale to pioneer (and own) really high-end technical capabilities (with a few exceptions—Samsung now gets almost as many U.S. patents as does IBM). Nor is their access to lower-cost manufacturing and R&D necessarily a long-term sustainable competitive advantage: TMNCs too can (and do) source their own manufacturing and R&D from their own low-cost locations. And the EMNCs naturally lack the large global organizations and the long historical knowledge base of their more established TMNC global competitors.

1

Choosing Consumer Segments and Expanding Internationally

As the Introduction points out, which consumers to serve—in which countries—is the most fundamental strategic decision that an expanding EMNC needs to make, as all other business decisions are contingent on this. Here in Chapter 1 we examine EMNCs' decisions regarding which consumer segments to serve and in which countries, decisions that can broadly be construed (as shown in Figure I-1 and elaborated in Figure 1-1) as a choice between serving consumers from other emerging markets who are similar to those served at home, or expanding to more affluent markets, where market conditions and consumers are relatively dissimilar. This chapter also documents how this choice—of which consumers to serve and in which geographies—evolves, as EMNCs gain an understanding of how to win in international markets. We end the chapter by documenting the evolution of Mahindra & Mahindra's automotive business in international markets. This case shows not only how Mahindra & Mahindra's choice of consumer segments and country markets evolved over time, but also how the organization's strategy changed from those of a Knowledge Leverager to those of a Global Brand Builder—the strategy that is the most complex and difficult to execute, but also the most profitable and sustainable one. The road map to the target-segment and country-market decisions is presented in Figure 1-1.

Choose Segments First, Then Countries

As depicted in Figure 1-1, we believe that the choice of which segment to target should come before considering which markets to enter. Among TMNCs, this is the dominant logic and is used by companies as varied as IBM, Procter & Gamble (P&G), and Pernod-Ricard. Yet in many of the EMNCs we talked to, the internationalization decision began with a discussion of which country or countries to enter.[1] For instance, Ravi Kant, CEO of Tata Motors, told us, "Before that [choosing customer segments], we need to choose our geographies very carefully."

We believe, however, that it is important to first begin with the choice of consumer segment(s) to serve. When using country characteristics as a proxy for segment attractiveness, countries that may appear unattractive (or attractive) may actually be very attractive (or unattractive) if one were to consider the attractiveness of the target segment directly. Consider Ranbaxy. Sanjeev Dani, senior vice president and regional director of Asia, Commonwealth of Independent States (CIS), and Africa, told us that emerging markets are generally more attractive for branded generic players as the use of branded generics is growing rapidly there. However, "although Japan is not an emerging market, branded generic penetration there is only 5–7 percent (compared to 25–30 percent in

Segment Choice		Country Choice	
Similar Emerging Markets	**Dissimilar Developed Markets**	**Opportunity for Profit**	**Ability to Profit**
• Following the ethnic diaspora • Price-sensitive segments • Segments that seek functional and reliable brands	• Niche segments • High-growth categories • Consumers accepting of new brands	• Market size • Geographic centrality • Market growth rate	• Similarity • Ease of brand building • Proximity • Relationships

FIGURE 1-1 Segment Choice and International Expansion

the United States), and Japanese consumers are turning big time to branded generics now." Ranbaxy expects the demand for branded generic pharmaceuticals in Japan to explode and achieve penetrations of 15 to 30 percent in the next 5 to 10 years, making it a very attractive market. Choosing countries first, as a proxy for segments, would have led Ranbaxy to miss the huge opportunity in Japan, an opportunity that Ranbaxy could ill afford to lose.

Choosing Segments

All the firms we talked to had clearly identified the target segments they served at home. Over the years, these firms have acquired dominant positions in these segments. For instance, Mahindra Tractors is the market leader in tractors in India, serving Indian farmers. It's sister concern in the group, Mahindra & Mahindra, dominates in utility vehicles (UVs) and SUVs, with over 50 percent market share, serving, till recently, the needs of rural Indians. Ulker dominates the Turkish market for biscuits and confectioneries, with a 60 percent market share; CEO Cafer Findikoğlu said, "All our products in Turkey are either number 1 or number 2. In the categories where we are number 1, there is a great difference between us and the follower." In Guatemala, the home of Pollo Campero, Roberto Denegiri (president of the organization's U.S. business) noted, "Everyone knows and loves Pollo Campero and we have a market share of more than 60%."[2] Café Britt's CEO, Pablo Vargas, told us that in Costa Rica Café Britt is "the number one player by far. We have over 80% market share."[3]

The dominant positions these firms hold come from their superior customer insights. For example, Mahindra & Mahindra, which started out some 60 years ago with a franchise from Willys USA to assemble Jeep-like vehicles, understands the needs of India's rural consumers from the lower socioeconomic strata. Given India's more than 500,000 villages, often not well served by the public transport system and connected by little more than dirt roads, Mahindra & Mahindra has developed a range of reliable, sturdy, economical, basic UVs and Jeep-like vehicles, such as the Mahindra Bolero and Mahindra Commander. These are typically acquired by small entrepreneurs and are used to offer point-to-point transport services for a relatively low price to impoverished villagers. To keep fares low, passengers are often crammed 10 or more to a vehicle designed for 5 to 8 passengers. Mahindra & Mahindra vehicles have a reputation for durability, reliability, and cost effectiveness among these consumers because it understands the needs of this segment and builds vehicles tough enough to withstand the difficult use conditions.

Mahindra & Mahindra has recently expanded successfully into the urban and middle and upper-middle segments with its stylish Scorpio, Xylo, and XUV SUVs; that move was preceded by an extensive exercise to generate customer insights into the more affluent urban Indian consumers' comfort, convenience, and power needs, as well as to understand the features required to build a sense of pride in ownership.

Given their deep understanding of the domestic consumer segments served and the resulting success in these segments, many of the firms we talked to attempted to leverage this understanding as they moved overseas, by looking for high concentrations of similar consumers in international markets. Targeting consumers overseas similar to those served at home helps develop a well-defined and cohesive consumer base that spans geographies, which is less expensive to cater to; builds economies of scale; is easier to manage; and creates synergies for leveraging their existing insights, capabilities, and product portfolio internationally. It also helps them to rapidly transfer new learning from international markets back home and vice versa, setting up a virtuous cycle of leveraging all the markets synergistically.

Not surprisingly, an obvious segment for these EMNCs to pursue first is their potentially large ethnic diaspora. A recent estimate put the number of Chinese and Indians living overseas at 60 million and 25 million, respectively.[4] The advantage to following their ethnic diaspora is that the firm already has a product or service portfolio that is likely to fit with this segment's needs and wants, creating economies of scale and reducing the need for expensive and difficult new product development. EMNCs in our sample benefiting from this strategy include Thailand's Vara-foods, Guatemala's Pollo Campero; India's Asian Paints, Dabur, Godrej, Marico, and Titan; and Turkey's Evyap. Following the diaspora has the additional advantage of benefiting from the diaspora's existing awareness and knowledge of brands in the home market, lowering the cost of building the brand in this segment. This segment is also likely to be more receptive to messages from home-country brands, as their perceptions are not colored by negative country-of-origin imagery—indeed, they might be bolstered by nostalgia for the old home country and old brand relationships. Older EMNCs with a longer history, operating in product categories where tastes and aesthetic appeals matter, are more likely to benefit from such a strategy.

Beyond following their ethnic diaspora, we identified two other ways in which EMNCs attempted to target consumers similar to the emerging-market consumer segments served at home:

- Targeting price-sensitive segments
- Targeting segments that seek functional and reliable brands

Not all the firms we talked to looked to target similar segments as those served at home. Many had taken the leap to serve distinctly new consumer segments in developed markets, as our strategic framework (Figure I-1 in the Introduction) suggests. This second set of EMNCs needed to meet the challenge of dealing with consumers about whom they had relatively less knowledge in a manageable and affordable way. They did so in three ways:

- Targeting niche segments
- Targeting high-growth categories, with "disruptively new" products

- Targeting consumers who are more accepting of new brands:
  - Going after non-mainstream consumers
  - Going after more knowledgeable consumers
  - Going business to business (B2B) to grow business to consumers (B2C)

We turn next to a discussion of each of these segment-choice decisions.

Targeting Emerging-Market Consumers and Others Similar to Those Served at Home

As noted above, EMNCs that focused on target consumers similar to the emerging-market consumer segments served at home followed two strategies beyond following the diaspora: they targeted price-sensitive segments and/or segments that sought functional and reliable brands.

Targeting Price-Sensitive Segments

Price-sensitive segments similar to those in EMNCs' home markets exist in other emerging markets, in certain developed markets, and always in B2B contexts. Since a key strength of EMNCs is their lower cost structure (see Chapter 2), EMNCs wield a sustainable advantage when serving price-sensitive segments.

In Other Emerging Markets. Price-sensitive segments exist in abundance in most emerging markets, making them a natural target. Thus Evyap, the Turkish personal-care brand, built itself a formidable reputation and market share in Russia by offering good-quality soaps with a broad range of scents, at competitive prices, when that market opened following the collapse of the Iron Curtain in 1989. Tata Motors CEO Ravi Kant reported that it has won strong positions in Turkey and South Africa because of its ability to offer a quality product at a very competitive price. He told us, "We are operating in the lower [price] segment and are reasonably placed by offering a lower total lifetime package cost, which enables people to buy our products. As a result, we have a 10% share in diesel pickup trucks in Turkey and about 11% in South Africa."

Mahindra & Mahindra's COO Rajesh Jejurikar also told us that the ability to target price-conscious consumers with competitive prices was a key reason for Mahindra's overseas success. Mahindra & Mahindra entered South Africa with an assembly operation in 2004 and today holds a 5 to 6 percent market share in the sub-300,000 rand category with just a single product, the Scorpio. Many other EMNCs too are moving aggressively into Africa, where they see a large and growing number of under-served consumers seeking value-for-money products and services. These include India's Bharti Airtel, Godrej, and Apollo Tyres; China's Huawei, in its new mobile phone business; and Turkish Airlines.[5] Godrej has recently acquired stakes in more brands in Africa, including Tura in Nigeria and the Darling and Amigos brands in 14 African countries.[6]

In Developed Markets. Price-sensitive segments are not the monopoly of emerging markets; they are present everywhere, including in developed markets, and tend to be large enough to be attractive, particularly in the less-affluent developed-world markets, like parts of Southern Europe. These are even more attractive because they are often under-served by the local players.

Not surprisingly, having expanded first in South Asia, then in Africa, Mahindra & Mahindra's first foray in the developed world for its UV and SUV business was in southern Italy in 2005.[7] Since 2005, Mahindra & Mahindra has expanded into other less affluent markets in Southern Europe, including Spain, Hungary, and Bulgaria, in effect encircling the southern edge of Europe. This global, price-sensitive consumer segment is important to Mahindra & Mahindra; to strengthen its portfolio of offerings and presence in this segment, the company recently acquired Ssangyong Motors of Korea, which is strong in this segment and offers a complementary range of products. Mahindra & Mahindra is now (2011) preparing to leap continents and launch its SUVs and pickup trucks in the United States. Chinese mobile handset companies Huawei and ZTE have now launched cheap and functional smartphones—selling for less than $100—in North America and Europe, sold through carriers such as Vodafone, Telus, and 3 Italia, as smartphone penetration grows into lower-income segments in those developed markets.[8]

In B2B Markets. B2B segments are typically price sensitive, as purchase managers are rewarded for achieving the lowest possible prices. Thus, there is a genuine opportunity for EMNCs to build a strong B2B brand by providing superior offerings at lower price points, as well as lower lifetime value, compared with what their TMNC competitors provide. Temsa, the Turkish truck and bus maker, competes successfully in Western European markets against home-grown giants like MAN, Mercedes, and Volvo by targeting the particularly cost-conscious segment of small-fleet operators. According to Temsa CEO Buldurgan, Temsa's business model enables it to achieve significantly lower component costs, compared with those of its competitors. Add to this Temsa's lower-cost but highly skilled labor force, and it is able to offer trucks that are of a quality comparable to that of MAN, Mercedes, or Volvo, its main European competitors, but at a 15 percent lower price and a lower lifetime cost. Chinese telecom network-gear maker Huawei and auto-parts manufacturer Wanxiang are among many of the Chinese EMNCs that have very successfully gone after B2B customers in both developed and emerging markets, because success there needs functional quality and value.[9]

Targeting Consumers Who Seek Functional and Reliable Brands

Our research suggests that lower costs are no longer the only or even the predominant capability that is being leveraged by EMNCs. Like the established TMNCs, they are competing on the basis of other world-class capabilities as well.

One such world-class capability that EMNCs possess stems from the demands at home that they face for functional and reliable products. EMNCs are leveraging this capability, in addition to their traditional cost advantage, to enter global segments that are looking for functional and reliable products. In doing so, they are becoming formidable competitors in the backyards of the developed-market multinationals.

A good example is Mahindra Tractors. Based on the needs of consumers served in India, the company has developed a full line of small, reliable, rugged, and fuel-efficient tractors. When it considered international expansion, it realized that the second largest concentration of consumers looking for such tractors was not in another developing country but, rather, in the United States, where hobby farmers and small landscaping firms make up two significant segments. Hobby farmers are weekend farmers who own farms that are typically five acres or less, and landscaping firms offer homeowners with large gardens initial landscaping as well as subsequent maintenance services. Both these segments want a tractor that is small, durable, easy to maintain, reliable, and economical, the same benefits sought by the Indian farmers whom Mahindra Tractors serves at home.

Mahindra Tractors entered the U.S. market in pursuit of the hobby farmer and landscaping firm segments in 1994, opening its first assembly plant in the United States in the process. Over the past decade and a half, it has built up the Mahindra brand as a durable, reliable, hassle-free, yet reasonably priced, brand in the minds of American hobby farmers. According to tractor division CEO Gautam Nagwekar, customer feedback suggests that American consumers today perceive Mahindra tractors to be "like a horse, very tough and robust, and one that definitely meets their requirements." In 2003, Mahindra opened a second assembly plant in the United States, followed by a third one in 2005.

Aside from the fact that certain segments desire durability and reliability, there are certain categories that are defined by these benefits. In these categories, EMNCs have the additional advantage of enhanced credibility. Thus, Mahindra & Mahindra's UVs and SUVs have been well received because "they are authentic and honest," according to Pravin Shah, CEO of international operations. The vehicles are truer to the heritage of these categories than many of the more luxurious vehicles marketed today in these categories by TMNCs.

Targeting Consumers from Developed Markets and Dissimilar to Those Served at Home

Not all the EMNCs we studied targeted consumers from other emerging markets who were similar to those served at home. As pointed out in the Introduction (Figure I-1), many EMNCs targeted dissimilar consumer segments using three approaches: targeting niche segments, spotting and targeting high-growth product categories, and targeting segments more predisposed to accept brands from unknown players. These three approaches enabled EMNCs to learn about new consumers and learn to manage in international environments without becoming overwhelmed by the costs, lack of knowledge of new consumers, competitive pressures, and managerial challenges of internationalization.

Targeting Niche Segments

When targeting customers in more developed markets, dissimilar to those at home, EMNCs (versus TMNCs) suffer from a lack of customer knowledge, weaker capabilities to compete internationally, and smaller financial resources. By focusing on niche segments, they are able to offset these weaknesses by avoiding a direct confrontation with TMNCs, as the latter typically do not compete in small niche segments, since they find them unattractive from the revenue-potential point of view. This makes niche segments safer havens for EMNCs in which to learn about new target customers, develop their capabilities, grow in size, and learn the intricacies of international business. The smaller size of these segments also means that the required marketing budgets are in line with what EMNCs can afford. Brazilian aircraft manufacturer Embraer— now one of the four biggest makers of commercial passenger aircraft in the world—grew by going after small and midsized niche segments, rather than competing directly with large-plane giants Boeing and Airbus.[10]

Marico illustrates this strategy among the EMNCs we studied. Following its initial entry into the Middle East, aiming at the Indian diaspora there, Marico quickly realized that a broader swath of local consumers needed hair-care products that would help them to deal with the impact of the much higher levels of chlorine in the local water on their hair, levels many times higher than elsewhere in the world. To tap this opportunity, Marico developed and relaunched its hair cream, which now had the ability to protect hair from chlorine. Given Marico's smaller size, greater flexibility, lower cost structures, and limited budgets, the small size of the segment suffering from highly chlorinated water made the segment more attractive to Marico than to the global giants Unilever, P&G, and L'Oréal, for whom the cost of developing and building brands for this specific opportunity was too high in proportion to the potential returns.

Since that time, Marico has developed an alcohol-free hair gel, taking advantage of the Islamic taboo on alcohol, again avoiding a direct confrontation with TMNCs. As Vijay S. Subramaniam, Marico's CEO of international business, noted, "Hair gel is a relatively small category; a niche segment, divided by geography and religion, within an already small category, is not interesting to the global majors. These segments [Muslim consumers] are below the radar for the large MNCs." Similarly, Titan watches had the consumer insight that, in the Middle East, waterproofing was very important (see Chapter 2). This insight, along with more locally appealing styling, high quality, and competitive price, has led Titan, according to CEO Bhaskar Bhat, to "displace Citizen and Seiko in the quartz category, to occupy the number 1 position."

Spotting and Entering High-Growth Categories

An alternative to targeting a niche consumer segment is to spot and target a category that is on the verge of growing dramatically. Thus, LG Electronics entered the U.S. washing machine space with a front-loading machine, a format that accounted for only 10 percent of all washing machine sales at the time of entry in 2002. However, this was a category that had just begun to grow rapidly—at over 20 percent a year compared with less than 5 percent growth in top-loading washing machines. The small size of the category had attracted only one established player, Maytag, which did not have the capacity to adequately serve the growing demand. By 2007, LG was the leading player in the front-loader category and among the leading players in the washing machine category more broadly, as by then front-loading machines had grown to account for 25 percent of all washing machines sold.

Haier's experience in small wine fridges is much the same. Haier brought to market a small, no-frills wine fridge in the U.S. market, a market where wine fridges had only been large, full-featured, expensive products targeted at affluent wine connoisseurs. Haier's efforts not only earned it a dominant 60 percent market share, but did so in a much-expanded category, as the lower price points tapped by Haier led the category itself to grow dramatically.[11]

Participating in these new categories has four important benefits beyond market share gains: easier sales, greater visibility, perceived innovativeness, and access to younger consumers.

Easier Sales. Given rapid growth, competing firms vie for a share of the growing pie rather than try to take share away from each other. LG Electronics would have found it much harder to grab a leading position if it had to take share away from established incumbents like Whirlpool and GE, rather than grab a disproportionate share of a rapidly growing category.

Greater Visibility. High-growth categories are more visible to consumers due to greater activity created by the rapid entry of new players. Thus, following LG's entry into the large-format front-loading washing machine category, Whirlpool, GE, and Samsung all entered too, creating significant visibility for the category, which LG, as an early entrant, benefited from.

Perception of Innovativeness. The perceived rapid innovation due to competitive activity in these emergent categories also leads to a positive rub-off on the pioneering brands in terms of being perceived as "innovative" and "modern." LG gained such imagery in North America from its front-loading washing machines.

Access to Younger Consumers. Relatedly, these emergent categories may also provide important opportunities to reach out to younger consumers, creating a defensible position for the future. LG Electronics entered the mobile phone business partly so it could reach out to young teenagers. LG hoped that this early relationship would benefit LG's other businesses such as white goods (durables and appliances), televisions, and the like, as these young consumers became young adults.[12]

Tata Tea provides another example. To energize, modernize, and rejuvenate its image, Tata Tea has made acquisitions in the herbal infusion space, acquiring the Good Earth and Jemča businesses. Growth in tea (the mainstay of its business) has slowed, and tea today is seen as an old-fashioned beverage, while infusions are growing rapidly, particularly among the young and trendy, creating an opportunity for the future.

Targeting Consumers Who Are More Accepting of New Brands
To reduce the challenges of serving customers quite distinct from those at home and located in developed markets that are quite dissimilar to the home market, several of the firms with whom we spoke searched for segments of consumers that were more open-minded and accepting of new brands. We identified three types of such segments: non-mainstream consumers, knowledgeable consumers, and B2B customers—primarily intermediaries who provided access to the end consumer. We describe each of these segments below.

Targeting Consumers Who Want to Make a "Non-mainstream" Statement. In every market, there are consumers who are looking for different and unusual brands. Almost by definition, brands marketed overseas by EMNCs are not the traditional and well-known brands in those countries, and thus these brands are likely to appeal to consumers seeking to distinguish themselves from the mainstream. For this target consumer group, the traditional weakness of emerging-market brands—their novelty and suspect country of origin, which turns away mainstream consumers—is attractive, making such consumers a desirable target group for EMNC Global Brand Builders.

We see two examples of this targeting strategy in our data. Asia Pacific Breweries has cleverly marketed Tiger Beer in Western markets as being a non-mainstream, exciting, "different" choice. It has gone after the youth market that it thinks will be responsive to such an appeal, using an "alternative" positioning in its media and creative choices by hosting performances by bands that embody this positioning in underground garages. Similarly, Mavi jeans from Turkey positioned itself as a brand for those consumers seeking an alternative choice—people who wanted premium-quality jeans at less than premium prices and who liked Mavi's message: "for people who want to feel youthful, not just for youth."

Such a strategy comes with natural caveats, however. Is this target market large enough to pay off? Is it efficient and effective to reach? Will this strategy make the brand liable to the fickle forces of fashion, such that it may be in favor today but be "old news" tomorrow?

Targeting More Knowledgeable Consumers. Just as targeting non-mainstream consumers allows EMNC brands to sidestep being handicapped by their typical liabilities, so too is the case when targeting the more knowledgeable consumers and customers. More knowledgeable consumers and customers are less likely to rely on stereotypes and imagery and more likely to focus on specifications and facts when making their purchase decisions. Thus, firms as diverse as Temsa, Bajaj Auto, LG Electronics, Infosys, Wipro, Haier, Midea, and Chigo have all focused on knowledgeable consumers and customers.

In the B2B space, Temsa and Tata Motors told us that knowledgeable fleet buyers are more willing to do business with them. These knowledgeable buyers understand the capabilities of the firm and the quality of the trucks and buses it manufactures. They are keen to take advantage of the superior price and lower lifetime costs, providing the initial toehold from which these EMNCs can develop their branded businesses.

Targeting knowledgeable buyers is even more important in the case of service providers, where quality is more difficult to judge prior to experiencing the service. Thus, while companies like Infosys and Wipro try to signal quality through certifications like ISO or CMM, at the end of the day, as Jessie Paul, CMO of Wipro noted, "Knowledgeable customers are much more likely to do business with us." With this in mind, Wipro targets the CIOs of Fortune 1000 firms as its primary target segment, as these domain experts are much more likely to have heard of Wipro, know of its capabilities, and be able to make a considered judgment based on the objective merits of competing IT providers.

Go B2B to Grow B2C. In the B2C space, the idea of targeting more knowledgeable buyers has led many firms to target distribution intermediaries first, rather than going after end consumers. As we learned from our research, such distribution intermediaries, compared with typical end customers, have greater awareness of established EMNC manufacturers, greater focus on functional benefits, and more knowledge that EMNCs can learn from. They also allow more focused deployment of limited resources and can create value through referrals.

Rakesh Sharma, CEO of international business at Bajaj Auto, noted, "Let's say we are entering Argentina or Mexico; we would not be bothered about the fact that no one among the end consumers knows Bajaj. The trade, the distributors, the people who would be setting up the service centers, they know that Bajaj is one of the top five two-wheeler manufacturers and produces some three million two-wheelers a year. This enables us to gain distribution access far more easily than acquire the end consumer. We leverage the distributors to offer differentiated products as well as a differentiated product experience, to build our brand in the initial stages."

Targeting intermediaries also enables EMNC Global Brand Builders to play from their strength, just as it did when targeting consumers who valued durable and reliable products, since this segment also values functional benefits (including price). Note that this does not mean that brand characteristics such as perceptions of quality and leadership, or feelings of trust and confidence, do not matter in B2B and commercial markets: they do. Wipro, for instance, told us that such trust (and brand awareness) matters hugely in the IT business and that Wipro still needed to raise its levels on these variables. But relatively speaking, the kinds of expensive-to-build non-functional brand imagery associations that matter significantly in end-consumer markets matter less in commercial and B2B segments.

Going B2B to grow B2C, moreover, allows the firm to tap the knowledge of the distributors about what the end consumers want and what is happening in the competitive space, without having to spend time and resources to acquire the information firsthand. Echoing this, Ulker's Findikoğlu noted that "when we go to a foreign country some of our products are more appropriate than others. Our distribution network tells us which."

Our data contain several firms following this strategy. When LG Electronics entered the United States in 2002, following its initial distribution with regional players, LG tied up with Best Buy as a strategic partner. This was critical, as it enabled LG to obtain information from Best Buy about the benefits sought by U.S. consumers in the various categories of white goods, including fit, feel, and finish, something that LG Electronics did not understand well.

Similarly, Taiwan's recently resurgent HTC benefits from its relationship with mobile phone service providers such as Orange and Vodafone, which are key distributors of HTC handsets. These operators share their insights into customer needs, as well as the future directions they themselves plan to take. This helps HTC to fine-tune its product development pipeline and quickly bring to market catchy smartphones that gain the consumers' attention.

Aside from the benefits accruing from these buyers' greater knowledge, targeting distributors and retailers has the advantage of reducing the magnitude of the customer acquisition task considerably, as it is no longer about reaching millions of individual consumers, but about reaching a much smaller number of at most a few hundred distributors and retailers. Thus, Chinese computer giant Lenovo prioritized the large and medium business segments, rather than the mass consumer market, as it expanded into new geographies beyond China. Much less money and effort is required to build brand awareness and preference for such a target market than is required for a mass consumer market. Indeed, fewer resources would also be required to set up after-sales service facilities for a smaller number of commercial customers than for more widely dispersed and larger numbers of end consumers.

Another advantage of targeting knowledgeable customers, which has a potential to reduce commercial costs, is their value as sources of referrals. Knowledgeable customers tend to have insights about the direction that markets are headed in, and thus they tend to be opinion leaders. As an example, the Lebanon-born market research firm, Integration, values its client relationship with P&G for its referral value. The same logic is applied by Infosys and Wipro, which are especially mindful of customers that can provide a referral. Such referrals can also be within the same customer organization: Chinese mobile phone brands ZTE and Huawei both are growing in Europe and North America by tapping into the consumer businesses of the network operators to which they already sell network gear, such as Vodafone and Telstra.[13]

Referrals also matter for B2C players as they attempt to penetrate organized distribution systems particularly in developed markets. Thus, Evyap CEO Mehmed Evyap noted that as the company attempts to gain distribution, it is asked for referrals; Evyap recounted that once the company was able to get a contract to manufacture private labels for Oriflame, it used Oriflame as a referral, which helped Evyap to bring in new business.

Country Choice

Once the segments to target have been identified, the firm has a lens through which to focus on the country-choice decision; i.e., which countries have a relatively high number and concentration of the target consumers? The countries where these segments are located can then be analyzed in more detail by layering on country-specific information to decide which of these countries the firm should enter with its brands, and with what priority. The country factors considered can be characterized as defining the size of the opportunity on the one hand and the ability of the given firm to profit from that opportunity on the other. We turn to a discussion of these factors next.

Opportunity for Profit

The factors that define the size of the opportunity are market size, geographic centrality, and growth. We discuss each of these below.

Market Size

Market size is the most obvious and standard country selection criterion. Not surprisingly, countries such as China, India, and South Africa were high on the list of many of the companies we spoke to, because of their size. MTS CMO Cynthia Gordon noted that MTS had just entered India, as it was a very large market. LG Electronics had entered India back in 1997 for the same reason, and by 2010 India had become its second biggest market after the United States.[14] Large countries can also serve as anchors or hubs for developing businesses in smaller neighboring markets, which by themselves may not be very attractive (see below).

On the flip side, smaller markets are less complex and can be less competitive. However, a small market size limits the upside potential and may not be large enough to warrant the cost of entry. Thus, Savola Foods CMO Tarik Hadi attributed the firm's poor performance in Jordan to the small size of that market. Importantly, Jordan appeared to be an attractive market for Savola

Foods on the other criteria that influence country choice, such as similarity and proximity, which drove the initial decision to enter.

Geographic Centrality

A second important factor that drives country choices is the country's centrality in a region. Centrality has two aspects: geographic centrality and image centrality. Both are important.

Talking about geographic centrality, Marico's Subramaniam said it "decided to move into Egypt because it's centrally located; it is the passport to North Africa." According to Dabur's Sunil Duggal, "The Gulf Cooperation Council markets are big; they are the hub of our international business. South Africa is increasingly becoming an important market, and serves as a hub for Southern Africa. Egypt is our hub for North Africa. And if you want to be a player in West Africa, you have to be in Nigeria." Geographic centrality stems from not only geographic location, but also the bilateral and multilateral trade agreements that the country has. This is another reason for Egypt's geographic centrality. According to Temsa's Buldurgan, "The second reason for entering Egypt was that Egypt has two customs union trade agreements: one with her fellow Arab countries and the other with the other African countries. Thus, when you produce something in Egypt and export it, you can easily reach these countries."

However, Marico entered South Africa in part "because other countries in Africa look up to South Africa," i.e., because of its image-building effects. Such image centrality can have regional or global implications, as well as implications at home. Temsa gained tremendously in the other markets it operated in, as well as the markets it planned to expand into, as a result of entering France. As CEO Buldurgan told us, Temsa is "now perceived as a European brand and the entire world respects us."

As another example of the importance of country image, following its initial expansion into neighboring Latin American markets, Natura decided to enter France. It chose France for a number of reasons, one being that success in France, or indeed even a presence in France, would play well at home in Brazil as well as the other Latin American markets it was already in.[15] For similar reasons, Bajaj Auto made a foray into Western Europe as early as 1990 with an adaptation of the domestic Bajaj Sunny moped. It established dealerships in France, Germany, and Sweden for the Bajaj Sunny and by 1992 had sold some 1,500 units in these markets.[16] While the sales volume of the Sunny was tiny, it helped improve the image of Bajaj at home at a time when it was faced with stiff competition there from its major global two-wheeler competitor, Honda.

Market Growth

Market growth rate is another key factor. Vitra's Hüsamettin Onanç said, "The Emirates, Saudi Arabia, North Africa, and Libya are priority markets for us. As long as oil and gas prices go up, these countries will develop fast and become wealthier. When they get richer, the first thing they do is construction: housing, hotels, real estate, etc." Likewise, low-growth countries are unattractive. According to Onanç, Vitra "used to put the US in the high priority category and made serious investments in the US for 10 years. But, following the mortgage crisis, we took the US out of our priority list, as growth prospects disappeared."

The position taken by Vitra with regard to the United States is interesting, as it suggests an important trade-off between market size and growth. Given that the United States is by far the world's largest market, growth seems to matter more once a critical threshold of size is met. It is not surprising that growth matters more than sheer market size. Growth markets allow firms to gain business from incremental market volume, instead of having to take business away from incumbents, a much more challenging task.

Ability to Profit

Three factors determine the ability of the firm to profit from a country opportunity. They are similarity with the home country, cost of brand building, and geographic proximity. It is noteworthy that while country similarity and geographic proximity are often correlated, proximity confers different advantages from those conferred by similarity, as we point out below.

Similar Market Conditions

Beyond the fact that they are targeting a familiar consumer segment, similarity in market conditions also enables EMNCs to leverage existing capabilities in distribution and their abilities to operate in volatile environments, and do so better than their TMNC counterparts.

Experience in emerging markets confers an advantage to EMNCs in managing distribution in other EMNCs. Evyap's Serdar Sarıgül, GM of international sales, commented that "the retail structure is not sophisticated and modern retail formats and a chain structure are not common in countries whose income level is low. In these countries, most of the sales are through traditional channels, which are highly fragmented. Our capability to access and manage this fragmented distribution is higher, compared to other companies, as a result of our experience in doing business in this structure at home in Turkey."

These capabilities can include proprietary technological solutions to help them manage such distribution systems better, which create significant firm-specific advantages. A case in point is India's Marico. To manage the fragmented Indian distribution system where retailers are often not fully aware of the stock (inventory) they have, Marico has developed an IT system that allows its salespeople, equipped with Internet-enabled PDAs, to quickly determine stock at a retailer and immediately place an order for that retailer over the Internet, increasing replenishment accuracy and timeliness. This helps Marico reduce working capital requirements and stock-outs. Marico is able to leverage this capability in other similar markets with fragmented distribution channels, such as Bangladesh.

Emerging markets also tend to be volatile environments in every way possible, often having high levels of inflation, variability in economic conditions, infrastructural volatility (e.g., availability of electricity, water, and communications), political and regulatory volatility, and the like. EMNCs are used to operating in such volatile markets, and they have both the skills and business models to adjust to these volatilities. For example, many EMNCs are family-controlled conglomerates, with decision-making power residing with the founder or family head, enabling these firms to make quick decisions and, thus, better able adapt to and manage volatility.[17] As Mehmed Evyap said, "Uncertainty is a very important factor in these countries. Compared to an international company which is used to doing business by the book, we have a structure which allows us to adapt more quickly to new conditions, make decisions more easily and faster, and implement them quickly. Turkish businessmen are accustomed to uncertainties; they can think of practical solutions and resolve issues that may give a hard time to their European or American counterparts."

Lower Cost of Brand Building

Another important consideration that favors entering other emerging markets is that the cost of building brands is lower, a factor that is significant for these relatively under-resourced EMNCs. Our research revealed several reasons for this lower cost: often no large TMNC is present in the local market, reducing the competitive intensity; there is a lack of strong preference and loyalty toward incumbent brands; and there are cheaper media.

In many emerging markets, major multinationals have only recently entered and thus have not yet built up strong brand preference or loyalty. Thus Chigo's Peter Liao, general manager of the overseas marketing division, said that "for small and middle sized companies, if they would like to have their own brand in overseas markets, it is better to choose markets in developing countries. They are easier because the local consumers mostly buy for price and do not have strong preferences towards the existing brands in those markets. Thus, one can more easily build awareness and influence the local consumers, and make your brand as famous as other international brands. For example, in Nigeria, we have been able to build up the Chigo brand to the extent that people take our name in the same breath as LG, Panasonic, or Samsung." Savola Foods' Tarik Hadi echoed the same sentiment, saying, "In our markets, the competitors in the food business are still not well developed, so we can play a very important part in the consumers' choice of cooking oil and sugar with our brands like Afia."

Acquiring customers is also relatively cheaper in emerging markets because the cost of reaching consumers is often significantly lower. For instance, the cost per thousand (CPM) reached by a 30-second TV commercial during prime time varies between $1.00 and $3.00 in China, depending on the CCTV channel on which the commercial is broadcast. By comparison, the CPM on the major U.S. TV networks during prime time is on average $22.65, a cost that is 10 to 20 times higher than in China![18] Given these radically lower costs, it also makes these markets attractive places to test strategies before fine-tuning and rolling them out elsewhere.

Geographic Proximity

Proximity to the home market is another criterion that is important in choosing which countries to enter, as we saw in the case of Godrej, earlier in this section. Asian Paints' Tom Thomas also noted that the focus of Asian Paints is on Asia and that the countries of Latin America are too far away to consider at this time. There are four reasons why proximity is an important criterion driving country choice for many of the firms we spoke to: higher brand awareness spillover, greater cultural similarity, lower supply chain and management costs, and stronger relationships.

Brand Awareness Spillovers. For several companies, brand awareness built from media spillover paved the way for entering neighboring countries: Savola of Saudi Arabia has rolled out its Afia cooking oil brand through the region, benefiting from the brand-building initiatives undertaken in the Saudi market. Similarly, India's Marico and Dabur expanded into neighboring countries of South Asia, taking advantage of the spillover awareness built up there for their Parachute and Amla brands of hair oil, respectively. The same reason drove Asia Pacific Breweries to expand into the regional ASEAN markets with Tiger Beer, from its home in Singapore. Ulker, Arçelik, and Vitra also pointed to spillover effects as having built up latent demand in markets neighboring Turkey, which then led them to enter these markets.

Greater Cultural Similarity. Brand preference requires more than awareness of spillover effects: consumers in those markets also need to find the brand values they learn from the spillover to be relevant for them. Thus, the fact that neighboring markets also tend to be culturally similar helps. Savola Foods CMO Hadi noted that "we are able to take advantage of spillover effects in building the Afia brand because both the types of foods cooked as well as the role that a woman plays at home is similar across most of the countries we operate in. Because of this, the Afia advertising in Saudi Arabia, seen in the neighboring markets, resonated with the consumers there, creating the latent demand that we were able to capture."

Similarly, the culture of oiling hair, prevalent across South Asia, helped Marico and Dabur take advantage of their advertising spillover. Had it not been for this cultural similarity, the awareness of the Parachute and Amla names would perhaps not have been of as much value to the brand owners in entering these markets. The importance of a similar culture in unlocking the spillover effects becomes clear in the Emirate countries. Here, hair cream, and not so much hair oil, is used, making the spillover effects of the advertising for the Parachute and Amla brands irrelevant beyond the ethnic Indian diaspora segment.

Similar cultures in proximate markets also are advantageous from the point of view of human resource management. The shared culture of locally hired managers makes the management task easier due to shared ways of conducting business and understanding each other. Ajoy K. Misra, senior vice president of sales and marketing at the Taj Group of hotels, noted, "Diaspora provides a work-force which is aligned with the philosophy of the service which the Taj brand stands for." EMNC managers who learn to succeed in the complex, volatile, resource-constrained, freewheeling (and often corrupt and bureaucracy-heavy) environments of their home countries find that their adaptive skills serve them well in similar market environments.[19]

The further one extends into disparate cultures, the more difficult the management problem. Thus, as Wipro and Infosys have grown with operations around the world, a clear challenge facing them is how to work in these disparate environments and, perhaps more importantly, manage the diverse workforce. Wipro CMO Paul said, "Japan, we've been there for over ten years, and we still believe it's a big a market, but it's not an easy market. The challenge there is language and we run an in-house training program for that. We also have a six-month intensive cultural program, where we only talk to Japanese, in Japanese, eat Japanese; that's worked to an extent." Thinking about managing the workforce as a whole, Wipro's GM for talent acquisition, Priti Rajora, noted that Wipro's biggest challenge was to develop a cadre of general managers who could lead the culturally diverse organization that Wipro had become, with a significant presence in places as distant and disparate as China, Japan, the Middle East, Finland, Poland, Romania, the United Kingdom, and the United States.

Lower Supply Chain and Management Costs. Proximate markets also lower logistics, supply chain, and management costs. Arçelik, Vitra, Evyap, Marico, and Asian Paints, as well as several of the other firms we talked to, noted that their cost advantage eroded as they expanded further afield from their home markets. This led some to focus on a limited set of neighboring geographies or to focus on categories with higher price points and superior margins, which justified the higher costs.

Talking about the lower logistics and supply chain costs of dealing with proximate markets, Evyap's Sarıgül noted that "our expansion is substantially and with priority in Russia, Ukraine, and the Central Asian* countries, and following these the Cauca-sian countries.† Right after these are Iraq, Iran, and Syria. Why are some countries prioritized? Due to our geographic location, we first expanded into nearby countries to benefit from logistics and supply chain advantages. Trying to do business in Latin America from here requires more resources compared to our activities in Russia, Ukraine, or Iraq." Also highlighting the cost of targeting distant markets, Arçelik's Hasan Subaşi said that "the first coun-try to come to mind was the US. But we saw that it was impossible to sell the goods we produced in the USA; the transportation costs make it impossible."

The only way to deal with these higher costs is either through building manufacturing capability in these distant markets, as Arçelik is actively considering, or by focusing on high-price categories to absorb the higher logistics costs, as LG Electronics did. LG entered the United States with front-loading washing machines, rather than the more conventional top-loading machines in vogue in the United States, because of the higher margins on front-loading machines—top-loading washing machines sold for as little as $299, while front-loading machines started at $999. The higher margins enabled LG to defray the incremental transportation cost of around $100 per washing machine incurred in shipping.[20]

Costs also increase with distance when it comes to managing, as many EMNCs are still in their early stages of expansion and their processes for managing are not adequately developed, leading to what might be called "managing by running around." Tarik Hadi said that Savola chose "geographies which are close to Saudi Arabia so that we can readily travel and go there. We are not yet so sophisticated as to be able to manage remotely." Consequently, Savola Foods currently limits its ambitions to the Middle East, North Africa, and Central Asia, and its top managers like Tarik Hadi manage the diverse country operations of its oil and sugar

---

* Kazakhstan, Uzbekistan, Tajikistan, Kyrgyzstan, Afghanistan, and Turkmenistan.
† Azerbaijan, Georgia, and Armenia.

business by physically visiting the different country markets on a routine basis. We discuss the issue of managing across markets efficiently in Chapter 8.

Stronger Relationships. A final important reason for making geographic proximity important is that, all else being equal, there are more likely to be relationships at the *personal, commercial,* or *government* level in such markets, and these play an important role. Indeed, personal relationships emerged as important in driving country choices in several cases. Temsa's Buldurgan explained the choice of Egypt as its first step in internationalization by saying that "the most important reason to choose Egypt was the connection Güler Sabanci [chairperson, Sabanci Holdings, the holding company of Temsa] had established with the Egyptian Yashin family." CMO Cynthia Gordon of MTS noted as a reason for its expansion into other CIS countries that "the CIS territories have an awful lot of people who work or have families or just have very strong connections across the CIS area." Dabur's Duggal points to historic trade ties between India and the Middle East, which led to established commercial relationships, as a driver of the success of Dabur in these markets. These ties were equally important to Godrej and Marico, two other Indian players operating successfully in this region. Government relationships can also be very important, as MTS's Gordon noted. According to her, these government ties "made it possible for MTS to get licenses to operate in the CIS markets or to buy local telecom players." Without the relationships, the rapid expansion that MTS has enjoyed would not have been possible.

Expanding the International Footprint over Time

Firms need not only to choose segments to target and countries to enter, but also to prioritize future expansion across segments and markets, in line with the resources and capabilities of the firm. This helps them to avoid taking on too much at one go, become overwhelmed by the financial and managerial demands, and fail.

Increasing their share of wallet within a country and segment and later expanding to newer segments and markets are two logical strategies for expansion over time.

Increasing Share of Wallet Within a Segment and Country

Increasing the share of business (share of wallet) of existing segments is a logical first step that the EMNCs we talked to often followed. Once a significant beachhead in the first segment had been established, they expanded to other segments, typically moving up price tiers.

A share-of-wallet strategy reduces costs, as it is generally cheaper than acquiring new consumers and segments. The desire of the Taj Group of hotels to gain a greater share of the hotel nights spent on business travel by its core segment, Indian business travelers, for instance, drove the Taj Group to expand into the neighboring markets of South Asia. Natura's expansion in France took a similar approach. Following initial entry using its Ekos skin-care brand, Natura quickly followed with the other brands from its portfolio, which included grooming and colored cosmetics, to broaden its share of wallet of the customers it had already acquired. It was only after this effort to gain a greater share of customers' expenditure on grooming and cosmetics products that the business in France became sustainable. Adding more brands and gaining greater share of wallet of each acquired customer defrayed the cost of acquisition. Moreover, by having a broader and deeper engagement with the customer through meeting her beauty needs more broadly, Natura also created a more loyal customer base.

A share-of-wallet strategy that relies on expanding the product portfolio can also be leveraged effectively by firms in their relationship with retailers and distributors. A prime example of this is LG Electronics in India. LG Electronics entered India late, after the likes of Whirlpool, Samsung, Sony, and others, making access to good distributors and retailers difficult. However, because of its broader product line, spanning kitchen appliances, washing machines, TVs, air conditioners, computers, and mobile phones, retailers found LG an attractive firm to do business with. Dealing with a single supplier reduced their transaction costs, and the broad product portfolio helped smooth demand at the retail level due to countercyclical seasonality across the different product lines. According to Shin B. Moon, CEO of LG Electronics India Limited, LG's wide portfolio was key to rapidly building up the broadest and most effective distribution system of any multinational in the consumer durables space in India, notwithstanding the fact that LG Electronics was a late entrant.[21]

Adding New Segments Within a Country

Once a sustainable business has been built within the segment(s) initially targeted, firms need to move into new segments within a country. For EMNCs this typically involves moving up price tiers, as initial entry and expansion are typically driven either by being an OEM supplier or by entering the low-price segments. Moving up price tiers is a necessary and critical move if one wishes to build a branded business, since in the higher price tiers, brands matter more in consumer decisions relative to price. This, however, is no easy task, and Chapter 4 discusses different ways of doing so, along with their advantages and disadvantages.

Adding New Geographic Markets

The thirst for growth inevitably leads firms to seek new geographic markets. Since entering new markets is resource intensive and, depending on the market, can take a long time to succeed, it is important to make such decisions judiciously and in a focused and step-by-step manner. Rushing into too many markets without adequate financial and managerial resources is a recipe for failure. As Titan's Bhatt ruefully noted about Titan's European efforts, "As consulting firms like McKinsey told us, an Eastern company would take around 7 to 10 years to succeed and the balance sheet has to be very strong. That's exactly what we didn't have, because our company launched three big projects at the same time, including launching watches into Europe, and the launch of our jewelry business. We made investments in all the three but we did not have the strength to absorb the initial losses." As a result, Titan exited the European business, having lost a significant amount of money.

Mahindra & Mahindra: Expanding Internationally One Step at a Time

Our research shows that successful EMNCs are strategic and take a long-term view. Such firms enter progressively more difficult countries in a focused and sequenced way, moving up the difficulty ladder and learning each time to prepare for the next move. They start with the easiest targets: similar consumers in neighboring emerging markets. The segments and markets are similar in terms of benefits sought and culture; proximity makes logistics easier and cheaper; relationships of various kinds are more likely to exist; media spillover is likely to have already built awareness of their brand and potentially created pent-up demand. These factors led Mahindra & Mahindra to first enter India's neighboring countries, the so-called SAARC (South Asian Association for Regional Cooperation) countries, with the rough-and-tough SUVs and UVs that it made, following what we call the Knowledge Leverager strategy (see Figure 1-2).

Next Mahindra & Mahindra developed and launched a more up-market SUV, the Scorpio, with tremendous success in India. With this broadened and more internationally attractive product portfolio and the confidence boost that came with Scorpio's success, Mahindra & Mahindra moved to Africa, setting up an assembly facility in South Africa in 2004 to sell the Scorpio and its light trucks. This move helped it to learn how to manage an assembly operation internationally, how to manage logistics at a distance (a key to offering proper service levels to customers), and how to deal with a more competitive environment and a demanding consumer base. In this second phase, Mahindra & Mahindra executed what we describe in our strategy matrix in the Introduction as a Niche Customizer strategy.

Consumer Segments and International Expansion			
		Focus on Similar Emerging Markets	Focus on Dissimilar Developed Markets
Strategic Competency Building	Mechanistic Extension	Knowledge Leverager	Cost Leader
	Dynamic Evolution	Niche Customizer	Global Brand Builder

FIGURE 1-2 Mahindra & Mahindra's Evolution

As its next step, Mahindra & Mahindra moved to Italy, in partnership with a local distributor. It focused first on southern Italy, as customers there were less affluent, like those at home or in South Africa; but it learned to adapt to a new and even more competitive environment and a regulatory regime that was much tougher than it had encountered before. This enabled Mahindra & Mahindra to expand around the southern rim of Europe, taking in Spain, Bulgaria, and Hungary, where it opened an assembly plant. Mahindra & Mahindra had now learned how to manage and operate in multiple countries and with multiple assembly facilities spanning significant distances and international borders with very diverse and sometimes stringent regulatory environments. Our Cost Leader strategy aptly captures Mahindra & Mahindra's entry and then expansion across Southern Europe, targeting the price-sensitive segment that desired a functional, rugged, and reliable vehicle.

Mahindra & Mahindra went to Uruguay next. This enabled it to learn how to manage at a very great distance and across a huge time zone difference, but the market being small helped the company to keep the potential downside low. Mahindra & Mahindra now had the capability to execute the fourth strategy in our strategy matrix: the Global Brand Builder strategy, beginning with focused innovation. Along the way to Uruguay, it launched a second up-market SUV in India, the Xylo, which like the Scorpio was designed and built entirely by the company. Importantly, the Xylo broke new ground in terms of the design process, as it was built inside out. That is, the interior was first designed based on customer insight, and only then was the rest of the car built around this interior platform and the performance deliverables wanted by the customer.

Now following the Global Brand Builder strategy, Mahindra & Mahindra is currently in the process of implementing both the focused innovation and acquisition strategy paths. Consistent with the acquisition-led Global Brand Builder strategy, Mahindra & Mahindra acquired Ssangyong Motors of Korea in the second quarter of 2011, to move up the technology curve, strengthen its R&D capability, and increase its international volumes by several orders of magnitude. The Ssangyong Motors acquisition boosts Mahindra & Mahindra's vehicle sales outside India from around 17,000 units in 2010 to an estimated 140,000 in the current year (2011). According to COO Jejurikar, the company is "on track" to meet this estimate.

Importantly, Ssangyong Motor's SUV portfolio complements that of Mahindra & Mahindra and enables it to offer a stronger, broader, and more up-market range of products in the South Asian, African, and Southern European markets it currently serves. In these markets, the broader portfolio can leverage the existing distribution systems to gain significant cost synergies.

In parallel, Mahindra & Mahindra is preparing to launch a new SUV and enter the United States with its newly augmented product and brand portfolio, narrowly targeting the UV and SUV categories. In our strategy framework, this is the focused innovation Global Brand Builder strategy.

Summary and Key Takeaways

For all the firms we talked to that today can be squarely categorized as following a Global Brand Builder strategy (e.g., Arçelik, LG

Electronics, Lenovo, Haier, HTC, Wipro, Infosys, Tata Tea, and Tata Motors), getting there has been a long journey through many segments and countries. While we did not find a common path across the firms we studied, each journey involved taking small steps, learning from those steps, and moving on using the newly acquired resources, skills, and capabilities, starting with one of the less difficult strategies: a Knowledge Leverager strategy (e.g., Tata Tea and Tata Motors) or a Cost Leader strategy (e.g., HTC, Wipro, and Infosys). Some of the EMNCs we studied are currently in the Knowledge Leverager strategy phase (e.g., Savola), others are executing a Cost Leader strategy (e.g., Chigo, Temsa, and Mahindra Tractors), and still others are following the Niche Customizer strategy (e.g., Marico and Dabur). Some, like Mahindra & Mahindra, are on the threshold of becoming Global Brand Builders, potentially threatening the hegemony of the TMNCs, as some of the others before them (such as LG and HTC) have successfully done.

The experiences of the firms we studied offer lessons for other EMNCs and for challenger firms more broadly. As a first step, aspiring EMNCs and challenger firms need to find segments ignored by EMNCs. This reduces the competitive intensity on the one hand and on the other is likely to be small enough to fit the resources of aspiring EMNCs and challenger businesses. Fast-growing segments and geographic markets are also relatively more attractive, as they too offer the opportunity for growth and for lower-cost customer acquisition and brand building, without head-on conflict with the giants. After identifying market spaces that are less competitive, it is important that challenger businesses and aspiring EMNCs recognize and focus on moving up price tiers, as margins in the higher price tiers are higher and more sustainable; the brand is more heavily weighted in these segments than is price. Figure 1-3 provides a checklist of questions that an EMNC can ask itself to guide the selection of which segments and markets to enter.

Keeping these three points in mind, challenger businesses and aspiring EMNCs need to focus on expansion in a step-by-step

- Does the segment or market already have high awareness and knowledge about us?
- Does the segment or market think positively, instead of negatively, of our home country?
- Are our capabilities in line with the potential target segment's desired benefits?
- Are the consumers in this segment or market more likely to try less-known brands?
- Is the segment size significant enough to be worth targeting?
- Is the referral or image value, of these customers and this country, high?
- Is the segment, and number of customers we need to acquire, small enough to fit the resources available?
- Is the segment uncontested or under-served by TMNCs? Do the potential customers have needs and wants we can understand, and serve, better than TMNCs can?
- Is the segment growing or likely to grow rapidly?
- Are brand-building costs here likely to be relatively low?
- Will it be easier here to take advantage of our existing distribution, supply chain, logistics, and management knowledge and capabilities?
- Will we benefit here from cultural similarity, physical proximity, and relationships?

FIGURE 1-3 Segment and Country-Choice Checklist

manner. Given their limited financial and managerial resources, reaching too far or biting off too much has severe consequences, as we saw it did for Titan. Flying below the radar and expanding capabilities sets the stage for the leap into a global branded business strategy, as we saw in the case of Mahindra & Mahindra.

There are lessons to be learned by TMNCs as well. Clearly, TMNCs cannot any longer afford to let aspiring EMNCs gain the scale and skills that today's Haier, Lenovo, HTC, Tata Motors, Mahindra & Mahindra, Arçelik, MTS, and others have acquired. With their lower cost structures, combined with the newly learned capability for lean innovation and branding, these firms can become dangerous competitors in bigger and broader markets. As GE's Jeffrey Immelt has noted, if GE is to be unseated, it will be by one of the new breed of EMNCs. TMNCs should not assume that these EMNCs that start competing in low-price segments in other emerging-market countries will only stay there. As can be seen from our case of Mahindra & Mahindra, and from the stories of ZTE and Huawei mobile phones from China we cited earlier, the long-term game plan for many of these EMNCs is to challenge TMNCs in the higher-priced, branded, developed markets as well. Just as the Japanese brands expanded upward and outward from single low-price entries in the 1950s and 1960s,[22] so too will many of these newer EMNCs in the years to come.

What then should TMNCs do? One clear option is to focus more on emerging markets, and instead of bringing products to those markets that have been designed and developed for the developed markets, spend the resources needed to study emerging-market consumers and, based on those insights, develop products that are more suited for them. The argument that emerging-market volumes are small can be overcome if TMNCs are more willing and able to use their cross-market coordination skills, since these emerging markets today are clearly very large collectively.

Some TMNCS have already understood this. Unilever has recently announced its desire to grow its emerging-market business from an already healthy 52 percent of revenues to over 70 percent. It has, through bitter experience, learned the need to develop emerging-market solutions and today has a portfolio of brands that speak to consumers in these markets, which Unilever leverages across emerging markets all the way from Latin America to Asia. GE too has recognized the need for more focus on emerging-market consumers and their needs and has developed low-cost ultrasonography and ECG machines that are being marketed across emerging markets, offering inexpensive diagnostics in third- and fourth-tier towns, gaining traction and becoming significant businesses. This initiative is not only bringing significant business for GE but also bringing competitive pressure on firms like Mindray of China, which have the potential to morph into very serious global competitors in the medical diagnostic equipment category if left unchecked.

2

Strategic Competency Building

In the Introduction, we saw how EMNCs seemed to be following four types of strategies as they seek to build their global businesses and brands: (1) Cost Leaders, (2) Knowledge Leveragers (leveraging primarily into other emerging markets), (3) Niche Customizers (also entering into other emerging markets), and (4) Global Brand Builders via focused innovation and selective acquisitions. The first two of these four strategies leverage "usual" EMNC home-country strengths of lower labor and manufacturing costs, their knowledge of emerging-market consumer needs, and their ability to identify such segments in international markets; we called this approach mechanistic extension. The last two of these strategies, using what we called dynamic evolution, also require the capability to innovate and to deploy consumer insights in their targeting of which customers' needs to serve.

These capabilities—capabilities that EMNCs need in order to expand internationally—serve as the second dimension of our strategy framework (Figure I-1) and are the focus of this chapter. Clearly, each of these four strategies requires its own enabling competency building of certain types of technologies, products, processes, and business models. Figure 2-1 provides a road map as well as a summary of the key points we discuss in this chapter.

Mechanistic Expansion		Dynamic Evolution	
Cost Leader	**Knowledge Leverager**	**Niche Customizer**	**Global Brand Builder**
• Continually lower manufacturing and assembly labor costs • Innovatively mix labor and capital • Convert fixed and overhead costs to variable costs • Lower raw material and supply chain costs • Lower R&D, distribution, and marketing costs	• Master a narrow but extendable technology • Learn to find other similar-needs markets	• Outlocalize using customer insights • Outcustomize via lower R&D and manufacturing costs and more flexible manufacturing	• High budgetary investments in R&D and technology— sharp focus, aim at growing new disruptive segments • Leverage lower-cost home R&D • Fill key gaps via acquisitions • Create needed organizational culture
		• Build customer insight capabilities	

FIGURE 2-1 Road Map to Strategic Competency Building

Cost Leader Competencies

Clearly, a continuous focus on cost cutting is an imperative if a firm is to become and remain a Cost Leader. We found that Cost Leader EMNCs were innovative in their approach to cost cutting; some managed costs through innovative combinations of labor and capital, compared to their TMNC peers; others innovated in the design process to achieve frugality; still others converted onerous fixed costs into variable costs, allowing for rapid expansion, notwithstanding the financial limitations typical of EMNCs; and, last but not least, Cost Leaders employed cost-cutting innovations throughout the value chain.

Continually Cut Costs, Everywhere

One comparative advantage (at least initially) that EMNCs usually possess is their capacity to compete on the basis of their lower costs and thus lower prices. So it is necessary for them to continue to have the lowest costs. One well-known reason for their low cost, which "comes with the territory," is low labor cost. While labor costs rise as EMNCs grow economically (pay for factory workers in China increased 69 percent between 2005 and 2010), and are likely to keep doing so, labor costs in EMNCs remain low. For instance, the cost of a labor-hour in the automotive industry in 2007 was an order of magnitude lower in emerging economies, compared with that in the developed economies—around $20 per hour versus $2 in India and China.[1]

This provides a significant comparative advantage, particularly in businesses where labor is a significant component of the total cost. As an (unusual) example, when consumers of premium jeans in Western markets began to seek fabrics that bore a pre-washed, pre-worn, and "distressed" look, washing and finishing procedures became an important part of jean manufacture. Mavi jeans from Turkey benefited from these demand trends because such fabrics require labor-intensive individual "aging" by workers using sandpaper and chemicals to produce the needed patina—and Turkish labor, while not the cheapest, was certainly cheaper than in many other supplier countries.[2]

When their own country operations cease to provide the lowest manufacturing costs, EMNCs seek out even lower-cost locations elsewhere for their production, just as TMNCs do. Turkish companies have done this in several industries: appliance manufacturer Arçelik now has a joint venture in China for this purpose, truck manufacturer Temsa has a new plant in Egypt, and denim jeans manufacturer Mavi does some of its sourcing from Asian locations. Even Indian IT providers Wipro and Infosys have, or are seeking, locations that have lower costs than India. So just because an EMNC begins by leveraging its home-country lower-labor-cost base does not mean it is limited to that home-country production location forever.

Importantly, we found that in their focus on costs, EMNCs go well beyond this country-specific labor-cost advantage they possess, as this does not provide any advantage over other EMNC firms and can also be eroded by TMNCs, which can themselves easily source from emerging markets to take advantage of the same low labor cost. EMNCs, we found, were using many other clever, innovative ways of lowering their costs in manufacturing and assembly, procurement of raw materials, R&D, supply chain operations, distribution, and marketing—*all* the elements of the value chain. These initiatives combined the country-specific low-cost-labor advantage with firm-specific capabilities of innovative cost reduction to create a sustainable firm-specific advantage.

Below we describe five particularly innovative ways in which EMNCs were lowering costs.

Mixing Labor and Capital in Innovative Ways to Reduce Cost
Not surprisingly, manufacturing costs are frequently lowered through high volumes of production (economies of scale, such as those of Arçelik, which has over 50 percent of the Turkish appliance market) as well as low labor costs. Turkish tile producer Vitra has much higher-volume throughputs than many of its competitors; thus it can run individual tile designs on individual production lines in larger and lower-cost volumes—"optimal lot sizes"—rather than needing to switch the designs per production line at higher cost. This lowers its costs per tile design considerably.

EMNCs are also able to develop lower manufacturing and assembly cost structures when they combine best-of-breed high technology with their lower labor costs through a systematic reexamination of their manufacturing processes, rather than blind adherence to the so-called best practice as implemented in TMNCs. For example, a recent Booz & Company estimate puts the all-in cost for a blue-collar worker at Tata Motors plants in Pune, India, at $5 an hour, versus $55+ for a U.S. automaker; even though greatly reduced automation means Tata needs 54 labor-hours to assemble a car, three times more than Toyota, this still allows Tata to make cars much more cheaply than TMNC automakers can.[3]

China's BYD substitutes low-cost labor in many steps of its process of manufacturing lithium ion batteries, where its TMNC competitors such as Sony and Toshiba use capital-intensive technology.

BYD is thus able to produce lithium ion batteries of comparable quality to that of its TMNC competitors, but at a lower cost,[4] reducing costs from $40 a battery to less than $12.[5] The result of producing high-quality but lower-cost batteries has led BYD to emerge as the dominant producer of mobile phone lithium ion batteries, a market in which it has an 85 percent market share. BYD has now launched an electric car, leveraging its battery manufacturing capability, at a price substantially lower than that of its competitors. (Indeed, BYD's success has led legendary investor Warren Buffett to acquire a 10 percent stake in BYD. This is not to say that EMNCs do not make mistakes. BYD has recently stumbled in its ambitious sales goals in the car business in China, and it is behind in meeting its electric car goals, according to recent reports.[6])

Using Frugal Design

To keep costs low, EMNCs have been innovative in developing and leveraging their frugal design capabilities. Consider the development of the Tata Nano, the world's cheapest car, which launched in India for a price of US$2,500. To keep costs low and be able to profit from its low-cost entry, Tata Motors developed a design in which components served more than one function. Cost saving, for instance, was achieved by having the horizontal brace that holds the front seats also serve as side-impact protection. Also as a result of this approach, the number of parts needed in the Nano was about 15 to 20 percent less than for a similar vehicle, such as the Renault Logan. Again seeking cost savings, Tata Motors outsourced 85 to 90 percent of the Nano's components using a reverse auction mechanism. Once a vendor was chosen, Tata Motors partnered with it to further reduce cost; thus 75 percent of the Nano's components are from single-source suppliers. The vendors were brought into the design process to come up with cost-saving ideas, such as the Nano's innovative two-cylinder aluminum-cast rear engine, again serving to reduce costs. Every aspect of the car was examined in this process to eliminate cost. The car only has one windshield wiper, no radio, and only three lug nuts to hold the wheel, rather than the traditional four.[7]

The Nano has seen sales drop for a variety of reasons, but it still illustrates the ability of determined EMNCs to innovate in coming up with greatly cost-reduced designs. The Indian slang word for such innovation, driven by scarce resources, is *jugaad*, and this style of innovation is now receiving a lot of attention in management circles worldwide.[8]

Many EMNCs are family-owned conglomerates that operate subsidiaries in multiple industries. Extending the idea of partnering to group companies, some have taken advantage of group companies' capabilities to design low-cost product offerings. Nano manufacturer Tata Motors is part of the Tata Sons holding organization, and its Tata Steel unit helped develop the Nano's engine cradle, which supports the Nano's entire power train. Tata Sons has cross-leveraged its diverse technologies to come out with innovative products such as its water purifier, Tata Swach, at a lower cost than that of its competitors, bringing together its Tata Chemicals and Tata Salt units on this effort. The word *swach* means clean in Hindi. This inexpensive water purifier, aimed at households that may not have electricity, won the top prize in the 2010 *Wall Street Journal*'s Asian innovation awards. Others of our EMNCs leveraged capabilities in one part of their business to innovate in others; for instance, Arçelik leveraged its washing machines know-how to create the "right" amount of foam in its high-end Turkish coffeemakers.

Converting Fixed and Overhead Costs to Variable Costs

The effort to lower costs also goes toward lowering the cost of up-front investments, as EMNCs often do not have the resources to make the necessary up-front investments to take full advantage of the market opportunity. One "outside-the-box" way in which EMNCs have dealt with this lack of capital is to convert fixed costs to variable costs.

WORKING ON THE PROFIT FORMULA

Consider Indian cellular operator Bharti Airtel. A key up-front cost in its business is the initial capital expenditure for installing the network, and it is traditionally paid to the supplier up front. Bharti Airtel did not have the funds necessary to build the network infrastructure in this way, an infrastructure it needed to take full advantage of the area it had been allotted by the government of India. It thus came up with an innovative solution: it outsourced its telecom network operations to Siemens and Ericsson; and rather than paying the typically large up-front fee with annual maintenance payments, a revenue-sharing arrangement was used, with carefully structured win-win incentive clauses, so that fixed-cost capital expenditures were changed into variable-cost annual operating expenditures. This business model innovation allowed Airtel to roll out rapidly in the geography it had been allotted.[9]

The model has benefits beyond converting a traditional fixed cost into variable costs. It also creates a compatibility of incentives between the network manufacturers like Siemens and Ericsson and telecom service providers like Bharti Airtel in terms of accurately forecasting demand, building the optimal capacity infrastructure, maintaining it, and augmenting it as needed, without repeated negotiations, all of which helps reduce costs. It also leads to more efforts in sales and marketing to build the customer base and capacity utilization to ensure that the promised minimum capacity utilization is met. The innovation led Bharti Airtel to dramatically lower its cost per minute, allowing it to offer the lowest per-minute pricing in the industry—and still remain very profitable, with incredible rates of revenue growth.

Bharti Airtel has extended this initial innovation of converting fixed costs to variable costs to other parts of its business: to IT services, retail stores, call centers, and passive infrastructure (cell tower) divisions, all of which it outsources. In September 2010, Bharti Airtel announced an agreement with IBM, very similar to the one it had in India, to manage its IT operations in 16 African countries, where Bharti Airtel had 45 million subscribers through its acquisition of the African businesses of Kuwait-based Zain. Under this reported 10-year contract worth more than $1 billion, IBM will oversee the management of all the technology operations, data center operations, servers, storage and desktop services, etc., once again allowing Bharti to lower its costs, and prices, for its per-minute phone call charges.[10]

Lowering Raw Material and Supply Chain Costs

The effort to cut costs affects every component of the supply chain. Firms for which raw materials are an important cost component look at this carefully and have developed the capability to extract maximum cost savings. Firms such as Asian Paints, Tata Tea, Natura, and Godrej, for whom raw materials are a significant cost component, have developed the capability to locate low-cost but high-quality suppliers and to create long-term relationships with them to reduce costs. Tata Tea, for instance, reduced the cost of its herbal infusions in Europe by acquiring a brand there (Jemča) with strong supplier relationships and then entering into long-term, low-cost supply contracts with that supplier. Natura was able to have significant cost savings during the currency crisis in Argentina by similarly agreeing on long-term supplier contracts. These firms also centralize buying to get the best possible costs, and some use innovative mechanisms like reverse auctions, as we saw with Tata Motors, to ensure the best possible prices.

Several of our EMNCs use vertical integration to lower their input costs. Thus Ulker, since flour variety and quality are crucial to its food business, owns flour mills to make its specialized flour products (and owns oil mills as well). However, vertical integration does not always yield the lowest-cost inputs, if one's own input facilities are not always the most efficient. So companies like Temsa build their trucks using components from multiple suppliers. They have developed their own design capability to mix and match components from various suppliers, as costs fluctuate, to yield the lowest-cost finished products (trucks and coaches). This enables them to achieve lower-cost production compared with that of their more vertically integrated European competitors such as MAN and Mercedes.

Lowering Distribution, R&D, and Marketing Costs

Some EMNCs seem particularly aggressive in using new IT capabilities to lower their distribution costs and improve efficiencies in distribution. Apollo Tyres uses IT aggressively to better service its tire dealers, carefully managing the stock levels of its numerous winter, summer, and all-year tire SKUs. To lower its R&D costs, Brazilian cosmetics EMNC Natura has found innovative ways to partner with university talent, rather than doing everything in-house. It uses an "open-innovation" model in which, in addition to its own internal R&D in Brazil and France (on which it spends 3 percent of sales), it partners with universities and research centers in Brazil and other countries to cofund equipment and project costs, as well as to obtain licenses for relevant patents and technologies (such as antiaging and antiaging-sign ingredients used in its Ekos Pariparoba and Chronos Passiflora lines). Haier too used university R&D, licensed from MIT, in developing its "no-tail," completely wireless TV sets launched in 2010, which use wireless power technology to get rid of video, audio, signal, network, and power cables—a world's first.[11]

Marketing costs can be lowered, too, in innovative ways; details of these are presented in Chapter 6 on the building of brand awareness. That chapter provides information about the "no-money marketing" tactics used by Wipro's then CMO, Jessie Paul, to build brand awareness at very low cost among very narrowly targeted audiences.[12] Lenovo's ex-CMO Deepak Advani told us how, instead of buying TV time in the United States through the traditional up-front or scatter buy systems, Lenovo instead bought greatly discounted—but still well-targeted—remnant time slots using Google's auction-based system.

When you are fighting for every penny of margin, every penny of cost counts, anywhere and everywhere in your entire cost structure.

Knowledge Leverager Competencies

For the Knowledge Leveragers, which expand existing products to geographically new but similar-in-needs markets, needed competencies include (1) the mastery of a narrow technology or skill set and (2) the ability to identify other markets where the EMNCs can win.

Master a Narrow but Extendable Technology

Mahindra Tractors focuses on the large (and geographically dispersed) segment of the market that wants tractors with engines of under 100-horsepower capacity, because that's where it has the design and engineering capability. Customers needing such tractors live not only in other emerging markets, but also on small hobby farms in the United States, as noted in Chapter 1. Mahindra Tractors has built a strong business and brand among these customers because of its mastery of designing and manufacturing rugged and reliable small tractors.

Mahindra & Mahindra, building from its expertise in manufacturing Jeeps and Jeep-like vehicles—the company has assembled and built Willys Jeeps since 1947—focuses on the specialized UV and SUV categories, going after customers who want functional vehicles at "honest" prices, not just in other emerging markets but also in parts of Southern Europe and now in Australia and the United States. Tata Motor's Ravi Kant told us quite clearly that its export strategy was to do a better job building vehicles that were competitively superior in the tough-and-cheap needs of other emerging markets. For Asian Paints, its competitive strength is a deep understanding of the issues surrounding paints applied in emerging-market conditions—climates, modes of application—and so that domain has become its technology forte. Temsa limits its focus to buses and coaches, not just for the Middle East and North Africa but also for Western Europe.

Such technology specialization is, in effect, creating economies of scale for these companies in those narrow areas—*narrow in*

technology but wide in their geographic or product applicability.
For India's Godrej and Marico, being the world's expert in black
hair and in pre-wash and post-wash hair care may be narrow in
product scope terms, compared with what P&G and Unilever can
manage, but it still leaves billions of people they can go after.

Value for Money
Because EMNCs are able to leverage their deep knowledge of
what it takes to succeed in their own home markets and their cost
advantages, one such targeted area of technical expertise, not surprisingly, is in the ability to create superior "value-for-money"
offerings. As discussed in Chapter 1, the EMNC auto companies we studied compete and win among those customers seeking not only rugged, durable vehicles and functional benefits, but
also lower life-cycle costs of ownership. Building products that can
be bought—and operated—cheaply is naturally an area in which
many EMNCs have expertise and credibility.

Having said this, it must also be noted that these EMNCs also
deliberately try to stay out of the very low end of their markets, a
point made to us by Haier USA, Tata Tea, and Godrej (see Chapter 1 on segment choice). And when EMNCs such as Asia Pacific
Breweries, Arçelik, and Midea do play in the really low end, they
use brand architecture carefully to launch separate brands for
the really low end, so as to not damage the brand equity of their
higher-priced offerings (see Chapter 7 on brand architecture).

Learn to Find Other Similar-Needs Markets
Aside from having low costs and mastery over a narrow technology or skill set, Knowledge Leverager EMNCs need to be able
to identify other—geographically different—markets where this
mastery can help them win. This is usually obvious, as Chapter 1
on segment and country choice showed: other emerging markets
are a natural choice for Asian Paints, Bajaj Auto, Dabur, Marico,
Temsa, and others. At other times, it is not obvious, such as the

discovery by Mahindra Group companies, Mahindra & Mahindra and Mahindra Tractors of the slices of the developed markets that would fit them too. Thus Knowledge Leverager EMNCs need to be able to understand and identify consumer groups that have needs similar to the consumer segments served at home, using the types of "consumer insight" we discuss toward the end of this chapter.

The competencies we discussed above—low-cost capabilities, mastery over an extendable technology, and customer-segment identification skills—are a necessity for those EMNCs and challenger businesses seeking to expand internationally in a mechanistic expansion manner. However, those EMNCs and challenger businesses desiring to follow the more sophisticated and difficult dynamic evolution growth strategies, in essence those of Niche Customizers and Global Brand Builders, also need to acquire additional, more sophisticated, skills. These more sophisticated capabilities include focused innovation, flexible manufacturing, and customer insight-generation capabilities.

Niche Customizer Competencies

As any textbook on global business or global marketing strategies will tell you, for most TMNCs the name of the game is selling huge volumes, wringing out economies of scale by ruthless global standardization (or near standardization). Naturally, this advantage of TMNCs means that some lower-volume, idiosyncratic local needs of consumers are not catered to as well by these TMNCs. It makes little economic sense for TMNCs to do so: the extra costs of localizing, for small incremental volumes, are outweighed greatly by the benefits of higher-volume, lower-cost, global standardization.

Outlocalize Using Customer Insight

What this TMNC strategy means is that it leaves open, for those entrepreneurial EMNCs that have good insight into customer needs (see the section below), market spaces in which they can win by outlocalizing these large TMNC competitors. Often, but not always, these market spaces are in other "peripheral" emerging markets, in which consumer needs (and maybe even distribution channel needs) are often different from those in the developed-market "economic center." The volumes may be too small to interest the large Western MNC players, but are sufficient for many EMNCs when such markets are aggregated together.

Examples of such insight-utilizing outlocalization abound in our data. The climate in much of Africa is very hot in the summer, so many Western chocolate brands melt in that heat. Turkey's Ulker developed a chocolate-biscuit product in which the chocolate sits inside the biscuit, which makes it melt less and makes the melting less of an issue for consumers when they eat it. Titan of India knows that Muslims wash their hands and arms before performing their Namaz prayers five times a day, which means their watches are likely to get splashed by water; and so superior waterproofing is an especially important attribute, one that Titan emphasizes in its Middle Eastern markets. India's Marico understands well some special needs of its Middle Eastern Islamic customers and creates hair gels for them that do not contain any alcohol. Moreover, Marico also understands that there is much higher chlorine content in the local water in these geographies and thus offers hair products that wash and lather well in such higher-chlorine water. Haier has gained U.S. market entry by creating innovative, high-quality offerings in niche areas such as compact refrigerators and wine fridges, and, today, half-keg beer dispensers and portable clothes washers, that no competitor realized had such demand. It also markets compact refrigerators for the student market that have locks for their dorm-room locations, and a washing machine without an agitator, which makes for larger loads and gentler washing and costs 40 percent less than a similar Whirlpool model.

Many other examples of EMNCs applying customer insight for market-winning localization appear in published research. LG, recognizing that power fluctuations were common in Indian households, leading to often-dim indoor light, developed a TV set with "golden eye" technology to adjust the TV screens' brightness and contrast accordingly (and came with circuits that resisted these dramatic voltage fluctuations). They also launched for cricket-obsessed India a television set with a built-in cricket video game. TV sets for rural Indian markets offered menus in India's 20+ major local languages.[13] For highly polluted Indian cities, it developed air conditioners with especially powerful air filtration systems. For Russia, it launched a hot-and-cold air conditioner for year-round use, a karaoke machine that comes with a library of popular Russian folksongs, and a microwave oven designed to meet the special needs of Russian homes. *To make all this customization possible, LG uses a deep network of local R&D facilities staffed with local experts.*[14] Unlike TMNCs, which are cutting back and closing their local R&D centers, albeit with their mostly "applied R&D" focus, EMNCs are opening R&D centers closer to customers in their important strategic markets. In our view, these localized R&D investments may separate winners from losers in the near future.

Outcustomize with Lower R&D and Manufacturing Costs

In addition, standardization-obsessed TMNCs are often simply not interested in creating too many customized local versions of their global products. But EMNCs, which often own their own design and manufacturing facilities (unlike the TMNCs, which often outsource their production to EMNC subcontractors), are more able, and more willing, to undertake such customization and localization, since it costs them less to do so. Mitac from Taiwan knows that personal navigation devices in differing national markets often have locally preferred feature sets (such as direct TV reception in South Korea). Because it has low-cost R&D and manufacturing capabilities to do so, Mitac designs and manufactures many such localized versions, more than its competitors, Garmin and Tom-Tom, are able to offer. These EMNCs are better able to do such customization than their TMNC competitors because they have the facilities, skills, and low-cost personnel to do it more easily and faster and at a lower cost.

In fact, this relatively greater inability and unwillingness to customize is not just a characteristic of large Western MNCs, but can even exist for larger EMNCs. Thus Haier (we were told by a competitor) did not look favorably upon the small-volume requests of air-conditioning distributors in certain smaller African countries; as a result, such distributors went to Chigo, a smaller Chinese manufacturer, instead. Chigo not only gladly accepted their smaller orders, but also helped them with their marketing efforts, such as designing their logos and brochures for free.

Now, for this lower-volume, more customized and localized strategy to pay off, EMNCs that practice it need to have a business model that fits. This means they need (1) cost structures that are low, in order to make money on smaller-volume orders and versions; (2) the design and technical capabilities to create these customized versions of their products; and (3) the ability to manufacture small volumes profitably, by having manufacturing systems that allow for quick changeovers of the physical setup and material routing, the parts or machines used, the production schedules and quantities, and even the operating instructions: so-called flexible (or agile, or reconfigurable) manufacturing systems. Whereas in developed countries these usually require, among other aspects, high degrees of automation and computer-reprogrammable controls, EMNCs may need to innovatively develop less capital-intensive ways of accomplishing these same goals.

Leveraging lower-cost labor while judiciously investing in cutting-edge technology can give EMNCs such flexibility at lower cost. Thus, United Distilleries of India, today the world's third largest purveyor of alcoholic beverages, is able to produce over 3,000 SKUs at a competitive cost—many more SKUs than the two market leaders, Diageo and Pernod-Ricard—enabling it to serve local tastes better. Its flexibility comes from using cheap labor to achieve low-cost, fast changeovers on production lines, which, combined with its use of cutting-edge technology in manufacturing, enables United Distilleries to maintain a consistent and high quality. Vitra's Onanç told us about how Vitra lowered production costs per SKU for its tile business. "Earlier, our acquired brand used small-volume production runs, in factories that were small and in different locations. Each time a production line has to be stopped to change tile colors, designs and materials, there can be considerable breakage, errors, sub-optimal results, and required fine tuning, which create costs for the company. Changing production for each SKU brought extra costs and extra waste. So they used to work with high-stock and high-cost. However, Vitra's production is very flexible, with much more automation, better factory management, and lower labor costs, enabling us to cut down the costs in half."

Mavi too is able to leverage its lower labor costs to offer an extremely large variety of sizes and designs, adapted to each country, called its "Perfect Fit" strategy. Natura lowers its new product testing costs by not doing formal, expensive new product launches. Instead, it releases new products and marketing initiatives continually and quickly to its direct sales force—10 new things every 21 days—and sees which ones get high consumer interest. Not only does this procedure save money; it creates a talking point for the sales consultants, which increases their productivity, while at the same time saving a lot of testing time.

Competencies for Global Brand Builders via Focused Innovation

While EMNCs often enter via low-cost positions and the Cost Leaders keep relying on these cost advantages, the Niche Customizers and Global Brand Builders need to develop the capability we called *focused innovation* in the Introduction. Whatever the market entry route taken, if an EMNC wishes eventually to market higher-quality, higher-priced products, it needs more than the low-cost story that is its door-opening calling card. Especially in businesses that are, or could easily become, very commoditized, this is the only way to survive long term.

The different trajectories of Lenovo and Acer illustrate this point. Lenovo's ex-CMO Deepak Advani has been quoted as saying, "The brand essence of Lenovo is innovation that makes a difference to customers."[15] Lenovo continues to innovate, launching its ultrathin, ultrasmall, wide-screen U260 Thinkpad notebook against the Macbook Air in 2011[16] and launching Windows 7 laptops that boot up 20 seconds faster than competitive models.[17] In early 2011, Lenovo's global market share exceeded 10 percent, and it was growing at over 14 percent annually (versus Dell's 4 percent rate).[18] Though Acer's market share is still slightly higher than Lenovo's, it has focused much more on a low-price strategy and spends only 0.4 percent on R&D; without a compelling product story, it has been struggling much more than Lenovo with declining PC sales. "If Acer thinks they can win customers in the changing PC market [just] by competitive pricing, it's not going to happen," according to an HSBC analyst.[19]

To successfully execute such a focused innovation strategy, we find several cases of EMNCs upgrading their R&D, design, technology, and innovation capabilities through organic (internal) means, acquisitions, partnerships, and joint venture deals. Competing with several other Android OS- and app-using smartphone players (such as Samsung and Motorola), HTC continued to build up the distinctive capabilities that keep it a step ahead in smartphone user-experience quality by acquiring two more mobile software companies in February 2011 (Saffron Digital and OnLive), which will enable it to deliver more "optimized video content" and provide a better gaming experience on its phones.[20] Five months later, it agreed to purchase U.S. graphics-technology firm S3 Graphics for US$300 million to enhance the multimedia capabilities of its phones. Then in August 2011 it acquired a majority stake in Beats Electronics, makers of Dr. Dre high-end headphones, to improve the sound quality of its phones.[21] HTC's revenues in 2011 were more than twice those in 2010.[22] HTC's innovation capabilities are evidenced not only in its world-leading new products, but also in its very rapid pace of new product rollouts, echoing the strategy of constant innovation used by Korean EMNCs LG and Samsung.[23]

This "upgrading of technical capability" is for such EMNCs a deliberate, long-term, strategic decision, born of—and creating— a vision and ambition to become high-capability global players. As Mahindra & Mahindra's Arun Nanda said to us, around 2002 Mahindra & Mahindra took upon itself a four-wheeler strategy to become the number one or number two player in a carefully targeted business, rugged SUVs. This "involved innovation and globalization; it was an aspiration. Prior to that we were doing incremental products. Around 2002 the Mahindra Scorpio product came out; this was our own product, which we had developed from scratch. It gave us tremendous confidence that we could become a global player in a small way; it gave us confidence that we knew how to make it, and attack global markets in a consistent manner."

The strategic decision to upgrade one's innovation capability is often led by visionary founders, as we heard from Haier, HTC, Lenovo, Ranbaxy, Ulker, and others. Ulker's Cafer Findikoğlu told us, "Our leader always advises us, 'Everybody can read and do what is written in the books.' What can we do beyond this to add value to our development? This is called 'competitive advantage.' Innovation and creating a competitive advantage have become of more importance in Turkey. We are always running after that. It gives us the opportunity to open new horizons and to be the leader in the places we go."

Building R&D and Technology Capabilities

What does it take to create such a successful innovation capability? Clearly, among other things, it requires investing resources in R&D capabilities—facilities, people, and organizational culture. It requires superior abilities to spot trends and understand latent needs and to create an idea-nurturing and -rewarding environment, with such ideas coming from in-company inventors, teams, and labs; from other companies, "crowd sourcing," sales personnel, and customers; from processes that efficiently manage and prioritize among multiple projects; and from successful new product forecast, test, and launch (commercialization) capabilities. And it requires the ability to identify the specific market areas in which that R&D effort can create the most customer value with the maximum competitive impact. We turn to these issues below.

Determination — and Budgetary Investments

Many of our EMNCs told us about this strategic, deliberate focus on R&D investments to build their "organic" ability to compete in higher tiers of their chosen product markets. As a result of its long-term strategic decision in the mid-1990s to invest very heavily in R&D, Samsung Electronics has now become second only to IBM in the number of U.S. patents it wins every year (in 2010, it won 4,551 patents versus IBM's 5,896).[24] On a much smaller scale, Arçelik established R&D efforts in the early 1990s, leading to its own unique designs, in part because its license agreements with European companies such as Bosch had clauses forbidding Arçelik to sell those goods in Europe. Thus it was forced to produce its own designs in order to sell to these countries. Today Arçelik believes it can count state-of-the-art technology as one of its core competitive strengths, reflected in its 2002 slogan, "Arçelik Means Novelty." A similar situation applied to Bajaj Automotive in India, which was forced by changes in government regulations in 1971 to terminate its licensing alliance with the Italian two-wheeler manufacturer Piaggio, owner of the Vespa brand, and to begin technology development itself. (It also allied with Kawasaki 10 years later when Indian government rules changed again.)[25]

Haier's CEO Zhang Ruimin too is determined that Haier not be just a low-cost commodity manufacturer and instead create innovative, differentiated products, built on local customer insights (see the section below on customer insight capabilities). Among Haier's innovations are washing machines that operate without detergent or water; another example is refrigerators that do not need compressors.[26] Haier's corporate culture stresses and rewards creativity and innovation in both products and processes; in 1996, it actually developed washing machines that farmers could use to wash sweet potatoes and other produce![27] Tata Motors now has six design centers in four countries and uses some of the world's most advanced testing equipment. Turkish bus and coach producer Temsa set up a Marmara Research Centre in Gebze in 2005, as an independent company, to give its employees independence from daily production pressure. Its 200 employees work full-time on Temsa's new and current products, raw materials, and alternative fuels projects. Turkey's Ulker food company invested in R&D to become the first to produce "transfat-free," unsaturated oil in Turkey.

It goes without saying that the innovation needed can come not only from the "product" side but also from the services or back-end processes side. Marico has developed a "Mi-net" system to better monitor retailer inventory so it can better maintain pipeline levels and decrease stock-outs. First developed for the Indian market, this system captures real-time transaction and stock-level information from most of its dealers and distributors. Aramex realized it couldn't compete with FedEx, UPS, and DHL—and set prices at their premium levels—until it acquired its own online shipment and tracking systems; so in 2004, it invested in its "InfoAxis" system to replace the Airborne Express "FOCUS" system it originally relied on.

Naturally, investing in such deliberate and large-scale innovation capabilities requires large investments in R&D spending. According to Bain & Company, the top 1,000 innovation spenders in the world in 2009 spent, on average, about 3.5 percent of their sales revenues on R&D. (These percentages are the highest in the pharmaceutical and software and related technology sectors, between 15 and 20 percent of sales). Patent-winner leaders like IBM and Samsung spent about 5 to 6 percent of sales each on R&D, as did 3M. Clearly, any company seeking to win through new and improved products and processes needs to be willing to spend considerable amounts on R&D: human talent, knowledge, teams, tools, structures, and processes.[28]

LG is one company in our EMNC sample that spends a lot on R&D every year. In LG's Michael Ahn's words, "We spend 4% of our turnover on R&D. With our 100 billion turnover this means 4 billion dollars a year. Our competitors copy us in six months in cell phones and in one year in home appliances. Keeping distance from competitors for six months is enough, as our R&D enables us to introduce new models every six months." Haier Europe CEO Rene Aubertin told us that Haier too spends about 4 percent of its sales on R&D; a 2003 book claimed a figure of 6 percent.[29] HTC is perhaps an extreme case, spending about 7 percent of its sales on R&D and having 25 percent of its employees working in that area. This percentage, however, is not unusually high for its industry; RIM too spends about 7 percent, Samsung Electronics spends almost 6 percent, while Nokia and Microsoft both spend about 14 to 15 percent of their sales on R&D, according to Bain's statistics. HTC's CMO John Wang told us that HTC also benefits greatly from its partnerships with Microsoft and Qualcomm, born of its "largest-customer" status (which is a consequence of its specialization strategy, see above).

Most other EMNCs told us they were spending less on R&D, however, typically 2 to 3 percent of sales. Naturally, when this smaller percentage is applied to their much smaller (compared with that of TMNCs) sales base, their total R&D investments can look puny. (Bain's 2010 numbers show 94 percent of the world's total spending on R&D to be taking place in North America, Europe, and Japan, and only 1 percent in India and China combined.) Even if you make adjustments for currency "purchasing power parity" and their lower R&D human talent costs (about which we have more to say below), it would seem that EMNCs can never outinnovate the TMNCs they compete against. So is innovation a hopeless cause and a losing strategy for EMNCs? We think not, for four reasons.

Focusing R&D Investments. For innovation investments to have an impact on marketplace results, the products and processes they lead to must not only be novel (original, unexpected), but also lead to useful benefits to targeted consumers.[30] Motorola Mobility's CEO Jha was recently quoted as saying "innovation itself is not enough—I sometimes call that corporate entertainment. Lots of things in [American] corporations are done in the name of innovation. It's wasted money unless it solves consumer problems. . . . It has to be unique *and* relevant . . . Very often, innovation is associated with being unique. Unique is not enough."[31]

Bain & Company's 2010 data and analysis also make the point very clearly that there is no significant correlation between innovation spending and financial performance: it is not how much you spend on innovation that matters, but how and where you spend it. Is it tightly aligned with overall corporate strategy? Is it aimed at meeting consumer and customer needs; is it based on an insightful reading of market and technology trends? Apple, widely regarded as the most innovative company around (and rated so in Bain & Company's survey), spends under 3 percent of its sales on R&D. Microsoft spends 15 percent, Nokia 14 percent, RIM 7 percent. Apple spent less on R&D during the entire 2000–2010 decade than Microsoft spent on R&D in the single year of 2010![32] Yet Apple's R&D and innovation spending are much more tightly focused on the one corporate goal that has led to its incredible market and financial success: building a deep understanding of end-user needs, so that it can create a user experience, through hardware, software, and user-interface design, that blows everyone else away. And these efforts are usually focused on one major update of its iPhone, or iPad, or Mac, every year. Nor does market-impacting innovation have to be patent-winning radical breakthroughs; it can consist of incremental changes as well. Apple barely makes the list of top 50 patent winners, winning 563 patents in 2010.[33]

The lesson for EMNCs and other under-resourced challengers, we believe, is that there is still hope to win through innovation *as long as (a) enough investments are made in it, (b) the efforts are tightly focused for maximum impact and are aimed at insight-utilizing ways rather than scattershot, and (c) the innovations leverage existing strengths.* Such focus and specialization in innovation is both more realistic and more feasible, allowing greater depth and leadership albeit in a narrower domain.

For HTC, this meant focusing on smartphones—*before* they became mainstream—and within that those with the Android (before it became big) and Windows Media OS. For Ranbaxy, it has meant investing not in new patented molecule discovery but in the development of drug delivery systems, such as patented technologies in oral controlled-release systems, allowing patients to take one daily large-dosage pill instead of several smaller ones. (Ranbaxy was even able to license this, for ciproflaxin, to Bayer AG for $65 million in up-front fees plus royalties on ongoing sales.)[34] For Godrej, such specialization has meant a focus on hair dye, and on powder-form technology. For Dabur, it is its herbal platforms; for Natura, cosmetics focusing R&D around a core of sustainably exploiting and extracting active ingredients from Brazil's biodiversity; for Marico, pre-wash and post-wash hair care. For Arçelik, this meant producing the most energy-efficient washer in the world in an effort to be "Respecting the World, Respected by the World."

Aim at Small but Growing, "Disruptive," New Segments. Such focused, specialized technology buildups also yield more market impact if they aim at (or create) "disruptive" strategic opportunities: technologically different areas of the market that are small currently—thus ignored by incumbent leaders—but show promise of rapid growth. As an example of going where the growth is: when it entered the North American market for washing machines in 2002, LG chose to do so via the front-loading category, then under 10 percent of the market, because of the higher growth rates (and premium) pricing there.[35] At an even more fundamental level, both LG and Samsung have capitalized on the technology "convergence" trends that today are bringing together the analog and digital worlds, an intersection where the two firms have long been focused, enabling them to use their integrated, crossover competencies, developed over the years, to bring new products to market that their narrower "old-world" competitors simply cannot. Using these competencies, they have been able to deliver on technology upgrade cycles and new product launch schedules that their competitors struggle to match.

Apple is another great example of creating disruptive new products: its iPhone, with its "apps" model, completely changed how smartphones were used, and its iPad, through its new tablet form factor, attacked laptops from a completely new direction. But in order to create or take advantage of such disruptive opportunities, EMNCs and similar challengers need to build up top-notch competencies in *consumer and market insight*, a topic that we return to below.

Leveraging Lower-Cost Home-Based Scientific Talent (Bang for the Buck). Many of our EMNCs take advantage of the lower-than-TMNC compensation costs of local design and engineering talent to partially compensate for their smaller R&D budgets. A Ph.D. employee definitely costs less in India than in Western nations, we were told by Ranbaxy, allowing the company to work on the necessary chemistry at a fraction of the cost in the West; many of Ranbaxy's scientists are actually foreign trained, returning to work in India because of the greater challenges involved. According to one recent report, India's scientists and engineers can earn less than 10 percent of what their peers do in Europe and the United States (leading to more investment of R&D budgets in emerging markets by many TMNCs such as Nestle, Bristol-Myers Squibb, DuPont, and General Motors).[36] HTC has strategically chosen to develop its own proprietary, easier-to-use TouchFlo and Sense user interface by setting up its own design studios in Taiwan—and Seattle. Similar stories were told by Mitac and others.

Filling Key Technology Gaps via Acquisitions. Several of the companies we interviewed have selectively used acquisitions to overcome technology gaps or build up technology leads; we discussed HTC's several acquisitions in the opening paragraphs of this section. Mitac bought Brunswick, one of its OEM customers, in part to gain access to GPS map engine technology. Apollo Tyres bought Dunlop Tires' Africa business in large part to become more capable in the radial tire business. Tata Tea gained tea blending and international brand-building skills through its acquisition of Tetley Tea. Tata Motors gained access to the medium- and large-truck designs of Daewoo Trucks and to the engineers of Jaguar via acquisitions of those two firms, and it acquired an 80 percent stake in Italian styling and design firm Trilix Srl in October 2010.

Others have chosen to selectively hire foreign technologists or engineers, such as Ulker, or enter into partnerships or joint venture agreements with other firms, such as did Chigo with its German partner. HTC built up its innovation capabilities through its hiring of Horace Luke, Microsoft's Xbox designer, and the other "wizards" in its "magic labs."

Creating the Needed Organizational Culture

Building a business around innovation requires more than hiring (or acquiring) lots of designers and spending more on R&D; it also requires creating and fostering an organizational culture of innovation. At HTC, CEO Peter Chou has created a work culture similar to that of a Northern California start-up, encouraging collaboration and open challenge in equal measure, so that innovation is rapid paced and exacting.[37] Haier promotes a culture of "Haier speed," of developing and bringing new products into the market at the fastest possible speed.[38]

Wipro makes huge efforts to build a culture of innovation. Its core values—which were developed with the leadership of the chairman, Azim Premji, and with inputs from a wide spectrum of employees—enshrine innovation; importantly, Wipro focuses on innovation that is valuable to its current and future customers.

To promote an internal culture around innovation, Wipro not only hires many people with a hard-core engineering background, but assigns them to R&D projects in areas such as semiconductor and chip design. Wipro has an internal Innovation Council, functioning like an internal venture capital firm, which employees can approach to get up to three years of time (if intermediate targets are met) to work on their own ideas. Around 800 Wipro people are working on such projects. "Our DNA is more oriented towards the engineering, technical way of life," Wipro's Jessie Paul told us. "It helps that many of the senior people at Wipro themselves come from an R&D background."

Wipro also offers innovation awards to its clients and encourages employees to report on the innovations that they have helped their clients achieve. Finally, the firm also honors leading innovators, including competitors, at an annual innovation awards event.[39] All these elements collectively focus on and continually remind, reinforce, and reward a culture of innovation, ensuring its internalization.

The Importance of Customer Insight

We mentioned earlier in this chapter the importance of strong "market insight" capabilities. For the Niche Customizers, strong market insight capabilities allow them to finely tailor product and service offerings to meet consumer needs better than can be done by a more standardized TMNC offering. To Global Brand Builders, it is such insight that tells them where—toward which customer needs—to focus their R&D and innovation efforts.

As discussed in the previous section, Apple gets tremendous value from its relatively low levels of R&D spending because it has the abilities to truly, deeply understand what its targeted consumers' frustrations and latent needs are with mobile computing devices—so that it can deploy its designers and technologies in a laser-focused way to improving its users' experience with its products and services. Superior objective quality and tighter quality control mean little if they do not speak to real consumer needs (and are consistent with the desired brand positioning). Thus, quality (and quality control) efforts must be expended only in directions that consumers really use to judge quality, in the touch points that really matter.

The precise meaning of *high quality* obviously varies with the nature of the product category, customer segment, and even geography. Creating high quality only begins with performance or reliability and durability attributes of the product; it usually goes beyond intrinsic, physical product attributes into the realms of customer service, delivery, financing, and warranty, or even hedonic, sensory, or imagery attributes. Figuring out what your target-segment customers want and need is not always an easy task: it requires the creation of the types of consumer insight capabilities discussed below.

For telecom operator MTS, such insight led it to focus not only on high-technical-quality service networks but also on a very high-quality retail experience and monthly bills that are timely and accurate. MTS relies on a thorough process of understanding the various drivers of customer satisfaction to decide where to focus its money and time. To achieve this type of in-depth understanding of consumer needs, EMNCs need not only R&D labs and teams of white-coated technicians, but also market research and customer insight staff—who live in, or travel frequently to, the markets where their customers live and who thoroughly analyze customer and market data.

Based on insights from such teams, Modelo's U.S. beers are lighter, more "drinkable," than European competitors', recognizing the taste preferences of its U.S. consumers. Asian Paints develops a wide range of coatings and paint applications that are better suited to emerging-market construction environments than their competitors'. Tata Tea creates localized breakthrough ready-to-drink tea drinks to better meet local needs. The insight-leveraging examples of Titan watches in the Middle East (adding greater water resistance to their watches) and Marico, also in the Middle East (counteracting the high chlorine content of the regional water), have already been mentioned. Godrej leverages the insight that hair colors usually require users to mix together in a bowl the chemical materials from two packages (such as a tube and a bottle), creating an impression of chemical artificiality. However, since its own powder products only require the addition of water, they seem more "natural" rather than "chemical," an advantage that it played up in its marketing. For Ulker, using liquid milk, instead of the powder used by competitors in their ice cream, enhances the customers' perception of the taste and nutrition of Ulker's ice cream.

Building Customer Insight Competencies

What does it take for a company to understand in such depth what consumers mean when they say they seek "high quality"? What does it take for a company to understand consumers' latent unmet needs and the signals and cues that consumers use to judge quality (see Chapter 6 on building quality perceptions)? Most companies (and their research and agency partners) are reasonably skilled in conducting both qualitative and quantitative market research of the more traditional variety: focus groups, in-depth interviews, market research surveys using questionnaires, with the data then analyzed through sophisticated multivariate techniques (regression, factor, and cluster analyses, for instance). Getting deeper insight into the hidden needs that can lead to out-of-the-box product and service features, however, often requires (1) more creative types of "ethnographic" research, in which consumers are observed using products and (2) in-depth and in-home work with lead users and user communities. The goal is to identify the "pain points" and "delight creators" that consumers do not themselves recognize and have difficulty articulating.[40] It also requires an enhanced organizational ability to gather, share, and use decision-relevant customer insights through intraorganizational and interorganizational networks: integrating data from different sales, marketing, product development, and customer service sources (connecting the dots) and collaborating better with outside insights partners.[41]

Many EMNCs initially learn about overseas local markets from their partnerships with OEMs and trade channel partners, their joint venture alliances, and their locally hired managers. Thus their sources of local market insight can include the following six avenues, the first three of which are self-explanatory:

1. Manufacturing for local OEM and private label customers; Apollo Tyres and LG Electronics are examples of this.
2. Hiring local staff, an avenue chosen, for example, by Asian Paints and LG Electronics.
3. Acquiring, or forming joint ventures with, local companies, utilizing their knowledge of local markets; a case in point is Midea's acquisitions in Brazil.
4. Using trade partners as information sources, as done by Midea and Chigo. Haier USA's Michael Jemal emphasized to us the importance of having good local partners, those with deep knowledge of local customer needs. LG Electronics's first CEO in India, K. R. Kim, spent endless days talking to dealers and customers to better understand the needs of the trade and end customers in India.[42] In Europe, LG sent teams of key personnel to observe customers shopping for durable white goods at retail outlets and also to talk to big-box retailers to acquire customer insight as the company prepared to ramp up its efforts.

Over time, however, the stronger EMNCs we studied developed their own internal, local capabilities for customer and market knowledge and insight. These include:

5. Forming locally based multidisciplinary research teams. LG discovered that its Korean-designed appliances weren't quite meeting the needs of its American customers, and so it set up its local market insight ("product planning") offices in New Jersey in 2003. There, it assembled experts from disciplines as varied as sociology, food science, kitchen design, home building, and consumer research to identify relevant consumer trends and segments and uncover unmet needs. It discovered there was a need for—and created in response—an innovative three-door design with better space utilization and consumer ease of use than the competition offered, which

became its very successful turnaround in the refrigerator category. It also learned that some customers wanted shiny black refrigerators with shiny knobs. Refrigerators, and washers, with cabinet colors of wild cherry, navy blue, and shiny black were very successful, as were refrigerators with built-in Internet connections and TV sets. LG also videotaped U.S. customers using their kitchens. These candid videos provided LG with the knowledge that customers open the fridge compartment 85 percent of the time and the freezer compartment only 15 percent of the time, leading first to the bottom-mount freezer and then later to the three-door fridge with the bottom-mount freezer.[43]

6. Creating locally based design and development centers. Haier's R&D personnel, in talking to U.S. customers, discovered that they liked to consume ice cream from freezers that was soft rather than hard; it developed a freezer with a separate compartment to keep ice cream at a slightly warmer temperature.[44] To garner such insights, Haier has established several local design and development centers in its overseas markets, staffed with local designers, to develop more market-responsive innovations. In Japan, Haier launched a compact washing machine for washing pet clothing, and in the United Kingdom, it introduced a refrigerator with upscale top lighting and a contoured wine rack.[45]

Summary and Key Takeaways

To summarize, what we are seeing now is that many EMNCs are choosing to compete not just on the basis of lower-cost manufacturing advantages. They are also developing and deploying new capabilities that were previously associated largely with TMNCs. These include leadership (or parity) in important (if narrow) technological areas, an emphasis on innovative products and processes, and the ability to understand deeply customer and consumer needs (using "insight"). These new capabilities are then combined with their lower costs of R&D and customized manufacturing to create potent and dangerous competition for the established TMNCs—not through a broad-scale frontal assault, but through narrow-slice attacks that have the potential to become, over time, wider and more problematic. TMNCs that thought that EMNCs could only compete on low-cost strategies need to rethink their game plans for the future. If EMNCs can now also innovate on the customer-benefit side, leveraging their lower cost of R&D, what changes must TMNCs themselves make?

Implications for TMNCs

The old TMNC model was one of taking advantage of economies of scale through large, globally standardized R&D and manufacturing outputs—physically located in the developed triad countries—and global organizational reach. To achieve lower manufacturing costs, manufacturing was often outsourced to contract suppliers (or to the companies' own plants) in low-cost locations. Today, some of the R&D function is also being moved to lower-cost locations, by companies such as GE, DuPont, Qualcomm, L'Oréal, Merck, and many others. Such TMNCs still possess the competitive advantages of larger-scale (and arguably higher-quality) R&D. But TMNCs that continue to pursue globally standardized product strategies at the expense of local responsiveness are leaving more customers with unmet "exact needs" in the numerous markets they operate. EMNCs, with the strategies we explained above, are leveraging these gaps to become more formidable competitors.

How might TMNCs respond? We see two possible pathways, which are not mutually exclusive. One would be to move to "even higher ground," ramping up the difficulty level of the technologies that they lead in, through even higher-scale R&D and even more complicated manufacturing processes, represented today by the likes of IBM and Intel. The other would be to do what the EMNCs themselves are beginning to do: move more of their R&D to emerging-market locations, do more localized product development (following LG's example in our chapter), and move to a business model that allows more customized, less-standardized, lower-volume production from low-manufacturing-cost locations. As an example of moving some R&D to emerging-market locations, P&G has recently struck an agreement with India's CSIR government laboratories for joint R&D efforts, to leverage the talent—and lower costs—of CSIR's scientists.

While theoretically feasible, the latter pathway naturally requires more wrenching and painful structural and organizational changes, and it imposes high intercompany coordination costs—which the EMNC counterparts do not face. It also requires taking new approaches to cost reduction, reengineering, and reimagining products and processes from the ground up, which might be too much to pull off for all but the very brave. GE is one TMNC going this route. It has rolled out around the world an ultralow-cost, portable small sonograph machine, developed in India, targeted at doctors in small towns everywhere, caring for patients with low incomes. Likewise, it has rolled out across the world a China-developed portable and ultralow-cost ECG machine that is helping those taking care of the poor, particularly in fourth- and fifth-tier towns, to save lives. To make these initiatives a success, GE had to make tough calls. It had to focus inexorably on world-class technical functionality while eliminating every non-critical nicety; it had to spare no effort to use less expensive components and source cheaply and locally; and it had to manage the organization, including the kind of people it brought in to run India and China, to get these innovations the visibility they needed within the GE organization to be successfully chosen by local markets for rollout.[46] These challenges are difficult to rise to, but GE seems to have done them.

For the EMNCs we have talked about, while the strategies and competencies discussed in this chapter certainly make sense, many challenges still remain. How do they step up to the "next level" in R&D scale and sophistication, for example? Selective partnering with TMNCs (such as Chigo's arrangements with its German partner), acquisitions of technology-enhancing firms (such as Mitac's of Navman), and the targeted utilization of foreign talent (such as that by HTC) are already being pursued. Other methods might involve more partnerships or licensing arrangements with national and international research laboratories (such as Haier's with MIT and Natura's with Brazilian and French universities) and possibly even cooperative efforts with other EMNCs to jointly fund larger-scale fundamental R&D.

For challenger businesses in developed countries that are seeking lessons from these EMNCs, we see three clear implications. The first is the need for a narrowly focused, narrow-slice strategy—a goal to be as good as the biggest firms in those narrow products or markets, possibly even better. The second—as we described at length in Chapter 1—is the need to identify unmet or poorly served or new and emerging (even if small in volume) end-consumer needs in those narrow market slices, using insight-seeking consumer research to identify the specific areas where they can create value through R&D or in some other way. And the third is to seek to radically reinvent ways in which business is done, to not take as unchangeable any element of the cost or organizational structure, product, or process—so that new ways can be found to strip away cost and enhance end-consumer value.

3

International Expansion
Through Acquisitions

Acquisitions and joint ventures are major vehicles for inter-nationalization used by the companies in our sample. A significant number of the companies we talked to, including Apollo Tyres, Asian Paints, Asia Pacific Breweries, Aramex, Arçelik, Chigo, Dabur, Evyap, Godrej, Haier, Indian Hotels, Lenovo, Mahindra & Mahindra, Marico, Midea, Mitac, MTS, Savola, Tata Tea, Tata Motors, Vitra, Ulker, and Wipro, have used one or more acquisitions in their expansion overseas. Many of the acquisitions have been small, local (one-country business) acquisitions, as part of a Niche Customizer strategy, as in the case of the acquisition of SCIB Chemicals in Egypt by Asian Paints or Kinky in South Africa by Godrej. Others, however, have been large and transformative for the acquiring firm, executed as a part of a multiple-market Global Brand Builder strategy, as in the acquisition of IBM's ThinkPad business by Lenovo, Tetley by Tata Tea, Miller Beer by South African Breweries, and Godiva by Ulker.

This broad use of acquisitions is consistent with the data that show that the use of cross-border acquisitions by emerging-market firms, as a percentage of cross-border acquisitions, has steadily risen from about 4 percent in 1987 to 20 percent in 2008. Companies

---

This chapter was cowritten with Professor Prashant Kale of Rice University.

from the four major emerging economies, i.e., the BRIC countries, have been the most active in doing overseas acquisitions in the last few years (see Figure 3-1).While the firms we talked to spoke positively about their acquisition experiences in most cases, research on cross-border acquisitions, based on the experiences of TMNCs, suggests that the acquiring firm loses value in more than 50 percent of the cases.[1]

Interestingly, the evidence from studies of EMNCs is mixed; some research has found that, as has been observed for TMNCs, over 50 percent of the cross-border acquisitions by EMNCs too did not lead to value creation for the acquiring firm.[2] However, others have found that acquisitions by EMNCs create significant value for the acquirer, and this is particularly the case when the acquired firm is from developed markets.[3, 4] We will discuss below the reasons for value loss and the ways in which it can be avoided.

In the remainder of this chapter, we discuss the following four questions that can help guide acquisition decisions and draw out the lessons we have distilled from the companies we talked to, for both EMNCs and challenger businesses as well as developed-world multinational corporations.

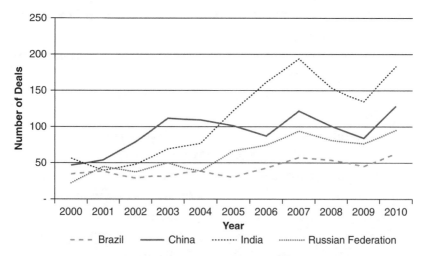

FIGURE 3-1 Overseas Acquisitions by Companies from BRIC Countries
Source: Developed from UNCTAD Data

1. During what stage of internationalization, i.e., when, should EMNCs pursue overseas acquisitions?
2. Why—and with what objectives—should EMNCs use acquisitions as a way to internationalize?
3. What is the process that EMNCs should use to select the target and make the acquisition?
4. How should EMNCs manage the post-merger management and integration of the acquired firm to best realize synergies and retain the acquired resources?

Figure 3-2 provides a guide to the discussion of these four questions.

Alliances or joint ventures are an alternative to doing acquisitions when it comes to internationalizing through inorganic means. This is because companies can achieve many of the same objectives (such as securing access to a distribution channel or supply chain, accessing technological or managerial know-how) through alliances, as well as acquisitions. In addition, alliances can be done much faster than acquisitions, and they also involve lower risk and lower cost for the concerned EMNC. EMNCs such as Tata Tea, Tata Motors, Mahindra & Mahindra, LG Electronics, and many others have done alliances with international players

When Should EMNCs Pursue Acquisitions?	With What Objectives Should EMNCs Use Acquisitions to Internationalize?	What Is the Process for Selecting the Acquisition Target?	How Should EMNCs Manage the Post-merger Integration?
• Already in multiple international markets • Ability to assess strategic needs and identify target • Financial resources to make an acquisition • Capability to integrate and manage the acquisition • Appetite for risk	• Faster growth with quick returns • Strategic role of the acquired brand • Access to distribution • Securing the supply chain • Knowledge acquisition	• Criteria for assessing acquisition targets • Balancing patience and speed • Specialist acquisitions group • Valuation: avoiding the winner's curse	• Leveraging the acquirer's capabilities • Leveraging the acquired company's capabilities

FIGURE 3-2 Guide to Acquisition Decisions

to accelerate their international expansion and to enhance their competitiveness. Generally, they have formed two kinds of alliances: alliances with TMNCs that are entering the local market (e.g., Tata Cummins, Hero Honda, TVS-Suzuki, GM-Shanghai Auto, Cummins-Dong Feng) and alliances with global players to help internationalize the operations or business of the EMNC.

Given the importance of alliances, executives of EMNCs need to be aware of various issues and challenges that have to be addressed in doing alliances successfully—because just like acquisitions, although alliances offer many benefits, they too are tough to carry out successfully, and research shows that more than half the alliances formed end up as failures.[5] Thus, in the website for this book, we have made available a discussion of the issues in managing alliances and offer some suggestions on how to deal with them.

When Should Acquisitions Be Used?

Most of the emerging-economy firms in our sample first achieved a certain degree of international presence and expansion in their core business and used acquisitions only at the second stage of their expansion. Consider Wipro as an example: it was already over a half a billion dollar company, with businesses across the world, before it made its initial acquisition, Spectramind, in 2003. Likewise, Mahindra Tractors was well established in tractors outside of India, including in the United States and Australia, before it acquired a controlling 51 percent stake in Yancheng Tractors in China. Turkey's Ulker had expanded broadly outside its home market before its acquisition of Godiva, and Lenovo had expanded out of China long before its much heralded acquisition of the ThinkPad business.

To understand why no company that we talked to had used acquisitions as a route to its initial internationalization, the comment of Vitra's executive vice president for building products, Hüsamettin Onanç, is instructive. Explaining why Vitra waited until 2006 to make its first acquisition, Engers, he said, "We reached a certain size; this means technological, infrastructural, and financial size.

If you lack the financial base, managerial and technical strength, and credibility, you cannot do this [make acquisitions]. We had the skills to assess whether the brand was good or the technology useful. We were ready for this as management. Your people need to be ready to go and manage the people there, to close those plants down if needed, be able to fight against the labor unions, and to do marketing locally there." Consistent with this comment, the EMNC acquirers we talked to all met one or more of the following four conditions, in addition to being in multiple markets, which gave them an understanding of the complexities of internationalization. These acquiring EMNCs had:

1. The ability to assess their strategic needs and identify suitable targets
2. The financial resources to accomplish their desire
3. The capability to integrate and manage the acquisition to extract value
4. The appetite for risk needed to go for it

Ability to Assess Needs and Identify Suitable Acquisition Targets

Identifying an acquisition target and assessing its suitability are steps that require several skills. First, the acquirer has to articulate the relevant criteria against which targets need to be screened, which requires the firm leadership to have clarity about its international strategy and needs. Thus, Tata Tea's Siganporia noted that it had "been very particular in realizing the inability to grow the Tata brand name outside India." As a result, from 1995 onward, Tata Tea searched for a brand that would enable it to have a global footprint that, according to Siganporia, would be "congruent with our strategy."

Second, the acquirer needs the skills to be able to uncover the potential target's strengths and weaknesses before the acquisition. Asian Paint's Thomas noted the importance of the company's capability to identify where the strengths and weaknesses lay in SCIB (the company it acquired) and, importantly, to assess its own capacity to leverage its strengths and address its weaknesses before making its successful bid for the firm. Without these skills, embarking on a strategy of internationalization through acquisitions is foolhardy.

Financial Resources to Act on Their Desire

Acquisitions require significant financial resources, and therefore two critical enablers are having the financial resources and having readily accessible cash.* Underscoring these points, Chigo's Liao noted that Chigo was waiting for its IPO to get the cash for acquisitions; sadly the financial crisis in September 2008 forced Chigo to shelve its immediate plans for an IPO and thus defer potential acquisitions, even though it had been approached several times with queries from interested potential acquisition targets. The fact that financial strength without the ready availability of cash can be a deal breaker is clear from comments made by Tata Tea CEO Siganporia. Siganporia noted that Tata Tea's initial efforts to acquire Tetley, when it first came up for sale in 1995, failed because of Tata Tea's inability to have the financial package ready to make the acquisition in a timely fashion, leading the Tetley shareholders to prefer a management buy-in over the higher Tata Tea offer. Tata Tea learned from this initial failed effort, an effort that was the first international acquisition attempt by the Tata Group at large, and made sure of funding support from Rabo Bank in advance of its successful bid for Tetley in March 2000.

Capability to Integrate and Manage
the Acquisition to Extract Value

Companies eventually do acquisitions to create incremental value by joining forces with the acquired company—thus after

---

* Due to myriad government regulations that govern foreign investors' ability to hold stock in emerging-economy companies, most emerging-economy firms prefer to use cash instead of stock to acquire foreign companies.

completing the acquisition, acquiring companies should be able to effectively manage the companies they acquire. This is of critical importance because the potential value in doing the acquisition is only realized during the post-acquisition management stage. But as many research studies show, companies often destroy value due to failure in this respect.[6] One senior executive of Tata Communications, which has done several overseas acquisitions, has this to say: "The rubber meets the road only if we are able to successfully integrate and manage the companies we acquire—if we don't do that well, there is very little reason to do the acquisition in the first place."

Appetite for Risk

International acquisitions are typically very large and significant investments for emerging-market firms. Consider Tata Tea's acquisition of Tetley. Tata Tea paid £273 million for Tetley, when Tata Tea's annual revenues were £120 million.[7] At the time, the major competitor brand, Lipton, owned by the global behemoth Unilever, had revenues of around US$1.6 billion, making it an order of magnitude larger than Tata Tea. For EMNCs, international acquisitions that are small by international standards can still be enormous and daunting. As Tata Tea's Siganporia noted, "International investments are too big to fail." Thus, appetite for risk is a significant influencer of emerging-market firms' acquisition strategy, and not all emerging-market firms have the large appetite for risk, as exemplified by Tata Tea's acquisition of Tetley. Consistent with this, Evyap, which has done few and very small acquisitions, has a lower appetite for risky acquisitions; Mehmed Evyap noted, "You pay a lump sum. A serious amount of money, all at once. If you believe that you may have a problem, you shouldn't buy." The comments of Dabur's CEO Sunil Duggal also reflect a much lower appetite for risk. He explained, "If you go wrong a large acquisition can cripple your company. It's a high stakes and very risky game and that is one of the reasons why Dabur has, as yet, not used the acquisition route as much as it might have."

At least two reasons could account for this difference in risk appetite: First, it could be because the more aggressive companies have belonged to groups that are much larger. For instance, while Tata Tea is small, it is a part of a larger group, consisting of over 80 independent companies. The group collectively has revenues running in the billions, and the group holding company, Tata Sons, supported Tata Tea's ambition to acquire Tetley.[8] Such a group structure is common to many emerging-market firms and can help spread the risk of an acquisition, making individual firms within the group exhibit higher risk tolerance. A second reason, perhaps, is that EMNCs are more often than not still family controlled (e.g., Dabur), with the family wealth significantly tied to the business, causing such EMNCs to be much more cautious in making acquisitions.

With What Objectives Should EMNCs Use Acquisitions to Internationalize?

Five key reasons emerged in support of growth in international markets through acquisitions:

1. Faster growth with quick returns
2. The acquired brand and its role
3. Access to distribution
4. The securing of the supply chain
5. The acquisition of knowledge—managerial, technological, and market knowledge

These reasons all revolve around speedily internalizing firm-specific capabilities that would enable the acquiring EMNCs to compete more effectively in international markets.

Faster Growth and Quick Returns

One of the significant reasons for taking the acquisitions route over building one's own brand internationally was that acquisitions were perceived as a faster way to achieve one's goals. Thus, Wipro's Paul noted that each business unit at Wipro is asked, "What are the gaps in your portfolio that you need to correct and then you can buy to satisfy the gap . . . As a company goal you need to catch up with the other guys . . . acquisitions are a way to speed up our goal."

The focus on faster returns could stem from the trading origins of many of the emerging-market firms that we talked to, as trading firms are used to earning quick returns on their investment. It is difficult for such firms, for which business performance is often measured using metrics like annual EBITDA, to wait for returns over long time horizons. Yet when building a branded business, a long time horizon is essential, as breaking even may reasonably take three years, and making positive returns may take even longer. Thus, acquiring functioning brands in overseas markets provides a way to expand internationally with a branded business while potentially realizing returns early. Highlighting this, Savola's Hadi said, "Acquisitions are a better option; that was always the assessment because we right away get a market position, brand, and market share, and you can turn this around very quickly into a business where you can put your added value and make it profitable. For a greenfield initiative, you have to invest, and in my opinion, invest for the long term. Waiting for a long time before you make profits is not embedded in the culture of companies like Savola."

The Strategic Role of the Acquired Brand

The second most frequently cited reason for expansion through acquisition was gaining access to the brand. Thus Arçelik, Asia Pacific Breweries, Asian Paints, Dabur, Evyap, Godrej, Indian Hotels, Marico, Lenovo, Tata Tea, Tata Motors, Ulker, and Vitra mentioned that the brand or brands owned by the acquired company were critical to the acquisition decision.

There were three reasons why these acquired brands were seen as crucial:

1. The brands allowed the acquirer to round out its portfolio of offerings to customers in the local market, typically—but not always—by adding higher-end brands.
2. The acquired brand shielded the acquiring firm from negative country-of-origin perceptions.
3. The acquired brand enabled the firm to build a regional or global brand "platform" for further expansion.

Rounding Out the Portfolio

As firms internationalize, their initial steps are not as strategic as they should be, and thus they often find they have unwittingly positioned themselves in the local consumers' minds in ways that are inconsistent with the desired image. For EMNCs, more often than not, this means that they are positioned at the low end of the market where competition is fierce and margins are all but absent. This initial low-end positioning was quite widespread, even considering today's global premium-brand successes from EMNCs like LG Electronics. Thus, one goal of many of the acquisitions was to move up price tiers by owning a more premium brand.

Consider Arçelik. When entering Europe, it did so in a somewhat haphazard manner, and its brands, e.g., Ned in France, occupied the low price tier. Arçelik's acquisition of Grundig, Arctic, and other brands stemmed from its desire to move up to higher price tiers. Tata Motor's Ravi Kant noted when discussing the Land Rover and Range Rover acquisition, "We already have a presence in multi-utility/sports utility vehicles at the lower end and we thought that Land Rover and Range Rover would be a great opportunity to create leadership in the top-end segment. Without the acquisition, Tata Motors would not have been able to move into the premium segment. With Range Rover and Land Rover it could, because Land Rover and Range Rover are the gold standards in 4x4 sports utility vehicles."

Acquiring brands to round out the portfolio is not just about adding premium brands through acquisition, although that is the more frequent need. Firms also acquire brands to compete in lower price tiers and use their existing, mainly home-market, brands to compete in the premium segment. Thus, in Egypt, Marico acquired two brands that could act as umbrella brands in the value-for-money and middle price tiers. In the words of Marico's Subramaniam, there was "still space at the premium end of hair care, where we have introduced Parachute," a brand owned and marketed by Marico at home in India. Likewise, LG uses the acquired Zenith brand in the low-price segment in the United States, while its own LG brand is positioned in the premium segment.

Negative Country of Origin

Emerging markets carry with them many negative perceptions that become associated with the firms from those countries. These associations often hamper the ability of EMNCs to build premium brands. Thus consumers buying a premium up-market SUV would probably not buy one they thought was made in India, while they would have fewer qualms buying Indian-owned, but British-made, Land Rovers. Similarly, the Turkish (Arçelik) ownership of Grundig and Arctic is reduced in salience when those European-origin brands are being considered for purchase.

Regional and Global Brand Platforms

Asian Paint's acquisition of Berger, Evyap's acquisition of Gibbs, Lenovo's acquisition of ThinkPad, Tata Tea's acquisition of Tetley, Ulker's acquisition of Godiva, and Vitra's acquisition of Villeroy & Boch, as well as several of the other acquisitions, were done with a view toward creating regional or global brand "platforms," which could subsequently be utilized in additional geographies. Interestingly, from this set, all but the Gibbs acquisition were judged as successful by the acquiring firms, and the publicly available data also suggest the same. According to Lenovo's ex-CMO Advani, the firm has successfully migrated the ThinkPad product brand to Lenovo from IBM. Lenovo today sells an innovative and up-market range of products under the "ThinkPad by Lenovo" brand globally. Tata Tea has successfully leveraged the Tetley brand and expanded the brand's footprint dramatically, bringing it into India aggressively as the premium leaf tea brand in its Indian brand portfolio and into other South Asian markets, where Tetley either was not present or was a relatively minor player prior to the acquisition. Subsequently, Tata Tea has taken Tetley to China as well as other new markets. Thus, Tetley has provided a global brand platform for Tata Tea.

Access to Markets and Distribution

Acquired companies are also helpful in providing access to distribution in new geographic markets, as companies as diverse as Vitra, Marico, Asian Paints, Tata Motors, Haier, and Lenovo noted to us. Thus, for Vitra, Engers and Villeroy & Boch provided access to showrooms that could display Vitra's products. This was critical because it enabled Vitra to showcase its offerings to key influencers, i.e., the architects and builders, among whom it had little visibility. Vitra's Onanç, referring to the Engers acquisition, noted, "The reason why we bought this brand was that it was a widespread brand and had showrooms. Our problem had been to get access to showrooms visited by key decision makers. If you put your products into a showroom, you are in a good position as the customers, subcontractors, and contractors often visit these showrooms, and make their choice there." Tata's Ravi Kant also mentioned the "loyal and passionate" Jaguar dealers who had supported the brand for the past several years (although they had not made much money doing so) as one of the reasons for acquiring Jaguar, along with Land Rover and Range Rover, the two main brands that Tata Motors was interested in. The common thread across these examples is that the acquired brand platforms provided the acquiring firm access to key customers and consumers.

Access to the Supply Chain

In certain industries, the battle for resources and the ability to have a strong and stable supply chain, one that can support the international organization, is another crucial reason for acquisitions. A case in point is Tata Tea's acquisition of Jemča, the Czech herbal infusions company, as it had a tie-up with the Martin Bauer Group, the world's largest supplier of the desiccated herbs that are a crucial input for Tata Tea in its ambition to become a global beverage company. Similarly, Tata Steel has acquired a number of companies in Australia and Africa to secure the supply of critical raw materials such as iron ore and coal to satisfy its growing needs. Other steelmakers, such as Essar and Jindal from India, Severstal from Russia, and WISCO from China, have also followed suit for the same reasons.

Acquisition of Knowledge

Acquisitions help the acquiring firm internalize three types of knowledge: knowledge about technology, managerial skills, and local consumer needs and behaviors. This knowledge is useful to EMNCs not only to strengthen their own competitive position in the face of growing global competition in their home markets but also to help them enter and expand into new foreign markets. The desire of EMNCs to acquire and internalize knowledge and build unique firm-specific advantages through acquisitions is validated by a recent survey that shows that acquisition of managerial and technological know-how is the most important reason for EMNCs to acquire overseas companies, apart from acquiring them to get access to their internationally recognized brands.[9] This is indeed an important reason, as research suggests that acquisitions by EMNCs to acquire knowledge have been successful acquistions.[10]

Technical Know-How

World-class technical knowledge and capability is crucial in enabling firms to bring innovations to market, which is central to building a differentiated brand perception in target consumers' minds. Thus, not surprisingly, many of the firms in our sample acquired firms to obtain world-class technological know-how. Consider Mitac: according to Mitac's Chris Wu, it acquired

Navman because "they have a development team in New Zealand that not only works on the user interface but also on the map engine. The map engine is very important for navigation and is one of the major reasons we acquired Navman." Apollo's Chattopadhyay noted that the Dunlop acquisition in Africa was primarily driven by the radial tire technology that Dunlop had. Tata Motor's CEO Ravi Kant, referring to the acquisition of Jaguar, said that Tata Motors "looked at their competencies, especially in the areas of engineering; we were interested in what they had in these areas," and that was one of the key reasons for agreeing to acquire Jaguar. It was again know-how in manufacturing heavy trucks, an area where Tata Motors lacked capability, which led it to acquire Daewoo's truck business, according to Kant. Ulker's Findikoğlu said, "When you look at the trend [in confectionaries] around the world, it is not biscuit alone or chocolate alone but there is a trend towards a mix. Of course, here is this successful brand—Godiva—that has achieved this much earlier than us. One of the factors that led us to the acquisition was that it would provide us a means to develop our knowledge and to catch that trend faster."

Managerial Capability

Aside from technological knowledge, a second area where an acquisition can help a firm is by providing managerial know-how for building and managing a brand internationally. Thus, for instance, Tata Tea did not have the knowledge of how to manage a global brand at the time it acquired Tetley. Through the acquisition, Tata Tea, among other things, acquired this know-how, and this has now become a critical source of advantage that the firm is leveraging to transform itself from a one-market tea company, with tea gardens and tea-growing technology as its main resource, into a global beverage company. Importantly, Tata Tea has since sold its tea gardens, which a mere decade ago were seen as a major source of its competitive advantage. It has also rebranded itself as Tata Global Beverages Limited.

Local Market Knowledge

A third area where acquisitions help is in providing local market knowledge. Thus Arçelik's Subaşi reported that understanding how appliances were used locally was a key benefit obtained from Arçelik's many local acquisitions. Marico and Godrej both noted the value of the local acquisitions in Africa, such as that of Rapidol in South Africa by Godrej, in helping them understand the local consumers' needs as a key reason for buying them.

What Is the Process for Selecting the Acquisition Target?

Having a sound and well-articulated process for selecting the acquisition target is crucial. Such a process begins with identifying the criteria to use in assessing potential acquisition targets. It also requires the careful balancing of the twin needs to be patient yet speedy, possibly by utilizing a specialist acquisitions group. Perhaps most important, it requires that a careful assessment be made of the value of the acquisition target so that the acquirer does not end up over-paying for the acquisition.

Criteria for Assessing Acquisition Targets

The five objectives for using acquisitions discussed in the previous section should logically be the criteria for assessing acquisition targets. Thus the acquirer has to assess whether a given acquisition target:

- Will help it grow faster, and do so with reasonably predictable returns
- Has brands that are strong and that fit with the brand portfolio needs of the acquirer
- Has the level and type of distribution access needed
- Has valuable supply contracts or assets
- Has valuable know-how and skills in the managerial, technological, and local consumer knowledge domains

Besides the above aspects, the acquirer also needs to assess whether the quality of the capabilities and know-how of the potential target is as per expectations, determine that the target company is available for sale, and ensure that there are no major regulatory constraints in the target's home country that might hamper the acquisition process.

Balancing Patience and Speed

It is important to note that getting the right acquisition target involves both patience and serendipity. For example, Savola's Hadi noted, "We have to be patient. I mean, in the case of acquisitions, it is counted in years, not in months. Basically, you start . . . and things may turn in one year, two years, or three years. This is what happened actually with us. The acquisition in Iran was voted down by the management of that company for a good nine years, but then their attitude changed and we were able to acquire it. We acquired the biggest Egyptian player in edible oils in 2008; that started in 2002. When we first bid for the same company, it did not work, and then we ended up buying from a third buyer that had acquired it in the meantime. So, a lot of patience; and you have to really be there, always be begging and pushing, until it works."

Dabur's Duggal also speaks of the need for patience, tying it to the risk of paying too much if one rushes into it: "The past few years have been very difficult. We believe that going forward valuations will correct and, so, it is a good time to be patient, sitting on your patch looking for a better value going forward, than to jump into something which is very expensive and then regret it later." Clearly and with 20/20 hindsight, many have commented that Tata Motors, in making its acquisition of Land Rover and Jaguar in early 2008, may have overpaid for these assets.[11]

Having said that, once the target is available, acquirers may need to be in a position to move very quickly in order to close the deal, in light of the regulatory and competitive pressures that exist once the potential target is in play. Thus, Marico's Subramaniam noted that "Marico has completed two overseas company acquisitions in Egypt—Hair Code and Fiancee—both within three months. We did that because speed was critical to a successful transaction." Highlighting the downside of an inability to act fast, a senior executive of the Avantha (formerly Thapar) Group commented how Avantha had lost out on a critical overseas acquisition because it could not move as fast as some of its rivals in completing the due diligence, securing the financing, etc. Tata Tea's experience is similar. As noted earlier, it tried to buy Tetley when it came up for sale in 1995 but was thwarted by a management buy-in that successfully acquired the firm, and Tata Tea was only able to secure Tetley when it came on the market a second time in 2000, having waited five long years for a second opportunity.[12]

Specialist Acquisition Group

Having a clear set of criteria with which to choose a potential acquisition target is certainly a good starting point. But companies also need to have a robust process in place to evaluate the targeted company in a systematic manner. Our research shows that some EMNCs have begun taking steps in that direction. For instance, most major companies in the Tata Group, such as Tata Tea and Indian Hotels, as well as other companies such as Mahindra & Mahindra, Marico, Tata Steel, Tata Consultancy Services (TCS), and Piramal, have created a dedicated mergers and acquisitions (M&A) team that is charged with leading and managing the acquisition process (we describe Mahindra Group's acquisition approach in detail in the final section of this chapter). These teams can develop a well-defined process and a set of tools, templates, and checklists to guide their evaluation and decision making during acquisitions.

In large, multibusiness groups such as Tata, there is also a group-level M&A team whose role is to support and advise individual companies in evaluating and negotiating acquisition deals. Such a group-level team can play a vital role in sharing lessons and best practices across individual companies in the group. A senior executive from TCS had this to say about Arun Gandhi, who is the group-level head for M&A at Tata: "It has always been very useful to vet any deal with Arun before we take a call. He not only pushes us to 'ask the right questions' before we do the deal, but more importantly, he is a great resource in telling us what mistakes or errors other Tata companies have made in earlier deals and how we can avoid making the same mistakes again. Without those inputs, I am sure we would have repeated some of the same mistakes others before us have done." To strengthen their in-house acquisition expertise and processes, EMNCs can also hire senior executives from outside the company (such as investment bankers, lawyers, consultants) who have subject-matter expertise or prior experience in doing acquisitions.

While it is natural that managers with a legal or finance background form the core part of a dedicated, firm-level M&A team, it is important that the team also have people from other functions represented when it evaluates potential acquisitions. If brand or technology acquisition is one of the most important objectives in undertaking overseas acquisitions, then marketing and engineering people should also play a role in the due diligence process because they can best assess whether the target brand or technology is likely to generate the expected value.

Some companies, such as Mahindra Group or Tata Sons, also strongly believe that HR executives are a critical part of the M&A team; this is not surprising because most EMNCs acquire overseas firms to also get access to their managerial know-how. The HR people on the M&A team can help not only in assessing the capabilities of the managers in the potential target but also, more importantly, in assessing whether their working styles, culture, and values are in synch with that of the acquirer; if the acquisitions are about people, carefully evaluating this "soft" aspect is very necessary. If some select managers in the potential target are vital to the continued success of that company after its acquisition, then the HR managers on the M&A team can help devise potential plans to retain and motivate the talent after the acquisition is completed.

Valuation: Avoiding the "Winner's Curse"

A lot of data show that many acquisitions destroy value for the acquiring company, and one of the primary reasons is that the acquirer ends up overpaying for the acquisition, so that value is destroyed the minute the deal is signed. So what can companies do to avoid this "winner's curse"? Apart from having a well-defined process to guide the acquisition decision making, successful acquirers also need to take a few other key actions.

First, each acquirer should recognize that the expected synergy it hopes to get from acquiring a particular company is often different in terms of its value than what another rival bidder might get by acquiring the same company—consequently the rival's bid might be different from (and even higher than) your bid for valid reasons. But in the heat of the deal, many acquirers simply forget that and decide the value of their own bid based on what others have bid! Mahindra & Mahindra judiciously pulled out of the bidding process for Land Rover and Range Rover when the price offered for these assets by Tata Motors no longer made sense from Mahindra & Mahindra's perspective, since it was primarily interested in Land Rover, but not Jaguar, which came bundled with it.[13]

Second, acquirers need to be savvy and disciplined about what synergies they take into account while valuing the target. The expected synergy in any acquisition can be one of two main types: revenue synergies or cost synergies. Revenue synergies exist when the joint revenue of the combined companies is likely to go up following the acquisition, either because of market and pricing power of the combined entity or due to cross-selling opportunities for the two companies. Cost synergies, on the other hand, arise when the two companies are expected to reduce some of their joint costs (in purchasing, manufacturing, distribution, etc.) due to economies of scale and scope from the elimination of duplication. A good example of these two types of synergies can be seen in the 43 percent stake taken by GE in Hyundai Card and Capital. GE saw huge opportunities on the revenue side stemming both from expansion of the credit card business, for which GE did not have a license in Korea, and from the massive base of auto loan customers that Hyundai Card and Capital had, which could be targeted for cross-selling a variety of financial products. On the cost side, GE's international visibility and reputation, and its AAA credit rating, helped Hyundai Card and Capital tap international capital markets to raise finance to support and expand its business, and to do so at a significantly lower cost of borrowing than it could have without the GE endorsement that the stake it had taken provided.[14]

Global successful acquirers like a GE or Cisco have an implicit rule that when they "value" any target, they only take the cost synergies into account (because they are more controllable or manageable to achieve) and leave the revenue synergies out of their valuation model (because they are comparatively much more difficult to assess as well as achieve). If revenue synergies do occur eventually, they are considered a bonus. This approach places an implicit cap on the price that acquirers pay for the target and thereby prevents unnecessary overpayment. EMNCs might want to heed this useful lesson in deciding their bid values. As we have discussed earlier, they often acquire overseas companies for their established global brands, their distribution assets, or their managerial or technological know-how. A big part of the synergies in such cases is likely to be revenue synergies, and not cost synergies—and if that is indeed so, EMNCs could potentially face a bigger risk of overpaying for their targets and thus suffer from the winner's curse.

The third factor in preventing the winner's curse is to have the discipline to walk away from a deal when the price you might have to pay exceeds the potential benefits you expect to get. One way to create this discipline is to follow the steps we have outlined earlier (in terms of putting together a well-defined process and having a conservative valuation approach). However, research shows that CEOs of companies often override these aspects and nonetheless buy the proposed target.[15] We believe that this risk may be particularly high in many EMNCs because the social and business setup in many of these situations is still much more hierarchical than in many Western countries. Consequently, due to their social culture or management style, senior executives may not be willing to openly disagree with the boss or CEO (who is also often the primary owner in many of the companies we talked to) if he or she is interested in doing an acquisition, even if the acquisition process and valuation suggest otherwise. One way to avoid this trap is for CEOs of these companies to recognize this threat and nurture an environment that allows for some dissent and disagreement, at least at the senior management level. A second way is to get inputs from outsiders whom the CEO might trust and respect, but who are not incentivized to get any financial or personal benefit from closing the deal, unlike most consultants or investment bankers. Advisory relationships with academic institutions or individual academics may be a good way to go forward in this regard.

Managing the Post-merger Integration: Realizing Synergies

The eventual success of any acquisition rests upon the acquiring firm's ability to manage the acquired company and realize the expected synergy benefits after completing the deal. In the case of EMNCs, post-acquisition management success is linked to the following two aspects: (1) how the acquirer leverages its own skills and assets to better manage the acquired company and (2) how the acquirer manages the acquired company to preserve and leverage the acquired company's assets and skills for joint benefits. We consider each of these aspects below.

Leveraging the Acquirer's Capabilities and Assets to Create Value

Our sample of respondents identified a broad set of capabilities and resources that the acquiring firm needs to have and draw upon, so that it can realize the full potential of the acquired brand. These capabilities were especially important when the acquisitions involved firms that were smaller, were in relatively small markets, and were in markets that typically consisted of local competitors alone—which was often the case with acquisitions done in other developing or emerging economies in Asia, Africa, or Central or Eastern Europe. These acquisitions, which are a key part of a Niche Customizer strategy, benefit from the acquirer possessing the following:

- Marketing skills and financial clout
- The ability to expand the acquired brand's footprint
- Superior buying skills, supply chains, and size economies in purchasing
- A strong and efficient manufacturing capability
- Sophisticated business processes

Applying the Acquirer's Marketing Skills and Financial Clout
Acquirers must have the ability to provide marketing know-how and financial support to leverage the equity of the acquired brand in the latter's domestic market when the acquired firms are smaller, are in relatively small markets, and are in markets that consist of local competitors alone. Such acquired firms often lack basic documentation on what their brands stand for, do not have organized processes for identifying their core customers and acquiring customer insight, do not have systematic marketing resource allocation tools, lack processes to coordinate the various marketing activities, and so on. For example, when Godrej acquired Rapidol in South Africa, the acquired company had a good portfolio of products but lacked the marketing skills described above as well as the deep pockets needed to take the brand forward. According to Godrej's Press, with its superior marketing systems and processes "Godrej was able to help Rapidol clearly identify and articulate the brand's core value proposition, assess the investment needs of the brand, and deploy both greater resources as well as deploy them more effectively."

Expanding the Acquired Brand's Footprint

Another important element is the acquirer's ability to leverage the equity of the acquired brand to take it into new market spaces. This expansion can take many forms. When Asian Paints acquired SCIB Chemicals in Egypt in 2002, it was the fifth largest coatings player in the country, with 80 percent of its sales coming from builders, that is, from the B2B segment. Given Asian Paints' broad product portfolio of decorative coatings as well as its knowledge of marketing to individual homeowners, i.e., the B2C segment, it decided to enhance the product portfolio under the SCIB corporate brand by adding decorative coatings and to enter the B2C segment of the coatings business in Egypt. By 2007, sales of SCIB had risen dramatically, moving it to the number three position in the market, with 70 percent of sales now coming from the B2C segment.

Entering new market spaces can also include taking the acquired brand to new geographic markets, including the acquirer's home market. Leveraging the acquired brand in one's home market is important, since the acquiring firm typically holds a strong position at home and thus is most strongly placed to leverage the acquired brand back at home, as Tata Tea did so effectively with its Tetley acquisition and Tata Motors with its Daewoo trucks acquisition. For Dabur, this ability to leverage the acquired brand back at home in India is a critical criterion in choosing an acquisition target.

Leveraging the brand in one's home market is one option, but acquirers can also expand the footprint of the acquired brand more broadly into the markets in which the acquirer is already present. Thus, subsequent to the Tetley rollout in India, Tata Tea has rolled out Tetley in other markets where it was present, such as the neighboring countries of South Asia as well as in the Middle East.

The acquired brand can also be leveraged to enter entirely new markets. Tata Tea has extended the Tetley brand to China, where neither Tata Tea nor Tetley were previously present. Apollo Tyres has expanded the presence of the Dunlop brand into new markets in Africa, and Asian Paints has expanded its footprint through the Middle East by leveraging the Berger brand, following its acquisition, and actually withdrawing the Asian Paints brand that it had already introduced in the Gulf countries.

Leveraging Superior Buying Skills, Supply Chains, and Size Economies in Purchasing

Acquirers can also help by being able to buy inputs at lower costs because of the larger scale of the acquirer or because of its more sophisticated buying capabilities. In businesses like edible oils, sugar, toiletries, and coatings, where raw material costs are a very significant element, the ability to compete is greatly affected by the ability to source inputs competitively. Companies such as Savola, Dabur, Godrej, and Asian Paints have developed sophisticated and centralized buying capabilities that allow them to source key ingredients centrally, thereby controlling the quality, timely availability, and cost of inputs, which in turn helps them to improve margins and frees up resources that can be used to support the brand through activities ranging from R&D to superior marketing investments.

Thus, following the acquisition of Kinky in South Africa, Godrej was able to score quick gains by bringing Godrej's supply chain capabilities to streamline Kinky's supply chain, making it shorter and more efficient, thus reducing supply chain management and inventory holding costs, as well as reducing stock-outs. It also brought its buying clout and superior supplier connections to improve input quality.

Improving Manufacturing Efficiencies and Capability

Acquiring firms also often brought more cost-efficient manufacturing capabilities. Thus, for instance, following Vitra's acquisition of the Engers and Villeroy & Boch brands, Vitra elected to shift manufacturing to its more efficient Turkish plants, which, because of multiple lines, were better equipped to produce the broad range of SKUs sold by Villeroy & Boch than were Villeroy & Boch's own plants in Western Europe, which it closed down.

Following its Engers acquisition, Vitra similarly made significant changes to Engers' manufacturing facilities, halving capacity, dismissing the expensive workers, and thus producing the same goods more cheaply.

Many EMNC acquirers not only possess superior lower-cost manufacturing facilities, but also know how to improve the efficiency and productivity of the acquired firm's facilities. For instance, at the time that Godrej acquired Rapidol, that firm was planning to invest in a new production line to increase capacity. Godrej was able to improve Rapidol's production capacity by more than was expected from the new line to be acquired, without investing in any new machinery. It did so by helping Rapidol better utilize its existing machinery through the implementation of superior planning and control processes.

Transferring Sophisticated Business Processes

Acquiring firms also take advantage of their superior business processes and tools in the staff functions such as HR, IT, finance, and accounting, when acquiring small companies in other countries. Thus going back to Godrej's acquisition of Rapidol and Kinky, Press said that Godrej "introduced processes such as 360-degree feedback, the identification of high performers, career planning, and the grooming of leadership," none which was systematically practiced there. Press also noted that "Godrej was able to introduce the ERP system that was in use at Godrej as well as key financial tools for both resource allocation and financial control." The implementation of these processes over time improved morale as well as productivity, helping the brand move to the next level. Similarly, various Tata Group companies ensure that key processes included in the Tata business excellence model are transferred to their acquired companies. The purpose is to not only improve business operations and strategic planning in the acquisition but also align its business and societal initiatives such as governance, safety, climate change, and innovation in line with Tata values. Over time, these business excellence processes have come to characterize the Tata way of enhancing and conducting its business endeavors, and to a great extent helped reflect the Tata brand.

Leveraging the Acquired Company's Capabilities and Know-How

In pursuing a Global Brand Builder strategy, EMNCs acquire companies in more developed economies to leverage those companies' capabilities to expand into new international markets and also to enhance their own skills and capabilities to compete more effectively against global competition at home and abroad. When making such acquisitions, acquirers need to address the following issues:

1. To what extent should they retain the resources of the acquired firm?
2. To what extent should they integrate the structure and process of the acquired firm with their own organization?
3. How quickly should they integrate the two companies?

Our research reveals that EMNC acquirers take a very distinctive approach in making these decisions, as compared with how TMNC acquirers traditionally approach them, with consequent best-practice implications.

Retention of Resources

When companies from developed economies (e.g., General Electric, P&G) buy overseas firms, they generally prefer to replace rather than retain many of the resources in the acquired firm, including human resources and brands. TMNCs typically prefer to replace the senior management team of the acquired firm with their own executives—this practice is quite consistent with the "market for corporate control" perspective widely prevalent in the United States, wherein the acquirer buys another firm to supposedly create value by replacing that firm's "ineffective management" with its own managers, who are expected to run the acquired company more efficiently and effectively. The replacement of resources is not just restricted to human resources—TMNCs also usually try to replace the acquired firm's local brands with their own global brands, as was the case when P&G first acquired a part of Godrej's soaps and detergents business in India and when Coke acquired Parle's soft drinks.

However, most EMNC acquirers take the opposite approach when they buy overseas firms. First, they retain (instead of replace) almost all of the senior executives of the acquired firm; in addition, they also give them a lot of freedom and autonomy in running their own operations. Speaking about Tata Motors' acquisition of Daewoo Commercial Vehicles in Korea, Ravi Kant said, "The Tata philosophy is to be seen as a local company rather than an Indian company. Hence we keep mostly local management and work to augment and support them." Anil Goel of Indian Hotels, which runs India's respected Taj Group of Hotels, commented, "We don't inundate the acquired company with managers from the Tatas. We demonstrate a lot of confidence in the management team of the acquired company from day one. The last thing we want to do is to 'Indianize' the company we have acquired." Second, EMNC acquirers also retain the brands of the overseas companies they acquire. For example, in acquiring Keyline in the United Kingdom, Adi Godrej said, "Ownership of strong local brands was a key driver of the acquisition—thus, we need to keep it because without it, it is difficult to penetrate markets such as the UK." The same approach was taken by VIP Industries when it acquired Carlton in the United Kingdom or when Tata Tea acquired Tetley.

For EMNC acquirers, this approach is not surprising, given their reasons for acquisition. If getting access to the acquired firm's managerial or technological know-how is one of the main motivations of acquiring overseas companies, then retaining their senior executives is critical, because they possess the invaluable industry and business know-how required to successfully conduct business in those markets. The social capital of the acquired firm also largely resides in the network of external relationships involving its top management. By replacing this valuable resource, the acquirer will find it difficult to deal with major customers, suppliers, and other stakeholders of the acquired firm. Replacement of top management may also create hostility among the rest of the managerial ranks and cause them to leave—which, if it happens, can again lead to loss of invaluable know-how from the acquired firm. Retention of the acquired company's brands is vital for the same reason. The acquired brand may have a strong cachet with existing customers, and replacing it makes it difficult for the emerging-economy acquirer to establish its own presence in that market.

Limited Structural Integration

When TMNCs do acquisitions, they often choose to structurally integrate the acquired company with themselves—they group the two previously distinct organizations into one common organizational and administrative entity. The two firms' structures become one, and the acquired company loses its separate identity in the marketplace. However, most EMNC acquirers take a different approach. They generally pursue very little structural integration; in other words, they keep the acquired company "structurally separate," with its own organization and identity intact. When Ulker acquired Godiva, Tata Tea acquired Tetley, Tata Chemicals acquired Brunner Mond, VIP acquired Carlton, and Hindalco acquired Novelis, they all followed this approach.

Structural integration can lead to the disruption of operating routines and resources in both companies, and it also implies greater complexity in leveraging the benefits of coming together. Both of these can adversely impact the operations and performance of not only the acquired company but also the acquirer company. Structural integration may also usurp the authority and status of some individuals in the acquired firm, which can lead to employee demotivation and turnover. Thus, by keeping the acquired company structurally separate, the acquirer company avoids the hazards typically associated with greater integration.

But then if the acquirer keeps the acquired company structurally separate, should this not adversely affect the realization of some joint synergies that can be leveraged by becoming one? EMNC acquirers attempt to realize these extant synergies by using some linking mechanisms to selectively coordinate activities or functions where joint benefits or synergies are involved. For example, when Tata Tea acquired Tetley, Tata kept the two companies separate. But the purchasing teams of the two companies formed a joint team to coordinate their tea purchases from the open market. Likewise, when Tata Steel acquired Corus, it formed temporary teams comprising employees from both sides to consolidate purchases of raw materials, reduce logistics costs, and share steelmaking know-how and best practices. When the Mahindra Group acquires an overseas company, it generally keeps that company separate with its own structure and management—but it selectively links some IT, financial reporting, and planning activities to share vital information and synchronize its overall strategic plans.

Gradual Integration of the Acquired Company

Most TMNC acquirers, such as Cisco, GE, Microsoft, Unilever, Diageo, and others, like to rapidly integrate the acquired company. Their logic is that rapid integration of the acquired company enables them to quickly realize synergies—especially in terms of joint cost reduction—that can be leveraged by coming together. In contrast, EMNC acquirers tend to integrate or coordinate activities with the acquired company slowly. This has two benefits: First, by moving slowly, the acquirer can get a better understanding of the unique processes and management practices of the acquired company, so as to make well-informed decisions of what to integrate or replace and what to leave as it is. Second, it also provides a sense of comfort to employees of the acquired company that their world is not going to change on a dime and that the new owner is willing to take the time to understand their concerns and thoughts before taking any drastic action.

The long-run payoffs of this approach are that it helps reduce costly mistakes and creates greater buy-in from the employees of the acquired company. These aspects are also perhaps more important for the EMNC acquirer than they might be for an acquirer from a developed economy. As we have mentioned before, firms from emerging economies are still relatively new to doing acquisitions, especially those of overseas companies; in addition, being new to the global stage and coming from less-developed countries, they are perhaps not yet viewed that positively by the companies they acquire—in which case, a slow and gradual approach to integrating and coordinating the combining companies might be a safer way to generate the desired long-term benefits from the acquisition.

Performance Implications

The distinctive approach to post-acquisition management followed by EMNC acquirers, especially when they acquire companies in more advanced economies, has been referred to as a "light-touch" or "collaborative" approach to acquisition management; this is because although these companies acquire an ownership control in the acquired company, they run it quite independently and interact with it just as they would with an alliance partner. Of course, this approach has invited criticism from some commentators since it slows down the realization of potential synergies from the acquisition. However, two recent large-sample studies provide some encouraging evidence to the contrary.[16] In general, overseas acquisitions by EMNCs have not necessarily destroyed value in the transactions that they have done. Importantly, these studies find that among EMNC acquirers, companies that adopt some of the above-mentioned practices to manage their overseas acquisition generate greater long-term benefits in terms of both creating value for their shareholders and achieving their desired business objectives. Our interviews with employees in acquired companies also revealed a generally high level of satisfaction with the acquisition. One senior executive in a large European company said, "Clearly we had concerns in the beginning. But, to be fair to them, they were very sharp and slick and had done a lot of homework. They have a very people-centric approach, which has been very good." Another person reported, "We have a just partnership with them. We have retained our voice; the company has grown and the employees have benefited."

A light-handed approach to managing acquisitions can also yield other benefits. Their considered avoidance of large-scale replacements and layoffs within the acquired company may be received favorably by their potential targets in future overseas acquisition attempts. If this begins to occur, they could become an "acquirer of choice" and could enjoy the advantages of that status, including the ability to attract more deals than before or the opportunity to buy targets at a lower cost. Thus, according to Godrej's Hoshedar Press, Keyline preferred to sell to Godrej over a local buyer because it believed that Godrej would retain most of the firm's employees. These reputational effects are important. Hemant Luthra, the architect of the Mahindra Group's successful overseas acquisition foray who refers to the partnering approach as a "light-touch model with the right balance between independence and control," says, "Now our management teams in the acquired companies have become my biggest salesmen. If people in any new company I am trying to acquire have concerns, I simply put them in touch with those managers."

How the Mahindra Group Does It

We conclude this chapter by briefly summarizing how the Mahindra Group successfully addresses many of the acquisition issues that we have highlighted above. Mahindra Group is a leading Indian EMNC that has grown rapidly through acquisitions in the last few years. The Mahindra Group has sales of over $12.5 billion with a presence across 18 diverse industries in over 100 countries.

The group has done over 30 acquisitions in the last decade to accelerate its overseas growth.

Why Use Acquisitions?

Mahindra Group companies undertake acquisitions, especially those of overseas companies, for the following reasons:

- To increase their presence in new product markets or geographies
- To procure superior technology or business processes to enable them to upgrade their products and practices
- To add to their pool of growing international management talent and become more competitive globally
- To create value in the acquired company by leveraging India's low-cost manufacturing base

Choosing the Acquisition Target

Based on its growing acquisition experience, the Mahindra Group adopts the following principle in scouting for potential targets: "It is always better for us to find the target and not let the target find us." This principle is followed so that the Mahindra Group companies get an opportunity to assess the target in its true form, before it has been "dressed up" for sale. Some of the other key parameters it uses in identifying potentially attractive targets are:

- Does the target company help us meet our strategic business objectives, and are there potential synergies with our existing operations?
- Is the target company located in a politically and financially stable country?
- Does it have a governance and cultural fit with our company or group?
- Is the quality of the management team in the target company excellent?

- Is the size of the target company manageable from a "digestibility" and "material" perspective?

The Acquisition Process

Over time, the Mahindra Group has established a well-developed process for undertaking acquisitions:

- Any group company sets up a *project owner* and a *process owner* for each M&A transaction. Together they, and their respective teams, constitute the *core acquisition team.*
- The project owner is a senior-level executive appointed by the concerned business unit; this person has full knowledge of the business and strategic rationale for the acquisition, has the necessary authority to deal with day-to-day matters arising out of the acquisition, and is responsible for overseeing the entire acquisition process, right through to the post-acquisition management phase.
- The corporate-level M&A unit appoints the process owner; this is a senior person with sufficient prior experience in guiding the acquisition process. In addition to guiding the acquisition, the process owner is responsible for ensuring regulatory compliance, appointing the due diligence partners, coordinating with the investment bankers and legal advisors, finalizing the optimal deal structure and ensuring overall process rigor. The process owner also acts as a devil's advocate in challenging the business assumptions of the business unit interested in making the acquisition so as to minimize "deal mania."
- The project owner and process owner, along with their respective teams, work closely together through the acquisition process. Once the acquisition is complete and the post-acquisition process begins, the participants from the corporate-level M&A team gradually withdraw so that the concerned business unit can assume full charge of this operational aspect.

- To prevent overpaying for the target company, Mahindra & Mahindra diligently pursues some of the following practices: relying on competent professionals for all decisions in the acquisition process, having executives from both the business unit and corporate-level M&A team work jointly on the deal, being willing to walk away from a deal at any time if the price or other requirements are not met, adopting its principle of choosing the target rather than vice versa, and initiating an internal review mechanism in the form of a Loans and Investments Committee that is composed of senior executives and board members before the acquisition is approved by the full board of directors.

Managing Post-acquisition Integration

The Mahindra Group follows a rigorous post-acquisition integration process so that the targeted benefits and synergies from the concerned acquisition are eventually realized:

- Mahindra Group companies have to mandatorily develop a 100-day plan that focuses on all key activities that need to be undertaken in the first 100 days following the completion of the acquisition, so as to begin the process of synergy realization; this plan has to be completed before getting board approval for the transaction.
- One-third of the members of the core acquisition team stay behind to hand-hold the acquisition during the first 100-day period. Usually most of them are managers from the business unit making that acquisition; these members could even be associated with the target company for two to three years at various levels till the post-acquisition integration process is complete.
- The value of the synergies to be reaped from the acquisition is closely reviewed in the "war room," which is an annual exercise undertaken by each business unit to formulate and review its overall business and growth strategy.

- During the integration process, maximum attention is paid to the communication between the acquirer and the target company so as to minimize uncertainty among personnel regarding their individual jobs, roles, responsibilities, etc.
- All Mahindra Group companies take great care in not behaving like a "typical acquirer," which might try to impose its will or throw its weight around the acquired company. Often, since Mahindra Group companies acquire other companies for the higher quality of their products, processes, and people, they need to recognize the value that resides in the acquired company. For this reason, Mahindra Group companies make a lot of effort to retain the talent in the acquired company and encourage employees to air their views in the new environment. The eventual goal is to make them feel an integral part of a globally growing group, where their inputs are appreciated and valued, rather than feeling they were "bought out" or "unwanted."

Summary and Key Takeaways

Acquisitions are widely used by EMNCs as they internationalize, and this chapter offers several takeaways for both aspiring EMNCs and challenger businesses, as well as for TMNCs. For aspiring EMNCs and challenger businesses, it is important to realize that they must first develop an internationalization strategy and accumulate the financial and managerial resources necessary to successfully acquire and manage international targets. The experiences of Evyap with the acquisition of Gibbs or the first attempt of Tata Tea to acquire Tetley back in 1995 attests to this.

It is also very clear that aspiring EMNC acquirers need to have a team as well as a clear process in place to identify potential targets, assess their strategic fit and value to the acquirer, successfully acquire the target, and manage the post-acquisition integration. A failure in any one of these steps reduces the chances of a successful acquisition, a consequence that EMNCs and challenger businesses can ill afford.

For TMNCs, our observation that acquisitions by EMNCs create significant value for them, as well as recent data from large-scale studies showing that the success rate of acquisitions by EMNCs is higher than that reported in studies of acquisitions by TMNCs, provides cause for reflection. One key difference between EMNCs and TMNCs, when it comes to acquisitions, is the light-touch approach preferred by the majority of the EMNC acquisition examples we discussed. Perhaps TMNCs can learn from this experience of the EMNCs as they consider acquisitions, since, clearly, the light touch seems to lead to superior internalization of the acquired firm's capabilities, which is the raison d'être for many acquisitions.

The light touch to integrating acquisitions is also an important takeaway for EMNCs, as not all are known for their light touch. Indeed, much has been written about the heavy-handed efforts to integrate and manage acquisitions by companies from China,[17] with attributions of failure to acquire in the first place due to negative stereotypes that have resulted from it.[18]

4

Brand-Building Strategies
and Road Map

In this chapter, we will offer a road map for building strong
challenger brands, learning from the global brand-building
experiences of the EMNCs in our sample. It should come as no
surprise that the building of global brands by EMNCs is a difficult
task indeed, given the enormous resources required and the intense
competition. The task might be somewhat easier in still-developing
countries, where consumer loyalties might be more susceptible to
change and where media expenses might be somewhat lower than
in developed markets. But a carefully thought-out strategy that
uses scarce resources wisely, building the brand step-by-step, is
still necessary.

Consider how LG built up its brand between 2002 and 2010 in
the U.S. market.[1] When it began in the United States, almost half
its sales there were going to OEM buyers, as a private label supplier; by 2009, this percentage had dropped to 8 percent. This
transition took many years, requiring tremendous patience and a
carefully planned and executed strategy. Founded as LG Electronics in 1958, it marketed a low-end Goldstar brand until 1998. In
1995, dissatisfied with the low margins and poor reputation of
Goldstar, and watching the rise of its main domestic competitor
Samsung in price and prestige, LG decided to become a premium
brand to obtain the margins and the respect it desired. To do so,

withdrew Goldstar in a phased manner from 1995 to 1998 and started rolling out the LG brand globally, entering the United States in 2002 with this brand. Based on the desire to build LG as a premium brand, LG Electronics carefully followed a rapid-fire strategy of launching technically innovative and stylish products, at high leader-matching prices, with high brand-building investments.

Given this "premium-status" goal, when it launched its own-brand products, it chose not to go after the discount-seeking mass merchandising channels (e.g., Walmart, Target, Costco). To avoid brand dilution, it tried instead to get its appliance and electronic products into the major retailers such as Sears, Home Depot, Lowe's, and Best Buy. But though these giant retailers recognized the quality of LG's products, they chose not to carry LG in those early years, believing an unknown brand like LG was too risky to carry. So LG turned instead to power regional retailers such as P. C. Richards and H. H. Gregg for its initial distribution push, incentivizing them with higher-than-usual margins and strong pro-motional, training, and sales force support and convincing them of the company's abilities through visits to Korea. Its high-price strategies provided the room for higher retailer margins and support. A year later, this initial toehold got it into the Best Buy chain and another year later into Home Depot—and into Sears in 2007.

Today, using the brand-building actions that the rest of this chapter will cover, LG is indeed a premium brand in the United States, carried by all the major retail accounts it desires, and it has finally elected to also move into the mass merchandiser channels it stayed away from in the beginning. In 2009, it was rated close to brands like GE, Whirlpool, Nokia, and Samsung on key brand metrics such as awareness, esteem, and liking, and even exceeded many of them on perceptual measures of being innovative, mod-ern, stylish, young, and sophisticated and having state-of-the-art technology. On some of these, it is still rated lower than Sony, but it is catching up. We will provide more details of LG's brand build-ing later in this chapter.

As this LG story shows, even EMNC brands that eventually seek—and achieve—premium-brand status often need to start with

OEM and private label production and a strategy of acquiring and satisfying targeted retail and trade customers. EMNCs thus often utilize a two-phase strategy:

In phase 1:

1. Enter via OEM or private label brands
2. Enter via brands aimed at meeting the needs of trade or retail customers, rather than those of end consumers
3. Enter by supplying the B2B or the commercial segment first
4. Enter with lower-priced or lower-end brands

And then in phase 2:

5. Add own-built higher-end brands—or go higher-end via the acquisition of existing foreign brands

In Chapter 1 on segment choice, we already presented the rationales and examples for targeting the needs of retailers and the B2B and commercial segments first. Thus steps 2 and 3 in phase 1 will not be discussed again here. And the logic and process of brand acquisitions was discussed in Chapter 3. Why, however, might going first after OEM and private labels make such sense? And what is the logic—and subsequent challenge—of following a strategy of low-price brands first and higher-priced brands later?

Private Label and OEM Supplier Entry Strategies

This is the oldest, most "standard," and most well-known brand-entry strategy, and it has been used by hundreds of companies (not just EMNCs) to enter new markets of all types. Samsung, for instance, used such OEM brand strategies in the 1970s and 1980s when it sold its microwave ovens, TV sets, and VCRs under the brand names of others, such as Sears and Kenmore.[2] Today, as appears in our data, a Chinese appliance manufacturer such as Midea may become the subcontracted manufacturer for a more well-known brand such as Electrolux or GE. Hon Hai Precision

(Foxconn) manufactures iPhones for Apple. As countries like China become the manufacturing foundries, or centers, of the world, this is an extremely prevalent business model.

The advantages of such a brand-entry strategy are quite evident: the supplier company simply needs to focus on the manufacturing, quality-control, cost-control, and supply-reliability aspects and does not need to spend any time or resources on end-consumer marketing and brand building or product design (if the upstream buyer provides designs and specifications for the manufactured products). By working with such an upstream buyer, manufacturer suppliers also get an opportunity to learn about better manufacturing techniques, quality-control procedures, product-design approaches (especially those involving world-class "fit-and-finish" or exterior styling aspects). They learn more about the tastes and needs of end consumers via the designs and specifications they are asked to manufacture than if they were collecting market and consumer research and investing in product design on their own. Such OEM and private label arrangements give them "incubation" or breathing time to consolidate their skills and abilities in the manufacturing, quality, reliability, supply chain, and other realms before they invest their time and money in building their own independent brands and distribution arrangements.

Such manufacturing suppliers also get, via these arrangements, toeholds in the markets of interest in terms of unit volumes, which can serve as a basis for later (phase 2) expansion and vertical spread-out. HTC, for example, which is now a big player in high-end smartphones under its own brand name, spent many years before that as a mobile phone supplier to many of the leading wireless carriers around the world (such as O2 and Vodaphone) and to many other cellular phone brands (it made Palm's Treo Pro); to this day, it still makes a small percentage of its phones under such arrangements, although it is now consciously decreasing that proportion. Navigation device manufacturer Mitac, which sells under its own Navman and Mio brands, also followed such a private label supplier route for many years.

Most importantly, from the perspective of resource conservation and return on investment, an EMNC following such a phased brand strategy does not have to spend hundreds of millions of scarce dollars to acquire millions of individual end consumers; instead, it simply needs to do enough marketing and personal selling to capture some fraction of the sourcing business of its upstream (OEM or trade) buyer. While this is by no means a trivial task, the ability to win such business is more likely to depend on cost and price levels, manufacturing and quality-control skills, and supply chain competencies than on marketing smarts and budgets. In some geographies, such as the United Kingdom and Western Europe, it may also require the ability to win the necessary approvals and certifications (such as the PL/ISO certification).

Hence, in many ways, such an OEM-sourcing strategy becomes a very feasible one for our EMNCs to follow to enter overseas markets. The downside of this approach—as vividly illustrated in the Introduction in the quote from Arçelik's Hasan Subaşi—is much lower margins than one could obtain in an "own-brand" strategy, especially if one's own brand is at the relatively higher end of the market or is more differentiated.

Starting with Low-Priced Own Brands

Many of the firms we talked to started at the lowest price tier with their own brand, as was done by Arçelik with its Ned brand in Western Europe. This low-end market-entry strategy makes intuitive sense. Starting out, most emerging-market Global Brand Builders lack the product features (including exterior styling and fit, feel, and finish), brand awareness, brand intangible and emotional associations and imagery, and brand trust and confidence—as well as sheer market presence—that strong brands usually need in order to extract higher prices and margins from end consumers. What they do often possess, however, are adequate (even if not superior) functional product capabilities for that low-end or price tier of the market, and very often a lower-cost manufacturing base and business model as well (see Chapter 2). So an emerging-market Global Brand Builder that may not be able to offer good value for money at the higher-quality, higher-price combination may be well equipped to do so with (relatively) lower quality at the lower price point.

Such a lower-end strategy also meets other needs for many emerging-market Global Brand Builders: it provides a crucial mechanism to grow and gain volume sales, enabling economies of scale, which are especially important in industries such as automobiles or even residential tiles (e.g., Turkey's Vitra), where continuous-process production lines require huge volumes for efficient operation. Such large volume and scale is also of value in itself since it gives the large emerging-market firms global visibility and prominence, which can serve as a signal or cue for trust and confidence, thus enabling a platform for future higher-end growth. Thus, Bajaj Auto of India benefits a lot by being widely known (in its business) as the world's fifth largest manufacturer of two-wheelers, as does China's Chigo in air-conditioning.

Climbing to Higher-Priced Own Brands

Our research suggests that starting in the low price tiers is a double-edged sword. While it allows EMNCs to leverage their strengths, the firms that started in the lowest price tier with their own brand, like Ned from Arçelik or Dopod from HTC, found it very difficult to generate margins or loyal customer bases. Such low prices and margins naturally do not create the resources to reinvest in the business (for R&D or brand building) and thus work against long-term viability: there is no takeoff to the "virtuous cycle" of higher prices, higher margins, higher quality, and stronger, sustainable brands. In fact, without such eventual building of a consumer franchise, even a "push," channel-oriented strategy is vulnerable to failure. Unless there eventually is adequate consumer "pull" for the brand, the trade too will wither in its willingness to carry and promote it.

As Arcelik's Subaşi noted in the Introduction, the combination of a lack of a distinct and differentiated value proposition and highly price-sensitive consumers makes it difficult for most players in this segment to make any margin. These low-end entries, in the experience of the companies we talked to, face consumer resistance at significantly higher price points. Thus, a new brand has to be launched to capture the mass segment in the middle price tier, as Arçelik did with its Beko brand. LG's experience is much the same. Having entered with the Goldstar brand in the low price tier, LG was unable to move this brand up, leading to the 1995 decision to globally withdraw the Goldstar brand in a phased manner and launch the LG brand later in the premium segment—using the Zenith brand it had acquired as a price brand.

Compared with margins of 5 percent or less in the low price tier, in the premium segment (with innovative products) LG was able to obtain much higher margins of around 25 percent in highly competitive categories like washing machines and refrigerators. Likewise, HTC went from being an original design manufacturer (ODM) in the smartphone industry (supplying the leading smartphone brand owners), to acquiring and (unsuccessfully) trying to leverage the low-end Dopod brand across Asia, to launching its own HTC-branded smartphones targeted at the premium global segment in 2006. The brand has now established itself in the premium segment, having garnered an 11 percent global market share in smartphones,[3] and recent reports put its margins at a fairly high 15 percent.

The Challenges of Climbing Price Tiers

Moving to the premium segment is difficult for emerging-market firms, as they suffer from poor country-of-origin impressions that need to be overcome. These firms also often lack branding capability and, importantly, the brand-building mindset. Additionally, emerging-market firms may lack the capabilities to create products with high and consistent quality, as well as the latest features, and can suffer in terms of creating better fit-and-finish, industrial, and user-interface design and exterior styling. These capabilities do not come easily to companies whose core skills are often in low-cost, high-volume manufacturing.

The firms we talked to fill this gap in three ways. One is by leveraging the learning and capability developed while selling low-priced brands. A case in point is LG Electronics. Much of its learning came over a 30-year period, starting with its entry into the United States in 1972, during which it struggled to build the Goldstar brand and extend it upward. LG leveraged these learnings to successfully launch the LG brand later as a premium brand in the white goods (durables) space globally.

A second approach is to leverage learnings from being a supplier to being a successful branded player (see the discussion above). An excellent example is Taiwan's HTC. HTC learned a great deal about designing, developing, and manufacturing high- and consistent-quality products by being a global supplier to leading mobile phone makers. As an ODM supplier, it also built up its innovation capability, enabling HTC to successfully burst upon the premium smartphone segment globally. LG Electronics' contract manufacturing agreement with GE similarly helped it in its journey to build a global brand in the premium segment. Its relationship with GE helped it to learn about the best materials to use to create the level of fit, feel, and finish that are a must for a premium brand of durable goods in the developed world, as well as helped it to learn about how to fine-tune its manufacturing processes to consistently churn out high-quality products.[4]

A third and final strategy, and one that is quite common, is to fill the knowledge gaps that emerging-market firms suffer from through acquisitions and joint ventures. We saw a large number of acquisitions by the firms we talked to, with the more visible ones being Tata Tea's acquisition of Tetley, Tata Motors' acquisition of Jaguar and Land Rover, Mahindra & Mahindra's acquisition of Ssangyong Motors, Lenovo's acquisition of Thinkpad, Ulker's acquisition of Godiva, and Vitra's acquisition of the Villeroy &

Boch's tile business. Chapter 3 discussed in detail the use of such acquisitions by EMNCs to build global branded businesses. And below, we discuss the case of Tata Tea's acquisition of Tetley, one of the earliest acquisitions by an EMNC of a well-known developed-world brand-owning firm, to highlight the potential of acquisitions and joint ventures in closing the capability gaps noted above.

The Tetley acquisition provided Tata Tea with the Tetley brand, which enabled the company not only to sidestep issues related to its country of origin, India, but also to obtain capabilities in branding, global management, R&D capability in tea-bag and packaging design, knowledge of the beverage market (beyond tea), and the like. The result has been that in the decade since its acquisition, Tata Tea has transformed itself from a tea garden–focused company that sold some of its teas in a branded format in India to a global-branded beverage player, with significantly higher margins, that no longer owns any tea gardens!

One consequence of moving up price tiers using acquisitions is the creation of a portfolio of brands, as the Tata Tea example also highlights. This raises important questions for how to manage the portfolio and create a manageable and yet meaningful brand architecture, a question we turn to in Chapter 7.

To get these higher margins from marketing one's own higher-priced "strong" brands, EMNCs need first to know how exactly to go about building such strong brands (in any market). Is there more to brand building than clever logos, catchy ad taglines, huge ad budgets, funny pass-along viral videos, and a company Facebook page? Is the "alchemy" of brand building simply "marketing smoke and mirrors," or does it involve something more fundamental? We turn now to developing a better understanding of what it takes to build a strong brand in any market. (Special considerations for the building of global brands and the building of global brand management organizations are presented in Chapters 6 and 8, respectively.)

Building Strong Brands: A Road Map[5]

Before we try to make our brands strong, we need a road map. While we will learn from the experience and strategies of EMNC brands like LG, Samsung Electronics, and others, let's first see what we can learn from the brand-building history of strong, established leader brands that TMNCs have built over the years. Think of these brands: Coca-Cola, Marlboro, McDonald's, American Express, Intel, Hewlett-Packard, Microsoft, IBM, Federal Express, Disney. Sony, Harley-Davidson, Apple, and Google. These appear frequently on various lists of "strong brands" that are put out annually by Interbrand, Harris (Equitrend), and BrandZ (Millward-Brown).

Now ask yourself, what makes them—and others like them—strong (among their target customers and geographies)? Here are some criteria that people usually give:

- Strong brands are widely known. People are familiar with them, aware of them.
- When you think of them, their logos or colors or package shapes come easily to mind. They possess attention-getting and memorable "visual identity."
- Such brands are perceived to be of high quality—they deliver well the benefits their targeted customers seek in the relevant category or segment.
- Even more, they are believed to be the *best* in their categories. They are perceived as *leaders*.

Many of them have some kind of non-functional imagery attached to them. They might have a brand or user personality or a cultural meaning or symbolism: Marlboro has its tough, rugged masculine cowboys; Coca-Cola has its Norman Rockwell–like American-ness; Apple symbolizes creativity, simplicity, fun, and "coolness." Let's call these types of imagery *brand associations*. For all these reasons, people trust and have confidence in these brands. They feel a kinship and loyalty to them.

Many of these strong brands have been around a long time. But such longevity may not be either necessary or sufficient to become a strong brand. It's true that Coca-Cola (Coke) is more than 125 years old (first formulated in 1886), but Dr. Pepper was also first sold almost that same year—and it is nowhere near as strong. (The Coca-Cola Company now owns the Dr. Pepper brand in most markets across the world.) Nike, clearly a strong brand, is only about 40 years old. Amazon.com and Google are even younger. Oldsmobile, over a 100-year-old car brand, became so weak that it had to be killed off by General Motors.

While Coke's longevity may certainly contribute to why it is number one on so many lists, that is far from being the only reason. Coke is a product that, even if it is not always the "best" in blind taste tests, certainly quenches thirst, refreshes people, and tastes good to many. The Coke formula is very secret, but even Coke executives say that the company's extremely broad and deep global distribution system—its "within arm's reach of desire" ubiquity—is the more important reason for its success.[6] Thus factors such as distribution or access to scarce resources (such as raw materials or patents) may also be critical reasons for brand strength in some cases.

Apart from being early and aggressive in building up its bottling and distribution networks around the world, Coke has also invested billions of dollars in all kinds of marketing communications: advertising, sampling, celebrity endorsements, sports sponsorships, PR. Some of these have had culture-changing effects, such as the "Red Santa" in early Coke ads. Red, of course, is Coke's color and is one of its strong visual equities, or branding elements, along with its script logo and its contour, or "hobble-skirt," bottle. Coke has very smartly leveraged all these in packaging, in-store merchandising materials, advertising, and even the sides of its trucks.

So what have we learned from this discussion? We think there is agreement that to build a strong brand, you must create one that has:

1. High awareness and familiarity in its target market, including awareness and recognition of its "identity" elements.
2. Perceived high-functional or high-benefit quality on attributes and benefits relevant to that segment. (This may be somewhat more aspirational than a perception of being the "best value," though that too is very important.) As we discuss in the next section, a reputation for high quality is arguably the most important brand-building ingredient.
3. A reputation for category leadership and dominance (including size and share, but also for innovation and being first to market).
4. High levels of trust and confidence—engendering high loyalty.
5. Imagery and associations concerning character, personality, users, deeply held values, consumption situations, and cultural and symbolic meanings.
6. Strong visual associations—visual equity.
7. Other brand-specific assets such as distribution and resources.

The order in the list is not meant to imply the sequence in which these characteristics need to be built up. We will turn to sequencing and the relative importance questions in a few pages.

If you compare this list with those of other well-known writers on brand building, you will find similar ideas.[7] And similar brand-strength components are tracked by the brand research models of Millward-Brown (BrandZ), Research International, and Young & Rubicam (Y&R) Brands (the Brand Asset Valuator, BAV).

The Relative Importance of These Brand-Building Elements

To build a strong brand, it is important to know not only the branding elements that need to be built up, but also the order or sequence or prioritization that is necessary. Above, we listed seven elements. What is their relative importance?

Just How Important Are Awareness and Identity?

A lot of marketers seem to think that building awareness, familiarity, and identity levels is the most important part of building a strong brand, for which high marketing budgets are needed. The people in charge of building the dot-com brands in the late 1990s certainly thought so, often spending most of their venture capital or IPO money on extremely expensive (and often creatively zany) Super Bowl commercials.

Do you agree? Just how important *are* awareness and identity for brand strength? It seems intuitively clear that if a brand is to become strong, it simply has to have very high levels of awareness—in its target customer and geographic markets. (It is obviously irrelevant if people you aren't aiming at haven't heard your brand's name before.) If there is no brand awareness, there is no brand anything, because you have to have a brand name in your head to attach other things to: perceptions of superior and relevant quality, leadership, trust, a personality, a visual equity element, whatever.

People usually don't buy brands they've never heard of before. Awareness implies and creates a sense of familiarity, leading to a basic level of confidence necessary to even be in the set of brands from which the consumer chooses. And as the level of awareness goes up, so does the perception of being the standard or default or safe brand in that product category, which usually helps increase the likelihood of purchase selection. (This is true except in certain fashion categories, where it may be seen as a negative: well known = safe = boring = uncool. Or among certain high-expertise customer segments, who take pride in and want to be seen choosing obscure brands.)

But now let's turn the question around a bit: to be a strong brand, is it enough to have very high awareness (along with a strong visual identity)? Put another way, in the relative scheme of things, just how important is a brand's awareness level? Does brand strength always parallel or track its levels of awareness and identity?

It may help if you thought about some high-awareness TMNC brands that come to mind. If you live in the United States, think of brands like Ramada, Kmart, Greyhound, Planet Hollywood. They are all brands with high levels of awareness. Would you call them all strong brands? Chances are that many of the high-awareness brands you will think of are clearly not high-strength brands. For others, like Apple, brand strength has clearly gone up over recent years—with innovative and high-quality products such as the iPad, iPhone, and its improved Mac notebooks and desktop computers— while its brand awareness levels have not changed much (they were already very high decades ago).

The intuition should be fairly clear: a brand needs some minimal levels of awareness and identity to be in the game, but these are in most cases not enough by themselves to make the brand strong and successful. *Brand strength and success depend much more on high quality and differentiated products and services, once the brand gets above minimally needed awareness and identity levels, than on the levels of brand awareness and identity themselves.* In fact, brand awareness increases as the brand gets more trial as word of its high quality gets around.

There is a lesson here: You must build high enough awareness and identity for your brand to merit purchase consideration. But you shouldn't overinvest in moving the awareness and identity meter. Once you've achieved "high enough" awareness and identity, you must make sure that you create the perception of a product that is relevant to the target market's needs, a product of higher-than-average quality—maybe even the quality leader— and that you are seen as "different" in market-relevant, possibly even non-functional, ways. Note that "quality" doesn't necessarily mean functional quality: in some categories and segments, imagery and sensory appeal may be the key perceptual drivers of quality.

We get confirming insight into the relative importance of brand awareness from an analysis done by Y&R on its BAV database.[8] It is a huge database, collecting 50+ measures on various brand perceptions on thousands of brands from hundreds of thousands of people in almost 70 countries for over the last 20 years. Y&R analyzes these brand-level data in terms of the constructs called Differentiation and Energy, Relevance, Esteem, and Knowledge.

Y&R claims that, according to its analysis, strong brands start out (in a small size) by creating margin-raising Differentiation; they then grow in size by increasing their Relevance (market penetration); this growth earns them Esteem (quality respect); and as they grow more, consumers become familiar with them (Knowledge). Brands with growth momentum also possess perceptions of dynamism and energy. Not all brands are strong on all these metrics, but the best brands (such as Disney and Coke) are, according to Y&R. And this is the confirming finding: there are many brands (e.g., Kmart, Ramada, Greyhound) that are high on customer Knowledge (familiarity, awareness) and possibly even Relevance (size), but no longer have Esteem (respect, liking) and, crucially, Differentiation and Energy.

Awareness and identity get you into the brand game. They are the cost of entry. They clearly matter (and we discuss ways of building awareness in the next chapter). But awareness and identity by themselves are not what win you the brand-building game. *Delivering and winning on perceptions of relevant quality—and earning the mantle of leadership, and trust, and loyalty—is what you need in order to win.*

Earning Respect for Quality—and Beyond

Creating perceptions of high quality (and value and differentiation) is not easy (we discuss this in depth in Chapter 6); it requires not just market-winning science and technology, but substantial insight into how these quality perceptions can be influenced—what are the quality cues or signals that consumers use to judge quality? Often these cues have nothing to do with "objective" quality—such as the sound of a car's engine and its doors or the feel of the door handle and turn signal levers—but you need to understand them and use them if you wish to communicate high quality. An EMNC we spoke to, Hindustan Pencils, told us that pencil users often judged quality not only by how well the pencil wrote but also by the "feel and finish" of the pencil itself (the lacquer and name print on the side, for example). So it requires a lot of psychological insight (and dollars) to communicate this quality edge to consumers, often in sensory ways that will drive engineering purists crazy.

But lots of good companies have access to the minds and specifications and raw materials and equipment to turn out very high-quality products. Fewer of them, but still many, can wrap high-level service packages around these products. Think about the companies in any business, such as yours. Aren't there quite a few that a buyer could reasonably choose among?

There are usually multiple high-quality competitors in any market. But there is always only one that is perceived as a leader (or maybe two). A leader, by definition, is singular (in a particular market space), though different brands can claim leadership in different things: different kinds of technology, for instance.

After you have created the necessary perceptions of high quality (and differentiation, and relevance, and value), you must create leadership perceptions for your brand, in *something*—something relevant that puts your high-quality brand way above the other high-quality brands.

When your brand is perceived as such a *leader*, you should be able to inspire the kind of trust and confidence buyers reserve for brands such as Intel (in microprocessor technology), IBM (in computing products and services), Apple (in consumer electronics), or Volvo (in the area of automotive safety). Among our EMNCs, HTC and Lenovo (and LG and Samsung before them) are examples of companies that understand and are going after this perception of leadership. Creating such leadership perceptions takes years, often decades, of credibly and vividly communicated rounds of innovation or first-mover commercialization of something. Key communication strategies seem to be the clever use of marketing public relations and a long-lived consistency of advertising messaging (think of how long Volvo has talked about its safety focus and innovation). Chapters 5 and 6 discuss these elements.

Quality, Leadership, Trust, and Other Brand Associations

High quality, leadership and authority, and trustworthiness and confidence are among the most important associations a brand can have, but they are not the only ones. In many product categories and customer segments, the "benefits" from the purchase often include ones that involve the customer wanting to *feel* or *be seen in* certain ways when they purchase or consume the brand or category. These can include feelings and imagery of being glamorous and sophisticated or down-home and authentic; of being smart and conscientious or playful and child-like; of being assertive and masculine or delicate and refined. A coffee-shop consumer might want to feel energized, or feel relaxed, or look sophisticated, or feel frugal, depending on the location and time of purchase (and the personality of the individual). Thus the brand may need to build associations (perceptions) that purchasing it and consuming it in fact not only will deliver functional quality benefits but will also make the buyers feel and look the way they want to.

In certain situations, such as for most B2B purchases, such brand associations are less relevant. In others, such as publicly consumed product categories that highly involve and highly reveal one's "sense of self," these may be all-important. When they matter, they often require sophisticated research and nuanced insight to discover and target. Once targeted, they usually require considerable creativity to evoke and consolidate. We will turn to these challenges in Chapter 7.

If the brand associations you create are strategically on target (relevant, unique, credible, etc.), they should succeed in getting customers emotionally attached or "bonded" to your brand. But brand loyalty can also be built up tactically through the kinds of databased "loyalty marketing" or repurchase methods that today are widely used as part of relationship marketing or one-on-one marketing (such as the customer loyalty program of our EMNC Taj Group).

Our Branding Pyramid

Since every framework about brand building needs a visual or mnemonic device to help readers remember a key point, we've created the branding pyramid in Figure 4-1 to help you remember what, in our opinion, is the appropriate prioritization and sequence of brand-building tasks.[9] A brand that is known mainly for its name and logo—has awareness and identity—is no more than a trademark. A brand that connotes quality and leadership as well, and gives its buyers a feeling of trust and confidence, has risen to the higher level of a trustmark. For most strong B2B brands, this is where they end up. A brand that, in addition, possesses brand associations that set it apart and make it something the target market aspires to, or identifies with, creates an emotional bond in the process that becomes (to use the term popularized by ad agency chief Kevin Roberts)[10] a "lovemark," similar to consumer brands like Apple and Harley-Davidson.

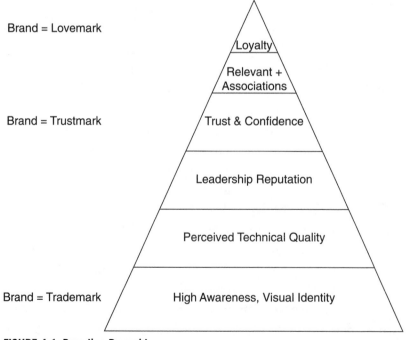

FIGURE 4-1 Branding Pyramid

This, then, is our road map to the creation of strong brands. If you think of the pyramid in Figure 4-1 in terms of jobs that have to be accomplished before going to the next higher level, then job 1, at the bottom of this branding pyramid, is creating high spontaneous awareness and familiarity, aided by a distinctive and clutter-breaking visual and naming "identity." We go into details on awareness building for EMNCs in Chapter 5.

Above that, job 2 is creating a perception of relevant quality, including related service elements, at the segment-relevant value point. There also needs to be something differentiating about the way this is communicated. This task is discussed in Chapter 6 for our EMNC global brand-building context.

Then we go to job 3, the next level, which is earning the mantle of leadership and the aura of authority. Chapter 6 also briefly discusses the creation of these leadership and trustworthiness perceptions. The perception of leadership should also get you to job 4, the next level of brand strength—establishing the feeling that you are a brand that can be trusted and associating your brand with confidence.

For job 5, you need to create for your brand—in some, but not all, situations—the other types of brand associations we discussed above (about linked feelings, values, and personality). The associations need to be targeted strategically, after a thorough analysis of the value needs of different consumer segments, competitive positioning strategies, and your own brand's strengths. And then they need to be communicated in a creative and impactful manner using every element at the brand builder's disposal, including product design, name and logo, price and warranty, choice of distribution channel, all kinds of marketing communications—indeed, every single brand touch point, including all employee and service interactions. "Everything communicates," as brand builders like to say, and the brand-building task is one for everyone in the company (including design and HR), not just the marketers. See Chapter 7 for a discussion of the association-building tasks for EMNCs, and also see the discussion there on the need for internal branding.

If the brand associations are strategically on target and well executed, creating such emotional "added value" should, by themselves, get customers emotionally attached to your brand. However, in performing job 6, EMNCs may need to reinforce such brand loyalty through other tactical means, such as through databased direct marketing and other tactical approaches mentioned earlier.

Brand Building in Action at LG

To see how this road map captures actual brand building by some companies, let's return to the LG U.S. case we opened with.[11] Before LG invested heavily in brand building, it waited until its product competencies were strong, its service network was set up, and its distribution (through power regional retailers) was in place.

To build and maintain high awareness levels, it has invested heavily in mass advertising in major media (with its "Something Better" and other campaigns). It was ranked 68 in the list of top 100 global marketers by *Advertising Age* in 2011, spending over $500 million in annual advertising.[12] It has also paid special attention to gaining public relations coverage through creating several newsworthy events. These include giving away 350 HDTVs and refrigerators to the audience of an Oprah Winfrey show, organizing a National Fastest-Texting Competition on LG handsets at both regional and national levels, and sponsoring a "top home chef" cooking competition. High-visibility sports sponsorships include those of various NCAA championship events and the skins golf game. Special attention is given to creating "one-voice" integrated brand communications.

To build a consistent and appealing brand identity, the LG logo—which at one time stood for "Lucky Goldstar," its early brand—now looks like a smiling human face, accompanied by an initial-fitting, optimistic slogan, "Life's Good."

To build a high-quality perception, LG treats high levels of reliability in its products as a base requirement (its "repair-or-return" rate declined by 45 percent between 2006 and 2009) and uses sophisticated customer-insight and R&D capabilities (see

Chapter 2) to embed highly valued and unique features and benefits into its products. It continually improves its after-sales service levels, reducing its average call-wait time by 75 percent from 2007 to 2009. It chooses high-quality retailers for its distribution, and it prices its products at category-leading levels to promote high-quality perceptions. It uses product placement with a leading brand at airports, providing the TV sets for CNN's airport network in 81 airports in North America.

Most crucially, however, it has carefully cultivated a leadership image through launching a never-ending stream of the "world's first and best" innovative flagship products: the first music phone (Chocolate) in 2006, the first steam washing machine in 2006, the first four-door refrigerator with an auto-close door in 2009, and even the world's first refrigerators with built-in TVs and Internet connections! It has won awards for its innovations (such as the CES Best innovation award for its Allergiane cycle washer and dryer in 2009). It proudly displays its logo prominently in New York's Times Square with other world-leading brands.

Now that we have our pyramid road map on how to build strong brands, the next three chapters will dive into the details of brand-building strategy and tactics, such as the tasks of building awareness, quality perceptions, and distinctive, relevant associations.

Cautionary Note for EMNCs Building Strong Global Brands

We have noted several times that building new global brands takes enormous resources, a long time, and much patience. This is due in part to the extremely competitive environments with which marketers must contend today—not only in the developed markets, but also in the high-growth developing countries in which every major player wishes to participate. The developed-country markets, of course, have the burden of very expensive mass media channels and pay-to-play distribution channels (which ask for expensive slotting fees, for example). Developing countries, on the other hand, have consumers who are less knowledgeable about many product categories, thus feel a higher sense of perceived risk in brands they do not know well, requiring large investments in advertising, branding, and communication. Brand-building expenses are also higher for new EMNCs that are still in the phase of acquiring new consumers (rather than striving to retain existing consumers or increasing their share of wallet from existing customers, which are usually cheaper tasks). For example, MTS, the Russia-based telecom operator, competing in large markets in the highly competitive wireless carrier industry, needs to (and does) spend lots of money on its brand building, because it is aggressively pursuing new customers who want to choose a carrier they can trust.

Given these investment needs, EMNCs have to carefully plan for, and accumulate, the financial and management resources they will need when they make a serious effort to build (or buy) regional or global brands. As Bhaskar Bhat of Titan told us, "You need to make sure you have the resources (both balance sheet and cash), and the stomach, for such brand-building." Many emerging-market companies are family owned (e.g., Dabur and Godrej in India, Savola in Saudi Arabia), or partly owned by state or province players (Haier in China, Titan in India), or publicly held but extremely cautious. The magnitude of brand-building investments we are talking about, and the long-term payback periods that they require, may not be what these stakeholders and decision makers are comfortable with. Thus EMNCs seeking to build their own strong brands (or even to acquire such brands) need to recognize that these investments, while holding the promise of greatly increasing margins, are long term and somewhat uncertain, with long payback periods. Changes may need to be made in how senior management and stockholders approach and evaluate these brand-building investments. The brand-building challenge lies not only in the wise spending of resources, but also in their accumulation.

Summary and Key Takeaways

While we believe the brand-building road map and framework offered in this chapter are of equal use to EMNCs, TMNCs, and under-resourced challenger businesses everywhere, some of the implications vary across these groups.

For EMNCs, we believe the key learning is the importance, to the long-term brand-building challenge, of first reaching and communicating very high levels of product or service quality. Given the enormous attention being given in marketing circles these days to the importance of branding, and the salience of branding success stories from the consumer goods, luxury products, fashion, and other industries—even politics and entertainment—it is easy to believe that to build brands one needs big budgets poured into clever advertising campaigns. While those certainly play a role, and are often necessary, we think it is much more important to get the "core quality" right first. This takes time and patience, and even long periods of low-margin status as unbranded suppliers to OEMs or large retailers, but we believe that the time is not ripe for significant marketing investments until that core quality has been established. Once it has been established, however, EMNCs must be willing to make the large and slow-payout investments in all the other elements of the branding pyramid presented in Figure 4-1.

For TMNCs, we see two possible implications. It is quite likely, we believe, that many of their EMNC competitors will slowly but surely achieve parity on the objective- and perceived-quality front. We believe that for TMNCs to maintain their brand superiority, they must therefore (1) stress and enhance their "leadership aura" and (2) build and bolster the higher-level aspirational and identification associations that create brands that consumers love, not merely like.[13] On both these fronts, global brands from the developed world (from TMNCs) often begin with huge advantages over brands that have their origins in developing countries (our EMNCs).[14] Yet these initial advantages are susceptible to erosion: a Nokia and RIM can give way to an HTC. To bolster their leadership perceptions, TMNCs might therefore need to invest even more in creating and communicating their unique dominance and mastery over key technologies and competencies in order to build the kind of market-winning confidence and trust that smaller-scale

EMNCs will find very difficult to match. And on the association-building front, TMNCs arguably have more "cultural capital" assets they can leverage[15] than EMNCs, since so much of global consumer culture today flows from the economic center to the economic periphery. These assets should be milked for all they are worth.

For under-resourced challenger brands everywhere, we think the key implication from this chapter is to first try to establish mastery of quality standards, even go for leadership status, in a narrow and feasible product market, before investing in any of the secondary tasks of brand building discussed previously in the chapter. Like the EMNCs, they too are vulnerable to investing too early and too much in the aspects of brand building that are less crucial and less effective. Once they build renown in their small initial markets, they should then try to grow market penetration and market size, letting their quality reputations do the brand building for them (through positive word of mouth), facilitated by targeted low-budget viral marketing techniques. They need to then build their levels of awareness, quality reputations, and brand associations in low-budget, guerrilla-like fashion—the subject of our next three chapters.

5

Building Brand Awareness on Limited Budgets

Creating a high level of brand awareness is the first major task facing any builder of a new brand, for without knowledge of a brand's existence (and of its identity elements, such as its logo), a consumer has no "anchor" in the mind around which to build brand associations (see Chapter 4). Brand awareness needs to be created not only among end consumers but also among intermediary trade partners, especially if they play important consumer-influencing roles, such as in appliances or paints. While high spontaneous brand awareness is never a guarantee of brand strength (since well-known brands can also have poor-quality and other negative associations), it is logically a necessary condition for it. High brand awareness also contributes to building brand trust and confidence, crucial ingredients for brand success, particularly when country-of-origin imagery is negative, as is often the case with emerging markets (see Chapter 6 on building quality reputations).

Unfortunately, most of our brands start out with very low levels of brand awareness in their targeted overseas markets: in 2006, Indian IT firms TCS, Infosys, and others, had awareness levels of 35 to 50 percent among Fortune Global 1000 decision makers, versus 99 percent for IBM and 94 percent for Accenture.[1] The Taj Group told us it had a 41 percent aided awareness, but just 1 percent unaided, awareness level in the United States, compared with 56 percent unaided and 100 percent aided for Ritz-Carlton! Chinese car companies like Geely and Chery only have aided awareness levels of 5 to 13 percent outside China, according to a global Interbrand survey in 2009.[2] Exceptions to this starting point are brands that have acquired high levels of awareness in contiguous countries because of broadcast and population spillovers or because of prior sales flows via independent distributors. Examples in our data include Savola's Afia brand in its neighboring markets of the Middle East; Turkish brands like those of Evyap in Egypt, Syria, Iran, and Iraq; Indian brands like Marico's Parachute or Dabur's Amla throughout South Asia, and Varafoods in Southern California.

Thus, most EMNCs face quite a challenge in building high levels of brand awareness for their overseas brands. Typically, new brands build their awareness levels through paid advertising campaigns, marketing public relations (MPR), events and sponsorships, direct mail, and the creation of "buzz" and viral word of mouth. These different forms of integrated marketing communications vary in the extent to which they require large financial resources. Paid advertising campaigns require the most, especially if they utilize national network TV (instead of local or spot TV), radio, online, print, or outdoor media, all of which usually permit smaller-dollar media plans. Thus awareness building typically requires lots of money—and the outcome is never assured.

Given these requirements and risks, several EMNCs have opted to *buy* (acquire) instead of *build* (their own) high-awareness overseas brands. This strategy for competing globally with acquired high-awareness brands was common among the EMNCs we spoke to, so much so that brand acquisitions is the subject of a separate chapter (Chapter 3) in this book.

The alternative to such acquisitions is to bravely make the large marketing investments needed to raise the awareness levels of one's own brands. A few EMNCs we interviewed—such as Dabur, Evyap, Mavi, and MTS—had followed this second path. Evyap, for example, says it never cut off its heavy advertising schedules in Russia and the Ukraine, even when those countries were going through turbulent political changes in the 1990s. Mavi Jeans spent significant amounts of targeted TV (e.g., MTV) and print (e.g., *Jane, Teen People, YM*) advertising money in 2001–2002 in the United States, in a campaign prepared by Leagas-Delaney of San Francisco, to launch its Mavi Amerika collection there. Dabur was perhaps the clearest case, with CEO Sunil Duggal telling us that the organization had extremely high advertising-to-sales ratios, attempting to match bigger TMNC players like P&G and L'Oréal in the markets in which they competed.

Ad budgets tend to be set in proportion to sales and revenue levels in most companies. Thus, as a first step, companies and brands new to a market need to be able and willing to invest in awareness building in advance of reaching high sales levels, accepting a payback period that extends years into the uncertain future. "You need to be brave and invest big," says Dabur's Duggal, but clearly very few of our sample companies have this attitude. Most of our interviewees were acutely conscious of the need to raise brand awareness levels, although they let us know in no uncertain terms that their organizations were only able or willing to invest very limited resources to do so.

As a result, most of the EMNCs we interviewed had fairly small brand communication budgets, especially when compared with the deeper pockets of their larger and more established TMNC competitors. As one example, Jessie Paul, CMO of Wipro, was faced in late 2006 with the task of raising Wipro's 35 percent level of unaided awareness among non-customers to bring it closer to the 95 to 100 percent level of competitors like IBM, with a marketing communications budget of $1.3 million versus the hundreds of millions spent annually by IBM.[3]

Building Awareness on a Shoestring

How then do most EMNCs manage to increase their brand awareness levels? We encountered several interesting strategies and tactics from which valuable lessons can be learned. It seems from our data that EMNCs have mastered methods not just of frugal manufacturing and technology innovation, but also of frugal marketing. Wipro—less than one-twentieth the size of IBM and one-quarter the size of Accenture—said to us, "The challenge has always been to build a brand which is going to compete with Accenture or IBM, but with a fraction of the marketing budget. To put it in perspective, IBM's marketing budget is roughly the size of our annual revenues! So the only way that we will ever make a mark is if we don't do what they do, and do things differently. And, secondly, if we spend far less than they do for the must-have things that everybody has to do." Or in the words of Aramex, "We didn't have the money to advertise to match DHL. So, we did different things: we were heavy CSR [corporate social responsibility] based, we invested in local sports teams, *we did a lot of marketing rather than advertising.*"

EMNCs thus try to build awareness frugally through (1) a concerted effort to *focus*, so as to enable them to attain an adequate impact from their limited budgets; (2) a relentless *cost obsession* to account for every renminbi, riyal, or rupee invested in building awareness; and (3) great efforts to create *multiplier effects* to gain outsized results from their small budgets by thinking creatively and holistically, leveraging partner resources, and getting opinion leaders to do their awareness building for them. Many such efforts pay off: Wipro claims to have raised its awareness levels fourfold between 2003 and 2009, and Infosys claims to have moved from a 25–30 percent aided awareness level a few years ago to over 60 percent today (in a quarterly survey of 150 CXOs).

TMNCs and challenger businesses can learn much from these firms' frugal approaches to awareness building. What follows is a description of the strategies and tactics adopted by the companies we talked to, organized around three themes: focusing (targeting), managing costs, and multiplying the impact of limited invested resources. Figure 5-1 provides a road map.

Steps	Activities
Focus	Narrowly define target segments and markets Focus on fewer intermediary customers Spend on only a limited number of products and brands
Relentlessly Manage Costs	Leverage channel-partner knowledge and clout Be willing to grab novel opportunities Leverage lower-cost emerging-market talent
Multiply Impact	Build buzz through creativity and innovation Leverage the reach of opinion leaders and editorial media Leverage member communications by partners Use Integrated marketing strategies

FIGURE 5-1 Building Awareness on a Shoestring

Focus

A strategy of tightly focusing their limited marketing resources was apparent from several EMNC awareness-building tactics:

- Narrowly defining target segments and markets
- Focusing on the much fewer intermediary customers
- Spending on only a limited number of products and brands

Narrowly Defining Target Segments and Markets

Our EMNCs often deliberately targeted smaller, more clearly defined target segments and markets. Thus, APB (Tiger Beer) chose to go after a niche market segment that rejects mainstream beers, "the earliest of early adopters." Thai Herbal targets just the older age demographic for its products. Grupo Britt targets tourists to Latin and Central America.[4] Mahindra Tractors focuses tightly on hobby farmers in the United States, and it initially focused geographically on only 3 of the 50 U.S. states. A sharper focus on a small and well-defined target group has the benefit of reducing cost not only through limiting the magnitude of the task, but also by enabling the firm to be more creative and effective in its awareness-building efforts through its superior understanding of the smaller segment.

Wipro offers an excellent illustrative example. Wipro decided that it only needed to target CIO- and CFO-type decision makers in the Fortune 1000 companies. Given such a clear and well-defined target segment, it was able to understand that this small number of individuals heavily frequented key airports and business lounges. Consequently, it placed its advertising at just Kennedy (New York), Heathrow (London), Frankfurt, and Narita (Tokyo) Airports. To target these same people, when they arrived in Bangalore, the hub for the Indian IT industry and the city where Wipro has its headquarters, Wipro designed "puzzle boxes" that it placed with the limousine companies that were frequently used to pick up senior executives from Bangalore Airport, as well as in the hotels in Bangalore that these executives were likely to stay in. Upon pickup or check-in, executives were handed information brochures and the puzzle box. The box, when opened, informed the recipient to go to the Wipro website to register to collect a prize, thus creating a second opportunity to build and cement brand awareness. These efforts, along with others such as exclusive advertising on the buses used to shuttle participants of the World Economic Forum, have helped Wipro significantly boost brand awareness levels.[5]

Focusing on Fewer Intermediary Customers

In the B2C space, building awareness among end consumers can prove to be a formidable challenge, even when targeting narrow segments. One way our EMNCs dealt with the challenge was to instead focus on the small number of channel intermediaries, particularly when they were in categories where intermediaries play an important role in consumers' purchase decisions. Thus, Chigo builds brand awareness and reputation among its narrowly targeted distributor target audience by focusing its advertising in *JARN*, a trade journal that is used extensively within the air-conditioning industry.

In its early days in the United States, LG Electronics used the majority of its marketing investments to build brand awareness with trade intermediaries. LG did so by investing in incentives, contests, and training for the floor salespeople that their final customers rely on for brand recommendations (a practice called *spiffing* in the United States).⁶ Indeed, LG waited until it had established broad distribution in 2006 in the United States to support its launch of the steam washing machine with TV advertising, its first use of the medium nationally. Haier USA followed a similar strategy. Since brand-building investments in mass media would go to waste in the absence of broad distribution, such a strategy is essential when building a brand from scratch. As Modelo's Gómez told us, Corona, its flagship beer that is internationally distributed, focuses on trade promotions and retail marketing first, only going to TV advertising when volumes reach critical mass.

Taking the focus on intermediaries a step further, Turkish tile producer Vitra uses extensive showroom networks that it owns to build awareness among architects, interior decorators, designers, and building contractors and subcontractors that are influencers and decision makers in their business. Vitra has acquired brands such as Villeroy & Boch to grow its showroom network.

Spending on Only a Limited Number of Products and Brands
HTC, like LG Electronics and Samsung Electronics,⁷ has a policy of concentrating its limited marketing communication resources on only a few high-potential star products, rather than dividing them evenly across all its new models being launched. Moreover, many EMNCs in our sample deliberately use only one global or regional master brand or power brand, rather than diffusing their limited resources across several brands or sub-brands. Thus, LG Electronics uses only the LG brand overseas, across products and markets, because it wants to focus its resources on the corporate master brand. (In Korea, LG uses different brand names for its different product lines. For instance, TVs are branded XCanvas, washing machines Tromm, and air conditioners Whisen, because in Korea its large market share allows it the luxury of supporting multiple brands.) In a similar vein, APB has decided to use the Tiger brand across markets, although it owns a large portfolio of

beer brands including Anchor, Baron's, and ABC Stout. The same is true for Mexico's Modelo, which (as noted previously) focuses only on its Corona brand beer in international markets. Other examples of building just one primary brand name across markets are Marico's use of Parachute across most of its African, Middle East, and South Asian markets and Savola's use of Afia wherever possible (but not everywhere).

Relentlessly Manage Costs

EMNCs try to wring every penny of cost from the awareness-building activities they undertake. Thus they use tried-and-true approaches such as *co-op advertising*, where the costs are shared with the retailers, or less expensive and more targetable and trackable media. As examples, both Tata Motors and Temsa use *direct mail* in markets with low volumes (especially in the B2B segments of their businesses), and Haier USA mines its customer service records to send out e-mail communications. Apollo Tyres makes extensive use of cheaper *online media* in Europe, since many customers there research and buy tires online, before getting them shipped and installed locally. Infosys focuses on *driving prospects to its own website*, where useful but free content helps communicate its thought leadership.

Turkish companies make significant use of *product placement* in the Central Asian, Middle Eastern, and Balkan countries (Turkish TV series are popular in 36 countries). We also saw the purchase of cross-national TV media, with lower cost-per-thousand regional footprints, by firms like Dabur and Godrej. However, our EMNCs went beyond these conventional tactics, cleverly leveraging channel-partner knowledge and clout, being willing to grab novel opportunities, and leveraging lower-cost emerging-market capabilities.

Leveraging Channel-Partner Knowledge and Clout

EMNCs are innovative in their efforts to reduce cost and increase effectiveness by leveraging the local market knowledge and media-buying clout of their channel partners. Large retailers like Best Buy or Carrefour have superior knowledge of what works locally, through access to data and years of local experience, compared with the recently arrived EMNCs. These retailers are also much larger businesses in their home markets as well as in markets where they are well established. As a result, they have much greater clout through their centralized buying of media compared with that of the EMNCs with their limited budgets. These larger media buys can lower media costs substantially, and so companies like Chigo leveraged their channel partners' knowledge and size to effectively lower the cost and increase the effectiveness of their own awareness-building spending.

Being Willing to Grab Novel Opportunities

EMNCs are also more open to grabbing novel opportunities that can reduce cost. As referred to briefly in Chapter 2, Lenovo's ex-CMO Deepak Advani proudly told us of a Google TV buy that the company made in fall 2007 (an experiment then for Google) in which it was able to buy at auction very cheap spot-TV time in the United States on Dish Network in specific markets in highly desirable shows (such as *Monday Night Football* and NCAA sports events). This opportunistic buy, which took quick advantage of this short-fused bargain availability, reduced Lenovo's TV costs by almost 90 percent! Lenovo used existing online video as the creative and customized the last 10 seconds of each spot with different promotional offers tailored to the programming. Tracking showed that 60 to 70 percent of those who came to the Lenovo website because of this advertising had never been to the website before. Google TV subsequently expanded its TV inventory beyond the Dish network to also include Bloomberg TV, Hallmark Channel, MSNBC, CNBC, and others.[8]

Leveraging Lower-Cost Emerging-Market Talent

While companies from all over the world locate or outsource their manufacturing, R&D, and customer support centers to low-cost emerging markets, some EMNCs try to also use the less expensive cost structures of marketing partners in emerging markets. Lenovo sources much of its marketing communications out of India and has created a global hub for such activities in Bangalore, because the organization recognizes that lower-cost India-based communication firms can come up with creative concepts every bit as impactful and imaginative as their West-based counterparts and achieve production values in implementing creative concepts that are also equally good. Lenovo's Advani told us how this led to very significant reductions in the company's worldwide expenses for advertising creative and production work, without in any way compromising the quality of the output, since it worked with the same kinds of world-class agency talent in India (Ogilvy & Mather) that it would have worked with in a developed-country location.

Indeed, Wipro's Jessie Paul argues[9] that the global delivery model that the leading Indian software firms like Wipro, Infosys, and TCL developed is broadly applicable beyond the software industry. Paul argues that any marketing service activity that is labor intensive but not culturally specific can be outsourced using the global delivery model. Thus, activities such as direct marketing, online marketing platforms, competitive intelligence, marketing analytics, and the like can also be outsourced to benefit from regional competencies in cost, time, and creativity. Like Lenovo, Wipro makes its video materials (TV and film) and does all of its high-quality printing, in addition to doing almost all of its creative work, in India.

Multiply Impact

In addition to looking for ways to lower costs, many EMNCs appear to be striving for and achieving "multiplier effects" of their limited investments in awareness building in these four ways:

- Building buzz through creativity and innovation
- Leveraging the reach of opinion leaders and editorial media

- Leveraging member communications by partners
- Using integrated marketing strategies

Building Buzz Through Creativity and Innovation

Marketing research over the past 30 years has repeatedly shown that the impact of marketing depends more on the creativity of the marketing activities than on the amount of money being spent.[10] Indeed, one of the key reasons that creativity increases impact is because it generates word of mouth, which is very influential.[11] We had several instances of our low-budget brands being very deliberate about creating high visibility, attention-getting products and creative messages, and in thinking outside the box in selecting media and designing promotions. We found two ways in which this was being done: more creative messaging and faster product innovation cycles.

High-Interest Creative Messages. EMNCs recognize the value of creativity and its importance for magnifying the impact of their limited budgets. Thus, they try to do things that are different, sometimes being controversial, as was the case with Mahindra & Mahindra's 2008 press campaign in South Africa about its 60-year Jeep heritage. Mahindra & Mahindra has the history and experience in building the original Jeep vehicle, under license from the original Willys company, since 1947, which gives it a special claim to knowledge about how best to build tough utility vehicles. The campaign involved a four-page spread of a mock New York daily newspaper dated September 2, 1945. The headline said "Victory! Germany, Italy and Japan Finally Beaten." The center spread showed a picture of a World War II army Jeep along with the Mahindra logo and the phrase "Since 1945." Various other articles on the spread detailed stories about Mahindra & Mahindra during this time. (See Figure 5-2.) The spread was put into the *Sunday Times* (South Africa). The campaign was disruptive; it won tremendous word-of-mouth attention for Mahindra & Mahindra. It made people understand that Mahindra & Mahindra was not

FIGURE 5-2 An ad created in 2008 by Mahindra & Mahindra for the South African market to illustrate its 60-year Jeep association.
Source: SP Shukla, President—Group Strategy and Member—Group Executive Board, Mahindra Group. Used with permission.

an inexperienced builder of rugged vehicles, but had decades of experience building them, even building some vehicles just like those used by the U.S. army in the deserts and mountains during World War II that beat the Japanese and German equivalents. Chrysler's Jeep division challenged this campaign in South Africa's local advertising council (unsuccessfully). Such controversial claims, particularly when they lead to unsuccessful counterattacks, can be hugely beneficial, as this particular campaign from Mahindra & Mahindra was.

In an interesting twist to this idea, companies like Infosys and Wipro try to promote a *novel or controversial point of view*. Leveraging the "flat-world" idea originally advanced by then-CEO Nandan Nilekani,[12] and later popularized by Thomas Friedman,[13] Infosys created a suite of products to help firms compete under this scenario. Its flat-world opinion on how the world was evolving, which was novel and distinct and offered ways for customers to win in such a world by creating more customer value, led to debate and awareness-building media coverage through both mass media reporting and word of mouth. Wipro promotes its own point-of-view approach with a *high-profile event* called "Stratagem" (now called "Sangam") that it hosts, at which clients, analysts, and other thought leaders huddle to debate important IT-relevant trends for the future, trends for the future advanced by Wipro as its point of view. These events are of broad interest to both IT vendors and customers and thus draw media attention, helping build awareness for Wipro, while at the same time building its reputation as a thought leader.

Some of the brands cleverly use brand-positioning strategies tied to *attention-grabbing aspects of their countries or regions of origin*. Leveraging country associations that are strong and positive, Wipro runs by-invitation parties at trade shows featuring Bollywood music and posters and Indian food, and Dabur uses Bollywood movie stars in its advertising. Modelo leverages its unique Mexican imagery for its beers—its beers are the only exported beer brands made in Mexico. Mavi has used Turkey's location on the Mediterranean to position its jeans around the "Mediterranean lifestyle."

APB takes this idea to the next level. It ties its creative executions closely to the Tiger name of its beer and the "tiger economy" imagery of its home Asian region. The region and its growth story are far more exciting than the home market of Singapore, and APB has cleverly leveraged iconic elements drawn from across Asia to build an exciting and cool image for its brand. APB mixes the animal visual of the tiger, the concept of the tiger economies of Asia, and the iconic sport of kickboxing from Thailand to stage kickboxing events in underground parking lots (with DJ music and Chinese food) in its Western markets. Such creative execution sparks interest, enthusiasm, and, more importantly, word of mouth among the target audience, multiplying the impact of the investments to far higher levels.

Faster Product Innovation Cycles. Several of the companies we spoke to relied on product innovation to garner attention and generate buzz through customer word of mouth, media coverage, and retail sales personnel. Every 21 days, Natura tries to do "10 new things," including new product launches, changes in packaging, and new offers, to excite its salespeople and give them new reasons to make repeat sales calls. This short innovation cycle significantly boosts its sales-force productivity and lowers sales-force turnover, huge competitive advantages for Natura. HTC and Lenovo are also good examples of this strategy: HTC's CMO John Wang told us that "the basis of our building brand awareness is not money, but our innovation." HTC launches 15 to 20 new products a year, focusing on innovations (such as the first smartphone with a dedicated Facebook button or the first 3D smartphone).

HTC's strategy is similar to that taken by LG Electronics earlier, when it launched the LG brand in the United States in 2002. At the time, LG decided to launch a new washing machine and a new refrigerator every 2 years, when the leading competitors launched new products every 5 to 10 years.[14] Leveraging this rapid innovation cycle, LG was able to build up a formidable unaided awareness level of 48 percent for the LG brand in the consumer electronics and white goods category.[15] A similar strategy has been used for flat-screen TVs and mobile phones by Samsung as well[16] and by LG Mobile for its Chocolate and Shine phones.

Leveraging the Reach of Opinion Leaders and Editorial Media

Opinion leaders and "earned media" (MPR coverage) can be used to extend the reach of a firm's own "paid media" efforts to build brand awareness. By favorably influencing respected, admired, and connected individuals, companies stand to gain favorable word of mouth, which not only is free but, according to research, is far more impactful than messages received through mass media.

Not surprisingly, EMNCs try to identify and target opinion leaders and then create opportunities and incentives for them to pass along messages in both the online and offline domains. Targeted opinion leaders for Infosys and Wipro are analyst and consulting firms such as Gartner and Forrester; Ranbaxy (pharmaceuticals) builds relationships with important doctors and nurses, creating value-added services (such as patient education and follow-up) they can talk about to others; Apollo Tyres goes after influential bloggers; and APB sets its sights on bar staffers and "cool" people to visibly use its Tiger Beer in bars.

The Mahindra Group has started an international recruitment program at the Ivy League campuses in the United States. According to S.P. Shukla, President-Group Strategy and Member-Group Executive Board, "This program not only helps in both increasing cultural diversity within the management cadre and bringing in fresh international insights, but also creates buzz for the company on these campuses, leading to high awareness of the firm among the graduating class every year." As the graduates of these prestigious colleges move into different firms across the world, the corporate profile of the Mahindra Group headquartered in India— with 140,000 personnel drawn from 100 countries, spread over 5 continents—travels with them and helps the Mahindra Group gain further global recognition.

To generate earned media (MPR) coverage, HTC creates (or takes advantage of) events where its innovative smartphones are featured (such as at Google's launch of the Android OS–based Nexus One or at a Microsoft launch event at which Bill Gates was holding an HTC-made Windows-Mobile smartphone). Aramex creates ads and events that celebrate its local and regional accomplishments and pride. Lenovo seeks and leverages positive (sometimes glowing) reviews and awards for its new products at forums such as the annual CES (Consumer Electronics Show) in Las Vegas. The Taj Group succeeded in getting media coverage of its annual convention of the Leading Hotels of the World held in its new Boston property (the former Ritz Carlton). LG "gave away high-end LG TV sets on Oprah's show and got incredible awareness at a fraction of the cost," according to Michael Ahn. And Mavi's brand awareness increased significantly when celebrities Cher, Daryl Hannah, and Chelsea Clinton were spotted wearing Mavi jeans.

Carrying out activities linked to CSR is a well-recognized tactic to get free media coverage. Thus, when consumers in the United States were keenly aware of the need to help victims of Hurricane Katrina, Haier gave away appliances to assist in rescue and rehabilitation efforts, gaining considerable media attention. Mahindra Tractors too donated tractors to nearby communities after Hurricane Katrina. While each tractor cost about $10,000, the resulting media coverage was worth much more. Mahindra's Arun Nanda told us that news coverage of the relief operations, which included footage showing Mahindra's tractors plowing through flooded areas in and around New Orleans, was equivalent to millions of dollars in paid-for advertising.

Leveraging Member Communications by Partners

Another way to "multiply" small ad budgets is to get the brand message out via existing organizations that have large memberships of brand-relevant consumers and send out frequent communications to them at the partner organization's expense. Thus many of the automotive-related brands we spoke to—such as Tata Motors, Mahindra & Mahindra, and Apollo Tyres—told us that they sought out auto clubs and driver associations to reach those clubs' memberships with product-related information as well as with test-drive opportunities. Taj Hotels entered into partnerships with credit cards and airlines, presumably with mutually beneficial member and customer offers. Infosys reaches opinion leaders by engaging with academic associations.

Using Integrated Marketing Strategies

It is well recognized that an integrated marketing campaign increases the effectiveness of marketing investments. Notwithstanding this well-accepted axiom, the majority of firms do not in fact successfully integrate the different elements of their marketing plans such as mass media advertising, product placements, sponsorships, events, and public relations.[17]

EMNCs, however, appear to take this axiom to heart and pay careful attention to developing integrated marketing programs. We saw such a careful integration of marketing activities by Lenovo as it integrated its Olympics, NBA, and Formula 1 sponsorships with its mass media campaign. Lenovo connected the activities through its value proposition of "computing strength." To get the most out of its NBA sponsorship dollars, Lenovo arranged to have its computers visibly present and used by on-air commentators to report a "Lenovo teamwork stat," a statistic it created that measured the extent to which each player assisted others on the team! These were, in turn, picked up in its mass media advertising to amplify the combined effect of the marketing investments. At the same time that Infosys launched its own "win in the flat world" messaging, it also publicized a blog on the subject, written by its CEO Nandan Nilekani and aimed at Fortune 500 CEOs; and it orchestrated a Nasdaq bell ringing from the Mysore, India, campus.

LG Electronics has tapped into the Indian passion for cricket. It has sponsored the Cricket World Cup and the Indian cricket team, and it has created a cricket video game that it builds into every TV set sold in India, some of which also contain a "time machine" that allows the consumer to go back a few minutes and replay events, a feature particularly useful when watching sports. The sponsorships, the built-in cricket game, and the time machine, combined with its advertising that leveraged these elements—featuring team captain Sourav Ganguly as the brand ambassador—significantly elevated LG's awareness,[18] making it a well-liked household name in India, according to K. R. Kim, the founding CEO of LG Electronics in India.

Summary and Key Takeaways

EMNCs thus appear to be building brand awareness effectively, notwithstanding their traditional resource constraints. They do so by meticulously picking their challenges, as in carefully and narrowly defining their target segments; focusing on one or at best a limited number of brands and products; and sometimes choosing to focus on the large but few intermediaries, rather than the many end consumers.

To make their budgets go further, EMNCs show far greater discipline and creativity in managing costs, and they do it continuously and relentlessly. They do so by leveraging the knowledge and scale of their trade partners; by being opportunistic in taking advantage of lower-cost options; and by thoughtfully locating activities wherever possible to lower-cost emerging-market contexts.

EMNCs then search for ways to multiply and amplify the impact of their marketing investments by creating and leveraging buzz; leveraging the reach of opinion leaders, earned media, and partners aggressively; and more thoughtfully integrating their various marketing activities to create a highly synergistic message.

These three steps collectively (see Figure 5-3 for a checklist) enable EMNCs to punch far higher than their weight level, allowing them to compete and win in the segments and markets they participate in, even against the more powerful developed-world multinationals.

- Have you identified your target segment carefully?
- Have you identified your opinion leaders?
- Have you chosen the best brand or product to put your communication behind?
- Have you considered targeting intermediaries and using them to become your advocates?
- Are you effectively utilizing the knowledge of the intermediaries?
- Are you effectively leveraging the clout of your intermediaries?
- Are you using the most targeted and influential touch points?
- Are you sourcing your communication development and design from a low-cost high-quality geography?
- Are your messages novel enough to gain attention and potentially go viral?
- Do your messages create opportunities to facilitate conversation?
- Do all the elements of your plan communicate consistently and coherently?
- Have you put in place tools and metrics for tracking outcomes?

FIGURE 5-3 Are Your Awareness-Building Efforts Optimized? A Checklist

The lessons of these EMNC awareness-building strategies and tactics for other EMNCs, and for other resource-challenged challenger companies, seem pretty straightforward. They too would be wise to aim their brand awareness-building at smaller and fewer segments and customers, for fewer products and brands. They too should try to identify partner organizations—suppliers, trade intermediaries, customer organizations—whose budgets, customer reach, market knowledge, and buying clout can potentially be leveraged. They too should use new products and innovation to win the attention and support of opinion leaders and buzz makers and media gatekeepers. They too should use the newer and cheaper online and digital media wherever possible and seek to be relentlessly cost-focused in all aspects of creative and production sourcing. And they should be prepared to push the envelope on messaging novelty and creativity to win attention and pass-along power.

What might the TMNCs learn from this? One response might be to harness their much larger budgets for "shock-and-awe" campaigns that EMNCs and other challengers could never hope to match, thus building and reinforcing the kinds of leadership and aspirational brand imagery that the last chapter said might be their forte. Examples of this might be sponsoring global, high-visibility events and campaigns with very global high-profile music, fashion, and sports stars. A totally different response (and this is not a mutually exclusive either-or option) would be to teach their own marketing managers and partners how to market in a lean, "guerrilla-like" manner, for example, presenting them with a scenario in which their budgets were slashed 50 percent and asking them to respond by using zero-base budgeting and planning methods, etc. Organizational theorists have long pointed out that large, successful organizations often develop tremendous slack and wasteful practices; learning how EMNCs do things can help TMNCs to identify and uproot these.

6

Building Perceptions of High Quality, Leadership, and Trust

As Chapter 4 pointed out, we strongly believe that having perceptions of high quality, industry leadership, and trust and confidence are much more important to brand strength than high levels of awareness or an attractive visual identity. Most of the EMNCs in our sample have low levels of brand awareness, made worse by negative country-of-origin imagery for most of them. A 2011 survey by GfK found that only one-third of vehicle buyers in the United States are willing to even consider Indian and Chinese auto manufacturers, versus 95 percent consideration for U.S. manufacturers, with poor (and slow-to-change) quality perceptions playing a major role.[1] Thus, it is not surprising that many of these EMNCs (e.g., Apollo Tyres, Chigo, HTC, Lenovo, Mahindra & Mahindra, Ulker) felt that raising their quality reputations was a major challenge. Increasing an EMNC brand's quality reputation is possibly the hardest aspect of its brand building because consumers are unlikely to uncritically accept a company's own claims about its high quality. And some recent research[2] has found that when perceptions lag reality, it can take consumers as many as six years to raise their quality perceptions to bring them in line with objective quality levels.

We present below the methods being used by the EMNCs we spoke to, to raise their brands' perceptions of quality, leadership, and trust, and we link these methods to some general principles. While the strategies and tactics used by our EMNCs can all fit into the general principles we will describe, the manner in which our EMNCs have implemented them again testifies to the fresh, low-budget thinking they are bringing to these brand-building challenges. We organize our discussion in terms of the need to first actually build high quality, next communicate this to create perceptions of quality in the target consumers' minds (overcoming the hurdles of low credibility that EMNCs typically suffer from), and then go beyond a credible claim of high quality to creating a leadership position in consumers' minds. Figure 6-1 provides a summary and road map.

First, Create High Quality

Building a high-quality reputation is not a marketing "smoke-and-mirrors" job; it first requires the real creation of objective quality through the application of R&D and innovation, and it requires superior manufacturing and quality control in the areas that matter to consumers when they choose a brand.[3] Every product and service element that contributes to the *experience* of quality by the target consumer needs to be carefully and objectively attended to. Several of our companies talked about their abilities to genuinely better satisfy their end customers than the competition does.

Materials and Features

Mahindra Tractors says its tractors are genuinely stronger because the company uses more and tougher steel in their construction. Asia Pacific Breweries says its beers use non-local (United States, United Kingdom, or Australian) malt and go through 250 quality-control checks, which its competitors do not do. Telecom operator MTS focuses on creating a competitively superior network

Create High Quality
- Materials and features
- Quality control
- Service and support

Create High-Quality Perceptions via Advertising
- Anticipate and refute reasons to disbelieve
- Position brand on high quality, not better value
- Compare your brand with the market leader, with proof

Gain Credibility via Third-Party Endorsements (MPR)
- Create newsworthy stories using tests, innovation, awards
- Target opinion leaders

Use Cobranding to Get a Rub-Off of High Quality
- Carefully choose and publicize customers, trade partners, suppliers
- Associate your brand with industry-leading trade associations
- Sponsor and leverage prestigious events

Use Quality Signals and Cues
- Use insight research to discover and leverage these cues and signals
- Leverage certifications, standards, ratings
- Use design to signal high quality

Change Perceived Country of Origin
- Create new global or regional brand identity
- Create a different, local, country-of-origin identity

Use Acquired Brands for Their High-Quality Reputation

FIGURE 6-1 Building Perceptions of High Quality

quality. Ulker uses vertical integration, with its own flour mills, to enable it to create and use special types of flour in its biscuits. HTC and LG Mobile both claim to be more flexible and responsive in meeting the needs of their mobile carrier customers than a Nokia can. Temsa builds buses and trucks that its fleet buyers in Western Europe find compelling because it better understands their unmet needs, including seats for their drivers that expand into beds. Titan, in its attempt to build a world-class watch for the European market, used the latest Japanese and German technology and machinery and European design.

Quality Control

High quality must not merely be designed into the product itself: it must also be implemented and enforced on the factory floor, and many of our EMNCs boasted about their high-standard quality-assurance systems. Haier is well known for its organization-wide attention to quality control: its CEO Zhang Ruimin once ordered his workers to destroy 76 faulty refrigerators, destroying the first one himself (it is now preserved in the firm's museum).[4] The Taj Group drops lower-quality properties (such as its New York Lexington Hotel) from its portfolio, so that those that remain are truly best-in-luxury-class, iconic properties (such as the formerly Four-Seasons Pierre in New York or the former Ritz-Carlton in Boston). It uses IT aggressively, such as its customer information and needs database, to deliver category-leading service standards. It also invests heavily in staff training and audits, and it prioritizes the delivery of a consistent "Taj-ness" in its customer experience worldwide. Chigo and the Taj Group both told us of their root-cause analysis of customer service calls and complaints to locate and fix quality issues so that they do not recur.

Service and Support

In many cases, companies discover that quality, to their customers, means not just the quality of the products purchased, but also (or even more so) the quality of the service after purchase. Lenovo sees quite clearly that its machines, no matter how well made, will at some point need such support, as do Haier USA, Chigo, and the auto companies in our sample (Temsa, Tata Motors, Mahindra Tractors, and Mahindra & Mahindra Auto). Consequently they aim to offer 24-hour, live, quickly responsive service networks, better than that of their competitors. In the case of Chigo, its service network is even better than that of the retailers for whom it makes private label air conditioners, an advantage it uses to try to get these retailers to stock Chigo-branded machines instead of the private-branded ones.

LG Electronic boasts a highly sophisticated customer service network. In the United States, it has dramatically expanded its service capability through investments in call centers and parts warehouses to coordinate and respond to customer service needs. In India, its second largest market after the United States, LG is aiming to be able to answer a service call within 1 minute and respond to it with an in-home service call within 1 day, from its current 3-3 level, making it the leader in customer service in the categories it competes in. Tile producer Vitra, because of its huge manufacturing scale, can be more flexible and customer responsive in how it schedules its production runs, even for limited-demand SKUs.

Service and support to create quality perceptions don't only apply to end consumers, but apply to trade customers as well. Apollo Tyres aims for competitive superiority in providing superior service to its trade customers via better logistics and IT support, a broader product portfolio, and higher service levels overall. Evyap, Marico, and Midea also aim to offer superior logistics and supply chain service to their trade partners, and we have described the IT-enabled infrastructure that Marico has created to ensure superior monitoring and replenishment of stocks across its vast network of retailers in India in Chapter 2.

In India, LG has opened over 100 branch and sales offices, a number that is about five times larger than that of its main competitors, to be able to offer its trade customers superior support and also to support its relationships with its customers through faster and more responsive after-sales service.[5] Ranbaxy offers added-value services to its physician customers, such as cholesterol checks and diet advice for their patients. It also offers physicians and hospitals a broad portfolio of therapies to make itself the easiest-to-deal-with supplier. Temsa quite clearly sees its pre-sales and after-sales support as crucial to winning business from its fleet operator market in countries such as Austria and France. It also tries hard to be a company easier to do business with than

competitor companies: customers value their ability to communicate easily with its CEO and senior managers.

Creating Perceptions of High Quality via Advertising

It is not enough for an EMNC challenger brand to simply achieve
high product or service quality in terms of technical and laboratory
tests and specifications. What matters is the extent to which you
create *perceptions* of high quality among the customer segments
that are most important to your business. Therefore a Global
Brand Builder's job is not only to actually create objective high
quality (in the lab or on the factory floor), but also to successfully
communicate this high quality to the marketplace.

A natural first effort in communicating the high levels of technical quality you've achieved would be to document your product's
technical specifications and publicize them in advertising and on
specification sheets and in brochures. Persuasive advertising can
anticipate, then refute, the reasons why consumers might disbelieve claims that the brand has high quality. In addition, consideration needs to be given to whether to position the brand as "high
quality" or "best value for the money." If you want to build a
truly strong brand, it might be better long term to be known as a
brand for high quality rather than for great value. Consumers may
feel emotionally unsatisfied knowing that, because of their limited
budgets, they had to settle for a second-best brand, even if it was a
better value choice. And if you compete on a value-for-money platform, you are probably more vulnerable to the next even lower-
cost supplier. South Korean brands like Samsung discovered years
ago that a quality-leadership positioning was more effective than
a second-best-but-more-value one.[6] The recent drop in Tata Nano
sales has been attributed by some observers to Indian consumers not wanting to own (and be seen owning) such a cheap car; in
such a visibly consumed product, a low price creates value but can
reduce pride of ownership.

Some of the companies in our sample did indeed put lots of
advertising money behind making quality claims, such as Titan for

its watch in Europe. Anticipating possible objections to its claims for a high-quality watch from an Indian company, Titan positioned its specially designed watch as a "best of breed" that had European design, French technology, and German engineering and was manufactured with Japanese equipment. The Taj Group too runs award-winning ads in some of the world's most prestigious (and expensive) media, showcasing its iconic properties and excellent service. Dabur is one of the few packaged-goods (or fast-moving consumer goods) companies in our EMNC sample that we found invests high amounts in advertising for its products. Chapter 5 (on awareness building) reviews many of the advertising-type brand-building efforts of Dabur and the other EMNCs we spoke to.

But such self-paid-for advertising efforts might not get noticed. One way to gain *attention*, if you are a market follower, is to compare yourself loudly and publicly with a market leader or two, in ads and collateral materials (brochures and spec sheets). To follow such a comparative attack strategy, you must be doing business in a country that allows such comparisons to be made publicly; not all do. You also must be factually and legally correct, with supportive tests by credible authorities or techniques, and have the backup documentation. Haier, in the late 1980s in Europe, paid for its products to be comparison-tested in Europe against competitive brands, with labels off, and was able to show better objective performance than major German brands, greatly helping its later distribution and sales performance there.[7] Mahindra & Mahindra enters its Scorpio SUV in competitions and rallies and uses its high performance there both for media coverage and in its own advertising.

Gaining Credibility About One's Quality Claims

Building *credibility* for your quality claims is a big challenge: the high-quality claims in your own paid-for advertising are unlikely to be believed. Assertions about quality are more credible if they come from an arm's-length, third-party source. Methods used by our EMNCs to make their quality claims more credible thus include garnering and publicizing *credible third-party endorsements* via MPR. Inferences about a brand's quality made by consumers on their own—rather than explicitly claimed by the brand—can also be especially powerful. Thus, EMNCs can build high-quality perceptions both by gaining credible quality "rub-offs" via *cobranding* techniques and by understanding and using the quality *signals and cues*—including *product design*—that the target segment uses to judge quality (often subconsciously). To the extent that an EMNC brand's country of origin contributes to its low-quality perceptions, EMNCs can try to find ways to alter or divert attention from their *perceived* country of origin. Finally, they can *acquire* brands with high perceived quality.

Gaining Credible Third-Party Endorsements: Attracting MPR Coverage

It is well known (and as we indicated above) that while consumers are unlikely to believe an advertiser's own claims of high or improved quality, they are much more likely to accept statements about these made by perceivably objective third-party sources, such as editorial media. Being featured and recommended in third-party editorial reviews in the media helps hugely (such as being declared the better product by the *New York Times* or winning the Editor's Choice award from a leading computer magazine). Such use of MPR also helps our EMNCs avoid head-on, high-budget confrontations with their better-endowed TMNC competitors.

Recognizing this, many of our companies went out of their way to seek MPR coverage to get the story about their quality, innovation, and feature or value leadership out to the public in a believable manner. As Chapter 5 on awareness-creating tactics made clear, third-party editorial media are looking for *newsworthy stories*. Apollo Tyres subjects its tires to competitive tests conducted by respected third-party sources, then makes sure its unexpected winning record gets covered by automotive and other media. Haier uses events tied to social responsibility to generate media coverage, as do Lenovo and the Taj Group.

Products with a high degree of innovation—getting a "wow" reaction for their novelty—are usually perceived as being worthy of attention and coverage by the media, and consumers find them to be worthy of pass-along (viral, word of mouth) communication as well.[8] Lenovo seeks out respected reviewers such as Walt Mossberg of the *Wall Street Journal* for its new laptops; its X300 laptop was the subject of a very positive cover story in *BusinessWeek* when it won awards at the Consumer Electronics Show in Las Vegas.

Winning and publicizing awards for quality is another frequently used quality MPR-generating technique: such awards get attention and media coverage. Among the companies that seek out and leverage such awards is Lenovo, which often wins them for its innovative notebooks. Mahindra Tractors publicized its Deming TQM award won in 2003. Temsa won and heavily publicized its European Producer of the Year award won in 2008.

Interestingly enough, a brand can become associated with quality not only if it wins awards for quality, but also if it *gives out such awards*. Wipro very cleverly created a series of awards for innovation in IT, given annually in conjunction with Forbes.com and two professional U.S. IT organizations. Winning entries were turned into cases and a book, and the awards event itself was conducted in a top-level hotel venue to prove that Wipro was no fly-by-night organization, but a top-class company.

Editorial media are not the only credible third-party sources one can tap. Infosys and Wipro target trusted *industry analysts* Gartner and Forrester. Wipro organizes Strategem conference-type events to which leading media and analysts, in addition to thought leaders from industry and academia, are invited; and it publishes case studies, white papers, and books based on them. Wipro also uses clippings from media such as *Forbes* and *BusinessWeek* in its sales calls.[9]

Using Cobranding to Get a Rub-Off of High Quality
Another useful technique to build perceptions of high credibility is to publicly associate yourself with other firms, products,

or organizations—in your industry or others—that are already widely perceived as having high standards in regard to quality. Such cobranding can benefit you through a rub-off of their high-quality image. In the United States, the Korean cell phone makers Samsung and LG both gained hugely in raising their quality perceptions as a result of their being suppliers to Sprint PCS, a leading service provider.[10]

To get such a cobranding quality rub-off, many EMNCs in our sample picked suppliers, dealers, distributors, and retail and OEM customers that are very well known and trusted themselves, and ran joint co-op ads with them. Mahindra Tractors told us it chose dealers that would help build the company's own high-quality associations. HTC ran co-op ads with mobile carrier customers such as Orange and Vodaphone; another boost came when Bill Gates showcased HTC's WindowsOS smartphone at a launch event, and HTC gained too as the maker of the first AndroidOS phone launched by Google. Haier USA benefits from the strong brands of its retail customers Best Buy, Home Depot, and Target.

Wipro leverages the strong reputations of the IT associations (e.g., the International Association of Outsourcing Professionals and the IT Association of America) and media partners (Forbes .com) with which it jointly gives out its innovation awards. Companies such as the Taj Group and Tata Tea that form part of the trusted Tata organization prominently mention that association. The Taj Group also prominently uses its strong partnership with the Leading Hotels of the World—to which it contributes 15 properties, among the largest of such contributors—and other such similar organizations. Lenovo acquired the Thinkpad brand from IBM, and concluded a five-year agreement with IBM to use its brand name and sales and service network, in large part to benefit from IBM's strong brand reputation. Temsa uses and publicizes crucial bus and truck components (such as engines) from suppliers such as Mercedes, MAN, Daft, and Cummins.

As part of such a cobranding effort, targeted *events and sponsorships* can also help to associate brands with high quality, such as Lenovo with the Olympics and Formula 1. Although expensive, these sponsorships can be very effective if used strategically: Lenovo used 30,000 pieces of its computing technology equipment at the Beijing Olympics, and it also showcases its computing products in Formula 1, using them in the starting and running of those exceedingly complicated pieces of high-profile automotive machinery. Korea's Hankook tires just became (in mid-2011) the official tire supplier to a prestigious European touring-car race called the Deutsche Tourenwagen Masters, and the company is bidding to become the sole supplier to Formula 1 teams when Pirelli's contract expires at the end of 2013.[11]

Using Quality Signals and Cues

Another technique to make your quality claims seem credible is to understand and leverage the psychological *signals and cues* that your target consumers use to decide whether a certain product does indeed have high quality. Digging deep into consumer perception-formation processes can sometimes yield insights that an engineering mind would never expect. Imagine you are a builder of car engines. You know that, technically, overall engine quality depends on having a strong "launch," having high passing power, being fuel efficient, requiring low maintenance, being reliable, having low emissions, etc. No surprises there. But is there something else that shapes consumer perceptions of engine quality? How about the nature of the sounds the engine makes? In a luxury car, an extremely quiet engine connotes high quality. (As David Ogilvy once wrote in an ad for Rolls Royce, "At 60 miles an hour the loudest noise in this new Rolls-Royce comes from the electric clock.") In a sporty muscle car, a high-quality engine is one that snarls and growls. Cultures can differ in their quality signals: Honda car designers ended up with very different engine "exhaust notes" for some of its Japanese versus American models.

Insights about cues and signals that convey quality to consumers were used by the EMNCs in our sample. MTS has recognized that bills that are on time, accurate, and understandable signal and reinforce the quality perception that the firm seeks, and so it takes pains to ensure that the billing is done correctly, is easy to understand, and is received on time. Evyap soaps use better-than-expected fragrances and formulations. Godrej's largest-selling powder hair dyes only need water, not smelly chemicals, to be readied for application; this serves as a signal of superior quality.

Infosys and Wipro show prospects and clients the clear and reassuring process maps created as a result of their Six Sigma processes. Wipro goes further and allows its clients to log into its systems to visually see their project tasks being tracked. To prove it is a serious long-term player, Mahindra Tractors set up its own dealer network in the United States rather than use a distributor network. Some EMNCs, such as Aramex and HTC, have consciously decided to move to higher levels of pricing to communicate their high levels of quality. Others, such as Haier, offer significantly longer warranties to signal their superior quality—1 year instead of the industry standard of 90 days. The Taj Group is acutely conscious of the quality signals it sends through the physical and sensory elements of its business facilities, services, and cuisine.

Certification and Standards as Quality Cues

Third-party quality standards and certification convey seemingly high objective quality and are used by Ranbaxy (FDA certification), Apollo Tyres (government standards), and Infosys and Wipro (CMM5 and Six Sigma standards, certification by SWIFT). Infosys points out that it gets third-party validation of its code and that it has a 95 percent on-time delivery performance record. In seeking private label business in Europe, Ulker relies significantly on the certifications it obtained from the British Retail Consortium and the International Finance Corporation.

Ratings as Quality Cues

Just as MPR builds credibility and gets attention, so do ratings and reviews. The car companies use this when possible, such as Tata Motors' use of the J. D. Power's ratings in trying to turn around the perceptions of poor quality associated with its acquired Jaguar brand. Haier USA and LG Electronics use the ratings produced by *Consumer Reports* magazine.

Utilizing Design to Signal High Quality

Sensory cues and product styling and design can play vital roles in creating a perception of high quality in all kinds of businesses. IBM uses design very strategically in shaping the perceptions of its servers and other computers, as do Apple, Sony, LG, and Samsung, to create a perception of high quality in the consumer electronics business.[12] Look carefully at the weight and feel as well as at the materials and textures, of a Gillette razor; it was designed to communicate masculinity and technical sophistication. The role of interior styling and design in communicating automotive quality is well appreciated: the feel and tactile shape of switches and materials, the use of leather and wood, are understood and used by all leading companies.

HTC, LG Mobile (e.g., with its Chocolate and Shine phones), LG Electronics, Haier, Lenovo, Modelo, and East African Breweries are some of our EMNCs that use shape and size and expensive-looking design, materials, and finishes to communicate high quality, reliability, and confidence. East African Breweries told us that the feel of the fatter bottle in the drinker's palm signaled a distinct quality to the Tusker Beer drinker, and the company has now launched this product across Africa, as well as in the U.K. market. Modelo's clear-glass beer bottle with a long neck for Corona Beer also communicates higher quality. We heard from LG Electronics that during its initial launch of LG-branded washing machines, it began with a machine that had European styling, to communicate high quality, since European products are perceived as high quality in the United States. Likewise, it used the name Tromm, a German word for *drum*, to reinforce the European association. It coupled this with demonstrating its novel direct-drive technology in retail display locations to underscore its high quality.[13] Following a similar logic, Haier uses European designers. Recognizing the value of design cues in subtly signaling quality, HTC has hired away Microsoft's X-Box designer, Horace Luke, to create and lead a team of "magic lab" designers in Seattle and Taiwan to create world-leading product and user-interface designs.[14] Lenovo's ultrathin, 1.3-kg U-260 laptop won plaudits in 2011 for its satin finish and svelte frame, leather-textured palm rest, and attractive colors.

Mavi jeans not only utilized a well-known European designer and consultant, Adriano Goldschmied, but also leveraged its lower-cost ability to create the kinds of fabric finishes preferred by its customers.[15] When the premium jeans segment began to take off in the late 1990s, washing and finishing procedures became a more important element of jeans design. Mavi was able to use its lower-cost labor to perform the labor-intensive job of using sandpaper and chemicals to create the patina desired by its upper-segment customers; this served as the needed "quality cue."

Changing Perceived Country of Origin

National Origin as a Quality Cue

Many of the home countries of the companies we spoke to still have an image of being under-developed and poor, with low competencies in technology and quality control, although these countries may admittedly have a more positive country-of-origin imagery in some narrow product areas (e.g., India as a source of tea, China for silk or low-cost computer manufacturing). Lenovo's ex-CMO Deepak Advani mentioned to us a survey in 2005 by PR consultants Edelman which showed Chinese products had a poor reputation for quality in many countries. Titan's Bhaskar Bhat explicitly said to us that his company thought its Indian country of origin was a major reason why its seven-year effort in Europe to market a global watch did not succeed (Titan pulled the plug on this in 2002), and China's Chigo said that China's poor image was a major reason why it decided to go the OEM route instead of marketing directly to overseas consumers. (There were, however, some other companies in our sample—Mitac and Midea among them—which did not feel their country of origin worked against them in their brand-building efforts overseas. Taiwan, notably, has had a nation-branding campaign in recent years focused on creating an image of high-quality innovation.)

If consumers doubt your quality because of the imagery of the country your company is from, it might help to downplay such country of origin by using either a global or regional brand identity or a local one. With today's wide Internet usage, no company can hope to keep its national origin a secret (as Lenovo's Advani reminded us), but it is still possible to reduce the salience of it through clever marketing. Alternatively, some of our companies target markets where their country-of-origin image is a positive rather than a negative: Evyap's country of origin, Turkey, is an advantage for its soaps in Egypt, as is Natura's country of origin, Brazil, an advantage for its biodiverse Amazon-sourced ingredients in France.

Create Global or Regional Country-of-Origin Imagery

The first strategy—of building global or regional brand imagery instead of imagery connected with the true country of origin—is used by Asia Pacific Breweries, which brands itself as a pan-Asian beer, communicating a larger pan-Asian mystique. Turkey's Temsa told us of how it went after European markets and sales first, before expanding into other Asian and African markets, in order to build and utilize a European brand imagery. Temsa is now a major player in markets such as Austria and France, and prospective Chinese customers view it as a European, not Turkish, company. Haier supposedly went into developed markets first, to build a reputation as a world-class competitor, before expanding further into developing countries. Interestingly, Haier also chose its company name because it sounded Germanic[16]—the same reason that LG chose the name Tromm (which, as noted above, is German for *drum*) for its washing machines in the United States.

Create a Different Local Country-of-Origin Identity

The second strategy—adopting a local brand identity—is used by Dabur in the Middle East and Nigeria and by Midea in Brazil, the former using local models and ad executions and the latter leveraging the local brand and reputation of its joint venture partner. Consumers therefore do not see (as visibly) the EMNCs' country of origin, with its possibly negative imagery. Marico uses a South African identity in much of Africa via its acquired South African brands, but it uses its strong Egyptian brand in North Africa. One of our Turkish EMNCs gave us the example of a Turkish beer, Efes Pilsen, doing well in Russia under a local brand name there, Stary Melnik.

Using Acquired Brands for Their High-Quality Perceptions

This last example illustrates the final strategy we uncovered of raising quality perceptions: when all else fails or seems infeasible, there is always the *brand acquisition or licensing* route to gaining an image of high quality (with linked country of origin). There are numerous examples: Tata Tea acquiring Tetley; Asian Paints buying Topman in Fiji and Berger in the Middle East and South Asia; Mitac acquiring Navman (number one in Australia); Haier USA obtaining a license for the Amana brand of air-conditioner products in some channels; Chigo using in Europe the name of its German partner, the Van group. But perhaps the clearest case is the acquisition of the Thinkpad and other brands by Lenovo from IBM in 2004.[17] Especially in the business end-user market, where confidence in product quality and service is key, it would have been hard for China-based Lenovo to assert these positives on its own, despite its dominance of the Chinese consumer PC market and its track record of innovation there.

Beyond Quality: To Leadership

We mentioned earlier in Chapter 4, while developing the branding pyramid, that after obtaining a high-quality perception in the marketplace, the best brands go beyond that to also build a reputation for *leadership*. Many competitors in an industry can claim to offer high quality, but only one or two can claim industry leadership.

How do leadership brands achieve that status? How, for example, did Volvo's perception of safety leadership get created, and what can we learn from Volvo? A review of the company's ads over the years in North America shows that (1) Volvo *genuinely* led in pioneering many safety features in cars and (2) although the ad taglines change over the years, for about the last 30 years Volvo ads have *consistently* focused on this one key message. The company also deservedly keeps getting tremendous PR coverage and winning awards for its latest-and-greatest safety features whenever it launches new vehicles. So the lessons seem to be these: First, if you want to claim leadership in some area, you must in fact *have* that leadership. Second, spend money communicating that leadership, persistently and consistently. Media coverage about a company's technical leadership can be crucial in building and sustaining such a leadership image (*example:* Intel), as can coverage of its patent-winning prowess (*example:* IBM). For consumers, *what may matter most in creating a perception of technical leadership is the general awareness that a company tends to be the first, and to be fast, in coming out with new products and new technologies.* Consumers infer from such innovations that the company behind them is smart, energetic, and dynamic—a leader.

Chapter 2 earlier gave examples of many EMNCs that are using this innovation route to leadership. As an example, HTC is, in both reality and perception, probably the farthest along of all phone manufacturers in pushing the envelope in Android OS phones: that's why Google itself chose HTC to make its own first Android-OS phone, the Nexus-1. HTC also innovates in creating its own proprietary, much more user-friendly touch screen and 3D user interface for its Windows Mobile phones. The sheer speed with which it launches new innovative phones—launching 15 to 20 new ones every year—also serves as a very important signal of its innovation. Speed of new product launch has also been used as an innovation signal by LG Electronics and Samsung Electronics[18] and by other EMNCs such as Bharat Forge.[19]

Wipro claims to own more patents in the chip software design space than any other IT services firm; it backs up (and makes "real") its positioning as a highly innovative firm by setting internal innovation targets (a goal of having 10 percent of its revenues come from new services launched in the last three years) and by funding research incubators, and it has its own internal research council. Lenovo, with its Beijing Innovation Center partnering with its R&D centers in Raleigh, North Carolina, and Yamato, Japan, leads in notebook computer technologies such as face recognition, roll cages, and Dolby Surround Sound, and it has some desktops that offer solar panels and recyclable materials. Ulker claims to be a world leader in biscuit and chocolate technology, investing heavily in this area; its expertise allowed it to market a competitively superior biscuit in hot African countries with the chocolate inside the biscuit, where it wouldn't melt.

Another interesting payoff from building an image of leadership came from our interviews with both Infosys and Wipro: to move up the value chain, these IT services companies needed to be seen as "thought leaders," not merely companies excelling in low-level execution. Infosys thus told us how it redesigned its entire website to make it an "opinion-based website," full of position papers on IT-related topics. Similarly, Wipro actively encourages its employees to coauthor books with influential academics. "We want to move from being seen as a descriptive player to being seen as a prescriptive player," Wipro told us.

Building Trust and Confidence

Our brand-building pyramid (Figure 4-1) in Chapter 4 pointed out that while a brand perceived to be a leader in its industry automatically gives a buyer a feeling of trust and confidence, brands can also take other steps to strengthen the levels of trust and confidence that consumers associate with them. Such trust and confidence are especially important in B2B and service businesses, as (in our EMNC sample) Aramex, Infosys, and Wipro pointed out to us. In Wipro's words, "When it comes to services, I can't show you anything tangible. So you're only going to listen through word of mouth, and trust matters a lot. So if I were Accenture, I would play on the fear factor: If you go with Infosys, or Wipro or TCS, and things go wrong, see what blame you'll get just because you tried to save a little money. Instead, if things go wrong with Accenture or IBM, it would be 'Who could blame me for choosing IBM?' So that [trust] is the factor that comes into play."

To build such feelings of trust and confidence, brands can play up aspects such as their size, service reputations, blue chip clients, impressive physical facilities, recognition by other leading institutions, etc. Thus, Mahindra Tractors, Marico, and MTS talk about their large size to create confidence and trust: Mahindra as the world's largest tractor manufacturer by units, Marico as the third largest MNC in Bangladesh, MTS as one of the largest mobile operators in the world. Wipro showcases its fancy headquarters building and campus, along with the "richest Indian" status of its CEO Azim Premji, to create an aspirational desire among its prospects and clients. Aramex uses its Nasdaq listing and Wipro uses its NYSE one to build confidence and signal stature.

Not only did both Mahindra & Mahindra and Mahindra Tractors choose to build their own company-owned distributor networks overseas to inspire confidence—that way customers could see they were in there for the long haul, not merely "here today–gone tomorrow" companies; they also paid careful attention to building up excellent service facilities (including offering roadside assistance, in the case of Mahindra & Mahindra) to give their customers confidence in the purchase. The role of service networks in establishing quality perceptions was also discussed at length earlier in this chapter.

Another confidence-building cue is to give customers their own 3D, physical brand experience via *tests, demonstrations, and trials*.

Tata Motors and Mahindra & Mahindra offer such experiences to members of auto clubs. LG Electronics showcases the technological features of its appliances in retail stores, and Haier USA as well uses road shows, trials, and demonstrations of its products to show off their quality. Grupo Britt went as far as to create and successfully leverage the Café Britt Coffee Tour, held on one of its coffee plantations and roasting facilities near San José, Costa Rica, to teach people about their premium coffees via learning and firsthand tasting experiences.[20] Many of our EMNCs, such as LG Electronics, Mahindra & Mahindra, Chigo, and the Taj Group, organize trips to their factories and facilities for their dealers and other trade intermediaries.

Summary and Key Takeaways

To conclude this chapter, here is a summary of what we've said so far about creating perceptions of high quality and leadership. First, using research, you must incorporate in the design those product and service elements that lead to perceived high quality, and you must create the quality-assurance systems to make sure this targeted quality actually gets created. Second, you have to gain attention for your higher objective quality, possibly via comparative advertising; and, you have to gain credibility for the quality in a number of ways: by using third-party endorsements, reviews, and awards; by utilizing cobranding strategies; by making intelligent use of the styling and design cues and signals that consumers use to infer high quality; and by altering country-of-origin perceptions.

Third, you need to build the perception that you go beyond expected quality levels and are actually the leader in some particular quality dimension. You do this first by creating real, lab-level innovations and then by communicating your technical leadership by bringing out a constant stream of high-visibility new products, by using focused, consistent ads that feature awards and patents, and by ensuring frequent editorial media coverage (PR) in high-impact media. You supplement this impact of perceived leadership on confidence by also talking about other confidence-building aspects of your brand or company, such as size, clients, and service.

These lessons apply equally well to other EMNCs and to small-resource challenger companies everywhere. Perceptions of both high quality and leadership are—we believe—the most important for building sustainably strong brands (see Chapter 4). Yet they are also the hardest to build, because customers will naturally view the quality and leadership claims of new and small companies with skepticism. This is especially hard for EMNCs coming from countries that are perceived to produce poor-quality goods and services. Simply asserting brand and company quality and leadership is obviously not enough when you go up against a skeptical market resistant to updating and altering its perceptions. Hence finding *proof points* and *quality signals* and leveraging them become very important to do, and our description of these and other tactics above can be very helpful. But there is another important lesson in this chapter: the quality *communication* challenge only matters once you actually have high *objective quality*. EMNCs and other challengers must first dedicate themselves to genuine, "real and verifiable," quality leadership before investing (smartly) in the quality communication task. There are no shortcuts. To help you examine if you are effectively building perceptions of quality and leadership, we provide a checklist in Figure 6-2.

What might some lessons be from this chapter for the challenged, incumbent TMNCs? Since most of these companies already have high market credibility, they often do not face the same uphill battles to create market perceptions of high quality and leadership. We pointed out earlier, in Chapter 4, the importance for TMNCs to maintain and increase their lead in "leadership" perceptions, drawing on their ability to leverage their larger scale and their budgets in game-changing R&D. Thus, one lesson for TMNCs would be to play up their leadership, not just their quality, in their communications, since EMNCs and challengers can more easily compete on the quality front than on the leadership one. A second

- Do you understand what are the signals of quality in your category for your target consumers?
- Does your product or service contain the signals that your target consumers use to infer high quality?
- Are your customer service and support communicating the same high-quality signals that your core offering does?
- Are you trying to shape a quality reputation actively through your communication?
- Are you generating media coverage in the form of public relations to support the paid communication?
- Do the media, institutions, and spokespeople who are generating and carrying your PR also have the same high-quality signals?
- Have you leveraged cobranding opportunities that can convey the same high-quality reputation that your product or service signals?
- Are you effectively diffusing any negative country-of-origin association?
- Are you a leader in your business, and if so, what are you doing to communicate it?
- What are the signals that engender trust and confidence in your target segment, and what are you doing to own and communicate them to your target audience?

FIGURE 6-2 Checklist for Building Perceptions of High Quality, Leadership, and Trust

implication is that market expectations about quality are obviously not static; they can change quickly with technology and feature advances. Thus, even while fighting EMNCs on the lower-price-and-cost front, TMNCs need to keep raising the ante on the quality front by aggressively adding features and benefits to their market offerings. As Chapter 2 pointed out, here the task is not simply one of spending on R&D and innovating—which TMNCs tend to do well—but one of ensuring that those innovations lead clearly to high consumer value. This is a trickier task, and so *how* TMNCs direct their R&D and innovation is as important as *how much*.

7

Global Brand Associations and Architecture

As mentioned in Chapter 4, a key element of building a brand's strength is to create strategically correct mental associations for it in the target consumer's mind. And each of the many brands in a company's portfolio needs to be both distinguished from and yet also linked to other brands of that company to leverage economies of scale and still go after different target segments. In this chapter, we first examine the process of strategically targeting and then building desired brand associations. We then examine the needs and trade-offs for different types of brand architecture (brand portfolios) and the options for how to best manage these trade-offs.

Brand Associations

Brand associations are a crucial component of strong global brands, as Chapter 4 pointed out. After all, a brand is really the intangible collection of thoughts and feelings that the consumer holds about the product, service, or company—it is what exists in the mind, not what exists in the physical world. A brand without many associations, regardless of what the associations are, is simply not a very strong brand. Even if it possesses brand awareness, which helps create some familiarity, it is only somewhat stronger than a faceless commodity. As India's Wipro said to us, "The problem is [that many of] them have just heard of our name, but they still don't know what exactly we do." Wipro's research indicated that it did not seem to be getting the market credit for all the innovative services it actually offered; innovation was not an existing brand association to the extent that Wipro desired.

As Chapter 4 pointed out, a strong brand first needs to be associated with quality—however quality is construed in that category and target market—and with leadership; together these help create the necessary trust and confidence in the purchase of that brand. We believe these associations are so important that we devoted Chapter 6 to them. Now we consider building associations that go beyond quality, leadership, and trust and confidence. These are the kind of associations that can help turn a brand from a trustmark into a lovemark (see Figure 4-1 in Chapter 4). The strongest global consumer brands, such as Apple, Coke, McDonald's, and IBM, all possess such associations.

If one of the key tasks facing a Global Brand Builder then is to create such associations for it, there first needs to be a strategic analysis that answers the question, what kinds of associations must I build for my brand? Next comes a tactical or executional analysis; this time the question is, how do I go about actually creating such associations for it? Decisions also need to be made about brand architecture: should the targeted brand associations be executed via one brand or many, via family brands or sub-brands or endorsed brands? And for a Global Brand Builder, there are additional important questions to address: which of the brand's associations need to stay consistent across countries or regions, and how do the executional elements of the brand's various communications need to reflect (or not) the cultural demands of particular countries or regions? We discuss each of these topics below.

Strategic Analysis and Targeting of EMNC Brand Associations

We believe a strong EMNC brand needs associations that are not just *positive,* but also *differentiating; unique, and ownable; relevant* to the targeted consumer segment; and *emotionally motivating.* They should also be *easy to communicate* in a simple and vivid manner and be capable of *unifying multiple brand communications and actions* around them.[1]

Differentiating

A frequent problem for a number of the EMNCs we spoke to is that many consumers in overseas markets tend to put them in the same perceptual category as their home or near-home competitors. China is today considered the world's factory, and many of the hard goods (such as appliances) sold around the world are made in China. Many Chinese companies are building global appliance brands; just in our own research, we talked to Haier, Midea, and Chigo, and there are undoubtedly many others. In the IT and business process outsourcing business, many corporate customers around the world today know of Indian suppliers such as Infosys, Wipro, and TCS. Thus, many consumers in developed economies seem, according to our data, to think of all Indian companies, or all Chinese companies, or even all Indian and Chinese companies, as being part of one large homogeneous category, just as some even today put Korean or Japanese companies into a group. Country of origin is often the first brand association that gets spontaneously evoked (and usually not in a positive way). There is clearly the danger that such EMNCs, in such industries and from such countries, could find their own company or brand imagery buried in such "country" imagery. It is therefore especially important for our EMNCs to differentiate themselves from other EMNCs that appear to be very similar.

The problem is even worse for brands that share the same industry or category classification as others, such as Indian IT firms
Infosys, TCS, and Wipro. If Infosys is seen to be the same as Wipro
and TCS and others, then this may benefit the companies among
them that in reality are weaker, but it will hurt the companies
that are actually the stronger players. The competitive playing field
between these EMNC players themselves will become too driven
by price considerations. So it clearly makes strategic sense for companies that find themselves in such clusters or groupings to try to
build differentiating brand imagery.

Wipro, as a consequence, has sought to differentiate itself on
the basis of its record of innovative services and practices, greater
expertise in R&D and technology, greater knowledge of emerging
markets (India and the Middle East), and even its organizational
culture—its "DNA." (Wipro also used pricing that was higher than
that of smaller and lower-quality Indian competitors to signal its
differentiation from them.) Such differentiation based on organizational culture makes a lot of sense for a service organization: the
reason is that a service or B2B brand is inevitably about the organization and its people and their values, and it is much harder for
a competitor to credibly clone an organizational culture than to
copy the specifications of a product or service. Wipro's competitor Infosys too has sought to build differentiating characteristics
for itself. In the early to mid-2000s, its messaging focused on its
"predictability" (its terrific record of on-time and on-budget delivery), evolving later to its "Win in the Flat World" campaign (with
a promise of a superior consulting and business solutions role as a
business partner). Infosys made these changes believing that talking only about predictability and reliability of performance would
not differentiate it from competitors TCS and Wipro. (In 2006
TCS launched a message of offering "certainty.")

Naturally, a choice of which differentiating perceptions to
create or make more prominent should be based on competitive benchmarking research. How do your target consumers currently perceive your brand versus the competition, and which of

these current or potential differentiators should you focus on? Such research, often called a study of the "brandscape" in which you compete, needs to employ qualitative, exploratory, insight-generating "projective" research, as well as larger-scale, representative, and market-projectable quantitative data. The Taj Group, for instance, found through such research that it was seen as possessing more warmth, personalization, and heritage and tradition than its peer competitors, which became potential differentiators for its brand-building strategy.

Unique, Ownable, Especially Credible

It is shortsighted to differentiate one's brand on a characteristic that a determined competitor can mimic and share in a few months' time, for then all the association-building investment made gets wasted. So it makes sense to pick something that is linked in some unique and ownable way to a core, non-imitable (or expensive and hard to imitate) strength or characteristic of your company or brand. (An exception might be a characteristic that you can preemptively own simply because you claim it early and spend a lot of money linking it to your brand). Thus, Tiger Beer, sold throughout Asia, plays up its "world-class" quality, proudly displaying on its bottle label (and in other communications) the many beer competition awards it alone—compared with other Asian beers—has won.

Hard-to-copy associations include those linked to the history or founder of the brand or company, for those are naturally very company specific. Thus, Mahindra & Mahindra leverages its history and experience in building the original Jeep vehicle under license from the original Willys company since 1947, which gives it a special claim to knowledge about how best to build tough utility vehicles, a 50- to 60-year heritage not shared by most of its competitors. As we noted in an earlier chapter, Mahindra & Mahindra highlighted this in a very attention-getting and impactful press ad campaign in South Africa, describing the Jeep as the U.S. army vehicle that in World War II beat the Japanese and German equivalents in tough desert and mountain terrains. The campaign won tremendous word-of-mouth attention for Mahindra & Mahindra. Mahindra & Mahindra also takes advantage of the needs of its target market to buy a tough, rugged, functional, "honest and authentic" (and not gussied up) vehicle. The company takes advantage of the common outsider perception that while an Indian automaker might not know how to make pretty cars with plush comfort, it surely should know how to make such rugged vehicles that are good enough for tough Indian conditions.

Thus, some of these unique and ownable associations might actually come from the brand's company (or region) of origin, to the extent these are not currently (or potentially) appropriated by other competing brands from the same location. Brazil is associated in many minds with the Amazon River and rain forests, and through that with the idea and ideal of biodiversity. The Brazilian cosmetics EMNC Natura has very cleverly capitalized upon this positive association in its product and brand development (and even in its choice of geographic markets, choosing to focus on France, where such a biodiversity brand position is likely to be highly appreciated).[2] It also has built up hard-to-copy ingredient sourcing arrangements and extraction technologies. Costa Rica's Grupo Britt leverages Costa Rica's association with coffee to market gourmet coffee throughout the Americas.[3] India's Dabur leverages its real and perceived herbal expertise. Similarly, the Turkish personal goods company Evyap has capitalized on the historically positive associations in Egypt of Turkey with high-quality soap making. Turkish jeans maker Mavi capitalized on Turkey's Mediterranean associations in positioning the Mavi brand as embodying the casual, relaxed, "enjoy life" imagery that is a part of (or consistent with) that origin, even using the term *Mavi-terranean* in its communications. Corona Beer from Mexico also plays up the sunny, temperate beaches linked to that country. While the place-of-origin positive imagery of Dabur, Evyap, Mavi, and Corona is potentially copyable by other brands from the same locations, the first brands to use such branding imagery are often able to preemptively own it, if they use it for long-enough periods and put large marketing communication budgets behind it.

Relevant

Naturally, targeted brand associations need to be relevant to the specific target segment the brand is going after (pertain to a benefit that potential customers value highly in the category). If a brand is differentiated in a way that has nothing to do with what the target customer seeks in the brand being selected, such differentiation is obviously pointless. Thus, Wipro thinks about the specific industry "vertical" sector it is pitching to (such as manufacturing versus retail versus financial services) in thinking about the characteristics it wishes to emphasize. Infosys believes strongly that customer benefit and value are the driving forces behind its choice of marketing messages. Mahindra Tractors realizes that while fuel efficiency and mileage mattered to its domestic Indian farmer market, they did not to the hobby and weekend farmers it was going after in the United States, and thus it adjusted its messaging accordingly.

Motivating (Emotional)

Strong brands often (but not necessarily always) mix in an emotional appeal as well, something that the target segment identifies with or aspires to at a gut level. Thus, Mahindra Tractors says it can help its targeted farmers "cultivate your dreams," while Tiger Beer says its brand essence is "all about winning" to its pan-Asian consumers in the high-growth and high-aspiration "tiger" economies, a claim made credible and real by its sales records and awards in the West. To its consumers in the West, on the other hand, Tiger Beer positions itself as the quintessential Asian brand, possessing an exotic coolness that its non-mainstream target finds alluring.

Anchoring a brand on strongly motivating associations can create the type of loyalty toward it that characterizes "love brands" like Apple.[4] Such associations include those that the target market either identifies with (deeply held life values such as cosmopolitanism, frugality, or environmentalism) or aspires to (not just prestige and status, but any missing-in-my-life quality, from male companionship to urban street credibility). Such deeply held or "higher-level" end values are often very similar for the same type of consumer segment across the world, even if the means by which they are pursued vary locally. Mahindra & Mahindra recently (in 2011) undertook a major rebranding effort, using "Rise" as its new corporate positioning, suggesting the upward trajectory and vision of both the company and its targeted consumers. In 2009, shortly after joining the Star airlines alliance (which includes Lufthansa, United, Singapore Airlines, and Air Canada among others), Turkish Airlines launched a "Feel Like a Star" advertising campaign starring Kevin Costner, strategically placing the ads in airports with heavy passenger traffic. The ad's emphasis on the star theme cleverly communicated both the new Star Alliance partnership and the enhanced quality of the in-flight service, particularly its award-winning cuisine. The campaign was very successful in raising both awareness and positive brand associations.

Despite the multiple criteria above, the most powerful brand associations are also those that are *focused and sharp*. In addition, the best brand associations communicate a strong idea that is capable of *unifying all brand actions* around them into a coherent, consistent thematic whole. Temsa describes itself as the "bus and coach master," and so everyone inside and outside knows what it does (and does not) excel in. Wipro used an "Applied Innovation" branding theme to connect together its diverse program and marketing initiatives. Strong brand associations are also *vivid and simple to communicate*—such as Tiger Beer's use of the word tiger as its name and the image of a tiger as its symbol to communicate its winning, powerful personality.

Finally, EMNC brands usually benefit by not changing their core branding ideas too often; the best ones may continue essentially unchanged (with advertising tagline and execution changes to keep them fresh) for decades. Volvo has used its key brand positioning of safety for decades, so that consumers the world over associate it with safety so strongly that it is often said that Volvo *owns* the safety association among vehicle brands. That being said, many EMNC brands and companies are growing rapidly in their scale, competencies, and product lines, and others are facing quickly changing markets or competitors; in either case, they need to evolve their branding messages to keep pace. Our Indian IT brands Infosys and Wipro have therefore each gone through several branding messages over the last 10 years. Wipro, for instance, has decided to link many of its capabilities to the contemporary search for sustainable, "green" business practices, under an initiative branded "Wipro Green," linked to more energy-efficient supply chains and computing and manufacturing practices.

EMNC Association-Building Tactics

Once a brand has decided on which associations to build, given the strategic criteria discussed above, it then has to undertake the tactical, executional programs that will create or amplify them. While we will discuss below examples in our data of some of the mechanisms that can be employed, it should be remembered that, as Coca-Cola's brand builders are famous for saying, "Everything communicates." That is, a brand gains its associations not only through its many forms of sponsored and unsponsored marketing communications—its advertising, PR, packaging, on-shelf, web, sales force, trade show, and collateral material communications—but also through the consumer's contact with the product or service itself and through the consumer's experiences with the company's employees, after-sales service programs, etc.

The brand manager therefore needs to be aware of all the messages that are explicitly or implicitly being sent out by the company and brand through these scores of customer touch points, and the brand manager also needs to ensure that the messages are the ones that are intended and that they are integrated and coordinated across these touch points. Some call this perspective "360 degree branding." Thus, the look and feel, via graphic design and content elements, of a website or a product package, or even a company's PR release, needs to be consistent with the strategic association-building goals of the brand and with all the other communication elements being employed.

Meaning Transfer

Naturally, paid advertising of various forms is usually the main vehicle used for building brand associations. Here, the associations sought for the brand are typically created by transferring meaning from some other entity that already possesses them—such as celebrity or expert endorsers, brand "ambassadors," places, and events (via sponsorship or cobranding).[5] As an example of transferring associations of tough masculinity through a linkage with a type of person, Eyvap uses a brand name and concept of "Commando" for its Arko male toiletries brand in Russia, and Asian Paints has considered taking advantage of the widespread associations of Indian professionals as being smart, intelligent, and educated to overcome otherwise negative "made in an emerging market" imagery. Asia Pacific Breweries, for its Tiger Beer, draws on the spontaneous imagery of a tiger. Titan watches were launched in Europe with a "world positioning," leveraging its use of French technology, German engineering, Japanese manufacturing equipment, and European designers.

Cobranding

Associating one's brand with another, and thus transferring quality and other associations from that other brand to one's own brand, was described earlier in Chapter 6 as a useful cobranding tactic. Lenovo and now Acer benefit from the world-class quality associations derived from their Olympics and other sports sponsorships. Infosys, Ranbaxy, and Wipro also gain credibility—and offer their customers a 360-degree perspective—by utilizing respected academic and industry speakers at customer events. The Taj Group creates events (such as the hosting of an annual convention) and partnerships with the Leading Hotels of the World and other leading hotel alliances (Virtuoso, Kiwi Collection, Fine Hotels and Resorts) and with luxury credit cards and top-ranked airlines.

Branding of Services

Special consideration needs to be given here to how services—such as airlines, hotels, retailers, banks, and IT service providers—build associations. While the usual communication elements (for example, advertising, web, PR) still matter in creating brand associations, of much more importance is the customer's actual experience with the company's employees, the operating processes they employ, and even the physical facilities and environment in which the service is delivered. It is commonly said that, for a service organization, "the brand walks around on two legs." Thus, the way in which employees are hired (recruitment criteria), trained, acculturated into the brand vision and values, evaluated, and compensated all matter hugely in delivering (or not) an "on-brand" experience to the end consumer through all touch points. Infosys believes, for instance, that its brand is built not only by its marketing efforts but also by its record for corporate governance and the actions of its very visible top management.

An excellent example in our data of an EMNC service brand paying a lot of attention to such association-building elements is the Taj Group, which aims to deliver the same top-quality level of "Taj-ness" around the world in its top-level Taj Group hotel properties. This demands very careful attention to staff hiring, training, culture building, performance evaluation, and service-auditing systems; to targeted enhancement and use of service processes including customer relationship management systems; and to a very critical creation and examination of the design and standards of the physical facilities and environment. In the words of the Taj Group, "Understanding the brand and its aspects are central in the induction process for every employee. This involves translating the brand definition into a distinct service philosophy, to bring the brand to reality. We conduct intensive employee training on these aspects as well as on creating an overall customer experience differentiated for each brand at each customer touch-point. . . . This is done via an employee engagement tool comprising of a brand spirit book for each brand, and a brand film, in which senior management of the company explain the similarities and differences across all our brands (our brand architecture)."

Internal Branding

For such service brands in particular, but also for other product brands, great attention needs to be paid to disseminating and gaining genuine buy-in for the brand's desired associations and standards *within the organization*. This includes, but goes beyond, the use of brand manuals and standards and web microsites (mentioned to us by, among others, MTS, Tiger Beer, and the Taj Group). It includes, especially, the alignment of performance goals and recognition and reward systems. Thus, Wipro makes sure its sales force knows:

- The details of all the innovative products and programs it has worked on
- The quantification of an internal company goal of the percentage of annual revenue that needs to come from efforts that can be called innovative
- The creation of internal innovation councils
- The internal and external web publication of white papers describing innovative projects
- The creation and publicizing of internal employee awards for innovation

And the list[6] would not end there.

Standardization Versus Localization: Decisions and Options

Adding to the complexity and challenge of building EMNC global brands are the usual phenomena of markets and cultures differing on the benefits and associations they value most highly in the product or service category in which the brand competes. Thus, as mentioned earlier, the farmers targeted by Mahindra Tractors in India placed more importance on fuel efficiency than the hobby farmers targeted in the United States. Such local-market variations can offset the various cost-reduction and speed-to-market advantages of marketing a brand in the same near-standardized way across multiple markets (creating a global or regional brand). These cross-market variations can also apply to a company's internal branding efforts: employee-related practices acceptable in one part of the world may not be acceptable in another. Wipro, for such cultural-variation reasons, decided not to use in Japan the same internal employee award competition for innovation that it launched in India.

There are several possible solutions. One is to weigh the trade-offs involved (see Figure 7-1)—by assessing the economies of scale and cost savings from greater standardization *versus* the revenue gains from greater localization—and then simply do what seems better in the aggregate. This calculation usually favors standardization in categories like appliances and electronics and leans toward localization in categories like foods, beverages, and personal hygiene products (though there are always exceptions). Indeed, EMNCs may strategically elect to limit their global or regional brand-building efforts to categories where, for cultural reasons,

Advantages of Fewer or Standardized Brands	Advantages of More or Localized Brands
Economies of scale in brand building and management	Greater segment, geographic, price, distribution, targeting and customization
Faster time to market	Potentially greater benefit relevance
Takes advantage of similar customer needs	Takes advantage of EMNC strengths

FIGURE 7-1 Trade-Offs Between Fewer or Standardized Versus More or Localized Brands

product and branding standardization seems more acceptable to the market. Savola, for instance, found that while standardization worked for sugar, it did not for cooking oil.

Here, one strategic competence advantage of EMNCS is that they can often do more cost-effective, low-volume, local-market tailoring than a TMNC can, and thus they can "outlocalize" a TMNC operating in the same geographic market. Several examples of such strategic localization emerged in our data and have already been mentioned (see Chapters 1 and 2): Godrej creating (or acquiring and building) hair coloring products and brands customized to the hair of African consumers, Marico developing chlorine-protective hair products for some of its markets, and Mitac customizing its GPS products to the needs of special local markets like Korea because of its ability to do such customization at low cost.

A second solution is to standardize and globalize at a more abstract, "core," level, but to allow and even encourage local-market tactical adaptations in elements such as advertising. This is the classic textbook solution to the standardization versus localization conundrum and is the path followed by most companies, TMNCs and EMNCs alike. Almost every EMNC we spoke to mentioned using this approach, and we will present these examples in Chapter 8, when we discuss managing global and regional brands. An example is Savola, which uses similar positioning concepts, but different local executions and products—even different brand names—in its various Middle Eastern cooking oil markets, for much of its brand portfolio.

A third option, building off the one above, is to allow the product itself (at the functional or specification level) to vary but the branding to stay the same. Thus, Dabur used the same Vatika brand, with the same herbal positioning and imagery, on hair oil in India and Egypt, but while the Indian hair oil is coconut based, the Egyptian one uses olive oil, "since coconut oil is an unknown proposition in Egypt," Dabur's Sunil Duggal told us.

A fourth option is to standardize across smaller markets but to localize for larger markets, where the higher cost of such localization more easily breaks-even because of the larger revenue upside of the size of that local market. Thus, P&G resists localization (in product formulation, pricing, and packaging) of its global brand Crest in most local markets, but makes an exception for a large market like China. Similarly, in our data, we saw several examples of EMNC brands adapting their products and brands for large markets like Nigeria (Dabur) and Brazil (Haier), while they still used more standardized versions in smaller countries.

A fifth option is to create regional, but not global, brands, limiting a company's standardized brand to just those countries that seem responsive to its brand positioning but not using that brand everywhere. Several examples of regional brands appear in our EMNC data, including Savola, Marico, and Asian Paints, discussed more fully in the "Global Brand Architecture" section that follows next in this chapter. It is important to realize that the set of countries suitable for a regional brand need not be geographically contiguous; they can be in diverse locations as long as they still share the important characteristics of consumer tastes, needs, and incomes. For example, some of our Indian automotive brands such as Tata Motors and Mahindra & Mahindra told us how they exploited pockets of demand in affluent Southern Europe, for instance in southern Italy, with the same brands and branding that they used in other emerging markets, because sufficiently large consumer segments existed there with the same consumer needs for products high in functionality and durability but low in price.

Figure 7-2 summarizes the discussion above, listing possible ways in which to manage the standardization-localization trade-offs.

Thus far we have discussed issues relating to how associations are built for individual brands. However, because EMNCs often market in lots of countries and consumer segments, and often end up acquiring brands (see Chapter 3), they also face the challenge of managing (coordinating) a large portfolio of brands. When does it make sense to have more, rather than fewer, brands? Should the same brand be used across price tiers? If a brand is acquired, should it be consolidated into other brands already being marketed, or

- See which option comes out ahead in an aggregate gain-loss revenue and cost assessment
- Standardize at the abstract, strategy, brand level; localize at the concrete, tactical, product level
- Standardize for smaller, low-upside markets; localize for larger, high-upside markets
- Create regional or other multicountry brands instead of purely local or totally global brands

FIGURE 7-2 How to Manage Standardization-Localization Trade-Offs

should it be left as is? These and other such questions are addressed in our next section on brand architecture.

Global Brand Architecture

Over time, when an EMNC expands across geographies and market segments, it may acquire some brands. When this is the case, it has to wrestle with the question of how to manage the multiple brands it ends up with in its brand portfolio, including:

- What is the optimal number of brands needed?
- How many segments (horizontal and vertical) should be spanned by an individual brand?
- How many country markets should be spanned by an individual brand?
- How should the multiple brands relate to one another (mono-brand versus independent brands versus sub-brands, etc.) and to the parent corporate brand?

There are only a few prior guidelines on this general topic,[7] and none that we know of that apply to our specific context—of building and managing global brand portfolios by EMNCs. Nonetheless, some general principles bear mention, illustrated below with examples and cases from our EMNC research.

Economies of Scale

Having fewer brands rather than many helps with brand-building economies of scale (such as in communications and media), facilitating the creation of brand awareness and associations. Thus, it obviously makes a lot of sense for low-resource EMNCs to try to greatly limit the number of brands or sub-brands they try to build across segments and markets. In the extreme, the EMNC may follow a strategy of having just one "branded house" (the same family brand used everywhere) or having very few power brands or family brands. As Infosys's Srinivas Uppaluri told us, "We can't sub-brand now: we have to work with limited funds . . . our mindshare is not much; when we are struggling on that mindshare, it is not worth it to have so many fragmented sub-brands."

The need to consolidate brands, because of limited brand-building resources that need to be concentrated for maximum impact, becomes especially relevant when outside companies or brands are acquired. When the acquisition is made for reasons other than the acquired brand's brand-name awareness itself (see Chapter 3 on motives for acquisitions), one common solution is to "migrate" or "transition" the acquired local brand into the larger, cross-national brand, as Aramex did with its acquired Irish TwoWay brand. It was initially hybrid-branded as TwoWay Aramex, and the "TwoWay" was later dropped once the local market became familiar with the Aramex brand. Wipro lets its acquired companies keep their original name (combined with the Wipro name) for a year (18 months in some cases), after which their name changes to a sub-branded division of Wipro. MTS, 6 to 12 months after it acquired mobile telecom businesses in Ukraine and Armenia, rebranded them as MTS. Such rebranding into the global brand being built up not only saves money in the long run, but also reinforces the perceived globalness of the brand, which research has shown can contribute significantly to consumer perceptions that the brand has world-class quality and status.[8] In some cases, where the local acquired brand's equity is significant and worth preserving, elements of its brand name or logo might be retained, as Infosys did with its France and Germany acquisitions. Asia Pacific Breweries does this with some of its local beer brands acquired in part for their local popularity, and Mahindra Tractors did this with the name of its Chinese Feng Shui tractor brand—which now is combined with the Mahindra "M" logo.

At the extreme, to gain the maximum economies of scale in brand building, a company may choose to use only the corporate brand name (or to play up its role as the master brand or endorser brand). Such corporate branding also makes a lot of sense in B2B situations for multiple reasons: the need for corporate-level trust and confidence is high; the company's culture and values can serve as a hard-to-imitate differentiating association; individual products and brands can have life cycles too short to justify making brand-building investments in them; and cross-selling can benefit from such corporate-level visibility and trust.

Greater Targeting

The obvious negative of the strategy just described is that it limits the ability of the brand marketer to create distinctive targeted brands for multiple segments with different needs, varying on either a functional or symbolic basis. For instance, a jeans manufacturer like Mavi markets to some buyers who want functional durability and value, others who want high fit and comfort above all else, some who want high-fashion chic, and still others who want an urban, street-savvy look. Can all these products and imagery fit comfortably under the same one brand? Similarly, Asia Pacific Breweries has analyzed global beer-drinking segments from a motivational and psychographic basis and recognizes the existence of one segment that drinks beer in a group, social, fun-and-friendship extroverted mode and another segment that drinks in a more introverted, individual-needs state. It then creates different brands for each of them.

Having just one brand also means that distribution channel conflict might arise, since the same brand is being sold across all channels: trade partners usually prefer to get different (ideally, exclusive) brands so that they don't have to price-compete with others on the same brand. There is also the possibility that negative associations or market failure might spill over from one category or country to others if only one brand is being used.

Price and Quality Tiering

A one-brand strategy also means that the same brand name will be used in different price and quality tiers, higher or lower than the initial price or quality tier used by the brand. This can often create problems since consumers of higher-priced products often do not feel they are getting sufficient "premium" quality and value if the product bears the same brand name as that of a cheaper-priced version (although consumers of the lower-priced version certainly gain psychological value by being able to purchase the higher-image brand at that lower price point). For this same reason, it is often hard to move to a higher price-quality tier with a brand name initially launched at a lower level. As Vitra's Hüsamettin Onanç told us, "We need a double-brand strategy almost everywhere . . . because there's a serious difference between the brand which the market calls premium and the brand that satisfies basic needs. It's hard to respond to both with the same brand. If you do, your perception goes down and the lower version cannibalizes the other. For this reason, if you are a premium brand, you should stay there. To satisfy more basic needs and to be widespread, you must have a second brand. This is the same almost everywhere. Vitra is our premium brand in the UK, and we use other brand names for our standard and necessity products."

Thus, it is usually considered smarter to use different brand names across multiple price tiers, rather than the same one, despite the diseconomies of scale involved. An excellent example of such price-quality tiered branding in our data is that of the Taj Group. After an exhaustive brand architecture analysis (assisted by brand consultants Landor), the Taj Group decided to align customer need segments with the quality and pricing of the properties using a three-tier structure, moving away from its historical usage of the Taj brand name across all types of properties. Going forward, only its very top, iconic luxury flagship properties will carry the Taj brand name. The Taj will also serve as the endorser brand for "upper upscale" (just below "luxury") properties. Merely "upscale" properties will bear the new brand name of Gateway (a nice figurative reference to the Gateway of India, Mumbai, the location of its key Taj hotel). And economy-level hotels will bear a new brand name, Ginger. Figure 7-3 describes the new Taj Group brand architecture for each targeted segment, showing the brand name, targeted audience, verbal and visual expressions and inspirations of each brand, desired brand associations, and price points.

Similarly, Asia Pacific Breweries uses multiple brand names in most markets, reserving the Tiger Beer brand for the premium segment and allocating other beer brands such as Crystal, Cana, Iceland, and King Star to the lower-priced segments in various countries. Asian Pacific Breweries knows well that beer drinkers often indulge in "repertoire drinking"; still, most of its consumers don't just drink premium beers all the time, and the company wants to make sure it has the product and brand for all the beer-drinking needs of all its consumers. Chinese appliance maker Midea uses the Royal Star name at the introductory level, and it uses Midea itself as a higher-level one—with further sub-branding under it to indicate price-quality variations (e.g., high-end air conditioners under Midea Virtue, lower-end ones as Midea Elite). HTC has only recently (in 2010) launched HTC-branded smartphones in China, where it has been selling Dopod-branded phones for years, a brand name it will keep using there for less sophisticated phones. China's Geely, whose parent company bought Volvo, plans to keep Volvo's production and R&D in Europe for the foreseeable future, thus separating the brand perceptions of these two brands and reducing the chances of Geely's lower-quality image pulling down that of the Volvo brand.

Brand	Luxury	Premium (Upper Upscale)	Full Service (Upscale)	Value (Economy)
Brand	Taj	Vivanta by Taj	The Gateway Hotel	Ginger
Target Audience	Authentic luxury experience seekers for whom luxury is a way of life	Work-hard, play-hard traveler seeking energetic and stylish experiences	Smart travelers, hassle-free and modern experiences	Budget travelers
Verbal Brand Driver	"Reinventing Tradition"	"Stylishly Spirited"	"Welcome Perfection"	"Smart Basics"
Visual Brand Driver—Architecture	The Louvre (contemporary styling, principles, and materials)	Apple Store, Fifth Avenue (contemporary styling, innovative, always available, engaging, leading)	Welcoming hotel entrance (warm colors, inviting, friendly, sheltering, natural, informal, comfortable)	Not defined
Visual Brand Driver—Animal	Bengal tiger (culturally iconic, powerful, swift)	Panther (agile, quick, beautiful, efficient)	Labrador (hard working, trustworthy, loyal, friendly, attentive, calm)	Not defined
Brand Strategy	Charming, passionate, progressive, attentive, responsive	Contemporary, radiant, agile, creative	Crisp, courteous, consistent	Smart, informal, fresh
Relationship with Taj Brand	Core Taj	Endorsed by Taj	Not linked to Taj	Not linked to Taj
Brand Play	Hotels, resorts, residential, outside hotel property, retail, grand palaces, small palaces, boutique hotels, safaris, private jets	Hotels, resorts, and residences, restaurants	Hotels and resorts	Hotels
Approximate Price Range	INR15,000 (US$300) and above	INR9,000 (US$180) and above	INR6,000 (US$120) and above	INR1,000 (US$20) and above

FIGURE 7-3 Brand Associations and Architecture of the Taj Group of Hotels

Source: Rohit Deshpande and Mona Sinha, Taj Hotels, Resorts and Palaces, case no. 9-511-039, Boston: Harvard Business School. Copyright ©2010 by the President and Fellows of Harvard College. (Reprinted by permission of Harvard Business School.)

Compromise: Sub-brands and Endorsed Brands

Given the trade-offs that are apparent between the greater economies of scale from fewer brands and the difficulties in providing segment-tailored benefits and imagery with these fewer brands, companies often compromise by using sub-brands (such as Midea Virtue versus Midea Elite) or endorsed brands ("Rebok Island Resort Langkawi Malaysia—A Taj Hotel"). Through this method, the endorsed brand or the sub-brand can provide targeted benefits or imagery while it still benefits from the awareness, quality, and trust associations of the endorsing or higher-level parent brand. Further, over time, the sub-brand—if it develops its own positive associations—can actually transfer these back to the parent brand (although a negative transfer is also possible).

One very interesting case of such transfer in our data is the use by Lenovo of the licensed IBM brand, which Lenovo obtained the right to use (for five years) when it bought IBM's personal computing lines in 2004. Ex-CMO Deepak Advani told us how Lenovo initially used the IBM associations to give its purchased Thinkpad notebook line credibility in terms of quality, support, trust, and innovation; it did this by rebranding what once was "Thinkpad from IBM" into "Thinkpad" by itself and then using the bolstered Thinkpad equity to help transfer these meanings to Lenovo, the corporate brand, via "Thinkpad by Lenovo."

Trade-Offs: Standardized Versus Localized Brand Architecture

The challenge of determining the most appropriate number of brands gets more complicated in our context of building regional or global EMNC brands. Fewer standardized brands can yield more media economies of scale, faster rollout, and higher "globalness" consumer perceptions. They may also be a necessity if the same global distributors and retailers are involved. As Arçelik told us, "When you leave Russia aside, we distribute via the same companies. There are retailers like Carrefour, which are Pan-European; they even have global distribution. If we position Beko as mass market in France, it cannot be a premium brand in Germany. They know at what price Beko is sold in France. If we tell them in Germany that Beko is expensive, they would laugh at us. They can actually sell what they bought for France, in Germany." Thus, there are many strong reasons why the same, similarly marketed global brands become necessary as an EMNC expands the countries it sells into.

However, as was discussed earlier, the brand associations relevant, motivating, and differentiating in one country or region might be less so in another. Income levels might differ; the physical infrastructure and distribution channels might not be similar; rules and regulations might vary. All of these argue for localizing rather than standardizing and for using multiple brands (varying across countries) rather than fewer. Some of the factors to consider—trade-offs involved and possible solutions—were already discussed above in the brand associations section of this chapter. In our EMNC data, we found cases fitting into each of our options and solutions.

Thus, some EMNCs believe in using just one global brand, such as MTS; this appears logical for MTS both because its consumers are likely to travel across national borders and thus seek the same global mobile carrier network (just as one would with Vodafone) and because with one-brand perceived globalness ought to communicate quality and strength. Other EMNCs seek to build their brands up as powerful regional, rather than global, brands, such as Marico's Parachute, used in South Asia, Southeast Asia, the Middle East, North Africa, and other parts of Africa. Savola uses a regional pan-Arab brand, Afia, for cooking oil, because the name *Afia* means health in Arabic and is thus appealing and suitable in all those countries. However, some of its other brands did not have this pan-Arab regional concept or name appeal, and thus Savola also uses many other country-level brands.

Other EMNCs in our data use multiple power or family brands, each aimed at a distinct global needs-based segment, as Apollo Tyres does (positioning its Dunlop brand for sportiness, Apollo

Tyres for premium comfort, and Regal for value). Lenovo now uses the Ideapad name for its more consumer-oriented notebooks ("different, edgy," Lenovo's Reid Walker told us), given the more corporate equity of its Thinkpad notebook line. Lenovo also used the Lenovo 3000 brand for its lower-priced "higher-value" line, so as not to dilute the premium associations for its Thinkpad range of products. Mitac intends to use its Navman global brand for personal navigation GPS devices and its Mio global brand for smartphone and other computing devices. Some EMNCs use the same family brand name globally but vary the sub-brand name for local reasons (e.g., Mahindra Scorpio is called Mahindra Goa in Western Europe to avoid confusion there with a previous vehicle of the same name marketed earlier by Ford).

Global Brand Management

Since global brand management requires a careful consideration of both the economies of scale and efficiencies that come with standardization, as well as the varying and different needs of important local markets, EMNCs need to set up management structures and processes that take into account both these sets of needs. We discuss some of these ideas in Chapter 8, on managing global and regional brands; and numerous books and chapters on the subject of global and regional brand management are available.[9] Global and regional brands are best created at their very inception by cross-country teams of brand managers, so that they contain brand elements that work in as broad a set of markets as possible.

Global brand management organizations often have global brand managers for their key global brands, as well globally centralized advertising agency responsibilities. Global brand manuals and handbooks need to exist that describe the global brand's core positioning platform and visual identity elements, outlining which brand and marketing elements are negotiable between headquarters and subsidiaries and which ones are not. Processes need to be put in place for approval and review to ensure compliance.

Processes are also needed for local markets to feel a P&L financial incentive to use global materials, and yet these local markets also need to be given the opportunity to modify the materials locally if the local-market revenue upside from such modification exceeds the cost of such modification. Readers are urged to consult Chapter 8, along with its notes section, for more detail.

Summary and Key Takeaways

To summarize, EMNC and other challenger brands need to build strength by adding brand associations that include, but go beyond, quality, leadership, and trust. These strategically targeted associations ought to meet the criteria discussed in the chapter (differentiation; credibility and ownability; relevance and motivating power). For EMNCs that all too often are lumped together in consumers' minds with other EMNCs from the same country or industry— such as Indian IT vendors or Chinese appliance manufacturers— differentiation is crucial, ideally in ways that are also emotionally motivating, so that the brand associations overcome (or put a positive spin on) potentially negative country-of-origin associations.

A competitive challenge faced by EMNC and other small-challenger brands is that they suffer in comparison with larger, established TMNC global brands on perceptions and inferences of quality, prestige, and cosmopolitanism.[10] Thus, these EMNC and other challenger brands too need to gain the quality and prestige connotations of being global and large scale. To do this, they might need to accompany their outlocalizing product strategies (see Chapter 2) with a brand architecture strategy that uses the same brand name or same family brand name in multiple markets even if the products sold under them differ somewhat, because the use of the same brand name everywhere is an important signal of being a global brand, with its consequent rub-off benefits. Or they could use sub-brands or endorsed brands, with a common parent brand name accompanied by more local-variant sub-brands or endorsed brands. Such a brand architecture strategy can give them the benefits of branding economies of scale (since the same parent or family brand is being used), can create consumer perceptions of a global brand (again, since the same parent brand is utilized everywhere), and yet can allow some local-market flexibility. Since it is hard to change brand names late in a brand's history, this means EMNCs and other challenger brands need to think and plan ahead and have a brand architecture strategy in place that deliberately tries to create global brand perceptions, even if local marketing and product needs will require market tailoring when market expansion actually occurs.

Incumbent global TMNC brands typically try to create and leverage economies of scale through as much global standardization of product and branding elements as seems feasible. This quite naturally makes them the prime beneficiaries of the global brand imagery that research has documented, as cited earlier. The challenge for them, however, is how best to retain these advantages while doing more localized marketing in large and important markets— to better fight EMNCs that are following an outlocalizing strategy or simply to better satisfy local market needs. Instead of seeing their choice set as fully globalized or fully localized brands, these TMNCs might benefit by a more strategic use themselves of sub-branding and endorsement branding strategies, which both prominently use a globally known parent brand, but also allow for (and signal) local-market responsiveness through the specific sub-brand or endorsed brand sold in that local market. Thus, brand architecture, not just brand associations, needs to become an important tool in the global branding playbooks of brands from EMNCs, TMNCs, and other under-resourced challenger companies.

8

Managing a Global or Regional Brand

As EMNCs move beyond the Knowledge Leverager strategy and execute on the Niche Customizer or Global Brand Builder strategies, expanding over multiple markets, they will likely use their own home-market brands, develop local brands, or acquire new brands. The challenge of managing all these brands across multiple markets then becomes a critical one. How does an organization manage them all in a decentralized enough way to keep these brands relevant and appealing to each individual local market, while still enabling the global centralization that permits economies of scale and the creation of a global (or regional) brand to occur? What kind of organizational structure and processes—and what kinds of people and culture—will allow the EMNC to reach the ideal state of being globally efficient but still locally responsive? Such questions are the focus of this chapter.

EMNCs typically begin expanding across markets without a long-term master vision in place. Brands are often marketed independently in different countries, resulting in the same brand name potentially standing for very different things in consumers' minds in different markets. Turkey's Mehmed Evyap told us, "Our skin care brand in Turkey is Arko. Arko is also the brand of our male products in Turkey; it's successful in shaving preparations. In Russia, however, Arko is only a masculine personal care brand."

Mahindra Tractors uses different logos in India and abroad for its tractors: at the time it entered the U.S. market, someone had made the arbitrary decision to change the way the Mahindra master brand was represented! Mahindra Tractors CEO Gautam Nagwekar told us, "There isn't a clear reason for that. But now we have agreed to have the same look and feel."

While a different logo seems trivial, and is relatively easier to harmonize after the fact, post-hoc harmonization is harder to do with different brand names or brand positioning across markets. Evyap eventually had to consider either using the Duru brand of its personal washing products to launch other skin-care brands in Russia, with the potential for overextension and weakening of what it stood for, or creating a new brand there for skin care at additional expense. Ranbaxy's Sanjeev Dani lamented to us that "many of the things which I have inherited that I am trying to change, like product brand names that are different across geographies, are very difficult to change now. Unfortunately nobody took interest in these issues when the products were launched."

As these examples show, independent brand positioning across countries during an EMNC's early expansion across borders allows for greater responsiveness to local-market conditions. But it reduces economies of scale in marketing communications and packaging, and it makes it difficult to create strong, consistently positioned global brands. As the degree of internationalization increases and EMNCs become more familiar with international business, the necessity of managing the multicountry brand portfolio in a more integrated and synergistic way becomes clear.

While few multinationals ever achieve the ideal global-local balance, and maintaining this balance requires constant adjustments, our research suggests that failure to manage brands effectively across historically independent national businesses can lead to duplicated costs, wasted economies of scale, and missed opportunities to deploy lessons and brands from one market into another. In this chapter, we discuss the different roles that central brand marketing might play in creating cross-market synergies and explore

Problems of an Uncoordinated Approach	Coordinated Management of Brands Across Markets	Implementing a Central Brand Marketing Team	Managing Talent in a Global Context
• Higher marketing costs due to overly localized marketing • Reduced quality of marketing due to uncoordinated programs • Inadequate sharing across markets	• Central team as facilitator • Central team as advisor • Central team as strategic driver	• Develop capabilities and experience first • Provide a clear brand vision • Engage the organization broadly • Get C-suite support • Have a clear structure with clear roles • Show results • Leverage regional or global agencies • Manage the evolution over time	• Rely on local talent • Recruit local talent • Manage local talent globally • Maintain and diffuse the organization's culture

FIGURE 8-1 Managing a Global or Regional Brand

how those roles evolve over time. We also look at ways to manage the challenges of implementing a central brand marketing effort, as well as other management challenges—such as dealing with people and cultures—faced by the EMNCs we talked to. We end the chapter with a discussion of the implications for the TMNCs competing with such EMNCs. Figure 8-1 provides a road map and summary of the key points.

Problems of Uncoordinated Marketing Across Geographies

Our research revealed three problems that resulted from the lack of coordinated brand marketing efforts across geographies:

- Higher marketing costs due to overly localized marketing
- Reduced quality of marketing due to uncoordinated marketing programs
- Inadequate communication and sharing across geographies

Higher Marketing Costs due to Overly Localized Marketing

Marketing efforts that are initiated and managed with a primarily localized emphasis have the potential to make many types of company costs much higher than they need to be, both because they create incremental costs and because they make it harder to achieve economies of scale.

Brand-Building Costs

The lack of a regional or global approach to managing brands across geographies can lead to brands acquiring different images in different markets, as our example from Evyap in Turkey and Russia showed. While adapting the brand image to the local market can initially increase revenues by making the brand more relevant to the local market, the longer-term brand-building costs in each local market can be significant, eroding profit margins (the primary reason for building a brand in the first place). Thus, Evyap's initial decision to launch Arko as a masculine brand in Russia with a range of shaving creams, aftershaves, etc., as opposed to a brand that catered to the entire family, as in Turkey, forced Evyap to later expand in Russia with an altogether different brand in its portfolio (Duru). Duru was originally an all-family personal-care brand in Turkey, but today it is a more feminine brand in Russia while Arko occupies a masculine image there. This extra brand adds more expense for Evyap in the longer run in Russia than if its Arko brand had been marketed there as a unisex brand from the beginning. Learning from this, according to Mustafa Arin, an executive committee member of marketing R&D at Evyap, the company has decided to maintain a uniform positioning for both the Arko and Duru brands across international markets in the future. This decision has already paid dividends, enabling Evyap to strip the number of SKUs under these two brands by more than 25 percent across international markets.

Media Costs

In today's media environment, many brand touch points are regional or global in nature; these include the Internet, call centers, events such as the Olympics or the FIFA World Cup, and TV networks such as Star TV, SKY, and CNN. Thus, excessively localized marketing programs not only lead to confused brand images in the minds of consumers but also fail to capture economies of scale in media buying. Dabur's Sunil Duggal talked about the benefits to the brand of the spillover reach of its advertising from India to some of the Persian Gulf markets, which meant that developing locally distinct programs for Dabur brands in those markets would be wasteful.

Manufacturing and R&D Costs

Excessive localization can raise costs not only in marketing but also in manufacturing, R&D, and product development. Thus, Mehmed Evyap noted that for his company, it was no longer interesting to look at brand offerings on a single-country basis; what Evyap looked for were new product opportunities that could be leveraged across markets under one brand, which led to the spreading of development costs over a wider region and enabled the company to capture economies of scale in manufacturing and product development.

Cross-market coordination also allows firms to invest in focused technology development behind opportunities that are potentially huge wins, enabling them to compete more effectively with their limited resources. Thus, in the appliances and durables categories, LG has focused its global technology resources on front-loading washing machines that it saw as a significant growth opportunity (developing direct-drive technology for its motors and revolutionary steam washing).[1] LG and Samsung are today also leading the charge in LED and 3D televisions for their worldwide products, while Natura has pioneered technologies to extract active ingredients from Brazil's flora for its flagship international Ekos brand.

Fragmented and Expensive Supply Chains

Brand localization also means an expensive and fragmented supply chain, as the minor local variations can require different ingredients, different packaging, different labels, and the like. Evyap's Arin thus noted with dissatisfaction how Evyap's very complex manufacturing structure led to inefficiencies and lack of focus on major brands and formats. He even characterized the business "as the management of complexity and inefficiencies."[2] Centralization leads not only to a firm being better able to negotiate superior prices due to higher volumes but also to it being better able to manage inventory and to deploy a more skilled purchasing team that can identify suppliers and work with them to get timely and stable supplies, as Godrej, Savola, Asian Paints, Asia Pacific Breweries, and others have done.

Reduced Quality of Marketing due to Uncoordinated Marketing Programs

Localized marketing programs can also lower the quality of the marketing efforts put behind the brands in these different markets; they can mean missing out on superior ideas, market intelligence, and human talent.

Superior Ideas

Speaking of the need for regional or global coordination, MTS CMO Cynthia Gordon observed, "If you're consistent, the higher quality and the lower costs you will have will improve your efficiency." As she notes, global or regional coordination not only can lower costs but also can lead to superior creative ideas (sourced and pooled across multiple markets), managed by a superior team with superior technological support, which can all lead to enhanced revenue. Moreover, larger centralized budgets can permit higher development costs for superior advertising and other marketing programs that are then shared across multiple markets. Ranbaxy's Dani noted that leveraging such economies of scale is a problem that has plagued him, as the "regional directors each have a different approach" to their marketing.

Superior Market Intelligence

Marketing today is no longer only about running advertising and promotion campaigns based on superior creativity and intuition. It also requires the use of sophisticated research that draws on ethnographic, survey, and behavioral data and that makes use of analytical tools ranging from simple correlations to sophisticated analysis of field experiments and analytical modeling of purchase data. Localized programs also have the potential to reduce the quality of these research programs because centralized programs can leverage the power of global service providers to uncover new and viable cross-market opportunities that may not be visible or viable when viewed at the individual market level. Thus, Mehmed Evyap noted that a $500,000 survey was under way at Evyap, sponsored by the central management, to better understand consumer needs and behaviors in the geographies outside Turkey. Such a broad pan-market survey of regional market trends and opportunities could simply not be undertaken on a local-country basis.

Superior Human Talent
To utilize such sophisticated data and analytics, marketing managers today require a broad range of sophisticated skills. At the individual market level, it is often difficult to get the full range of human capabilities, due both to lack of availability of skilled personnel in a given market and to scale and cost limits on the organization's ability to pay for top talent.

Noting the shortage of skilled personnel in many geographies, Marico's Vijay Subramaniam noted, "The general management and marketing skill levels of managers in specific geographies are often not up to par due to the less competitive nature of their markets, which means you have to look harder to locate top talent there." The shortage of talent in specific geographies was also noted by Edmond Neo of Asia Pacific Breweries and Ranbaxy's Dani. The latter explained that when trying to strengthen "brand marketing ability, I mean the people . . . I am trying to strengthen our capability by bringing competent people. I am also trying to improve people's competency through training sessions. Then you take the best people you have trained to another country and stabilize there." The reliance on local programs led by local talent reduces capability relative to those competitors that leverage their best talent from across the organization.

Taking a pan-market view also allows firms to locate, hire, and retain top talent to manage their brands. Thus, Savola's central marketing team was (at the time of our research) led by Tarik Hadi, who had almost two decades of brand-building expertise, acquired both at Savola and from a decade-long stint at P&G. He also brought to the table firsthand knowledge of several of the markets in which Savola operates. Such deep talent can have a transformative impact on the brands the firm owns, far beyond anything that can be garnered from local brand management teams.

Inadequate Communication and Sharing Across Geographies

Too much decentralization also reduces valuable cross-market communication. Since success in marketing depends on the early detection of customer needs and trends, cross-market communication helps firms more easily detect new opportunities and better assess them for economies of scale. The firms we talked to recognized the need for cross-market communication but noted that they are only in the early stages of executing on this. Thus, Marico's Subramaniam commented that "we try to consciously promote cross-sharing of ideas between not just various businesses but also between geographies. We try to pass on best practices through cross country learning forums . . . this is, however, something we will have to improve substantially." Firms seeking to increase such cross-market communication need to put in place a variety of mechanisms, including frequent meetings and visits, the use of multicountry teams and committees, the creation of both formal and informal knowledge-sharing networks, the hiring and rotation of managers with a global mindset, and the use of performance evaluation and incentive systems that reward sharing.

The companies in our sample thus recognize the challenges stemming from the history of pursuing independent multilocal approaches in their initial forays into internationalization and are searching for answers. Mahindra & Mahindra CEO Pravin Shah noted that "the question that you are raising, as to how do we now graduate to being able to look at the brand globally and manage the brand globally in a consistent manner, is important . . . we are in the process of doing exactly what you are asking."

Coordinated Management of Brands Across Markets

Not surprisingly, the usual response of our EMNCs to dealing with the challenge of having fragmented businesses and brands across geographies was the establishment of a strong centralized team. Such a team could then provide a broad range of support and services that included doing centralized market research, articulating the brand identity, formulating marketing strategy, developing and providing collateral materials such as TV and print advertisements for local deployment, and so on. However, while the importance of such centralized management of marketing was recognized, many of the firms in our sample were yet to adopt such a structure. Thus, Aramex's Fadi Ghandour noted that the company's regional directors were "completely empowered to run that region and every country manager is also a local CEO in our view." The earlier comment from Ranbaxy's Dani about such decentralization echoes the same point.[3]

Those firms in our sample that had already adopted some form of central management of marketing differed in the role this central group played. We found three types of roles that the central groups played:

- Facilitator
- Advisor
- Strategic driver

Over time, we saw that the roles sometimes changed, the evolution being from facilitator, to advisor, to the strategic driver role. We discuss them below, and the key points are summarized in Figure 8-2.

	Facilitator	Advisor	Strategic Driver
Evolution over time	➔	➔	
Control of marketing processes to create standardization	**Medium** • Disseminates a common vocabulary to assess and manage marketing and brands • Develops, provides, and encourages the use of a common planning process • Develops and maintains IT platforms • Organizes events and meetings to enhance competencies • Facilitates cross-group communications • Builds and makes accessible databases and knowledge pools • Country marketing head reports to country head	**High** • Creates and ensures compliance with common planning processes • Develops and maintains IT platforms • Participates in and potentially leads the analysis to identify opportunities and threats in the different markets • Collects and disseminates cross-market customer insights • Dotted-line relationship with in-market, marketing head	**High** • Serves as custodian of the brand globally • Is responsible for generating and acting on customer insights • Decides on strategic direction and marketing strategy • Marketing heads in countries report to central marketing head who heads the team
Control of marketing program to create standardization	**Low** • Marketing programs developed and implemented locally	**Medium** • Recommends strategic directions and marketing activities • Helps to fine-tune strategic initiatives coming from the markets	**High** • Is responsible for producing marketing programs • Local markets have some say over adaptation of materials • Final sign-off on adaptations with central marketing team • Local markets only implement programs

FIGURE 8-2 The Role of the Central Marketing Team

Phase 1. Central Team as a Facilitator

The central team acting as a facilitator engages in developing, providing, and encouraging the use of:

- A common planning process
- A common vocabulary to assess and manage marketing and brands
- IT platforms
- Events and meetings to enhance competencies and cross-group communications
- Databases and knowledge pools that can be accessed by the various brands, businesses, and geographies

This role appears to be the first and easiest step for firms operating on a multilocal basis, as it does not threaten the local fiefdoms. Thus, Marico has created a centralized hub at its Mumbai headquarters to support the regional groups that are currently based in multiple locations, in addition to the South Asia group that is also based in Mumbai. Marico's Subramaniam observed that "our role here is more of a support center. We're in the early stages . . . in a launch [of the company's Parachute brand] in Egypt [and] while our support center will have a view on positioning and packaging, all other aspects of the mix would be fundamentally anchored by our Egyptian country team."

Interestingly, the central brand marketing team seems to play no more than a facilitator role at Corona as well, even though Corona has been engaged in international markets for quite a while. This may be because Corona's expansion outside Mexico and the United States is relatively recent, making coordination of the brand across far-flung markets a relatively recent challenge. Corona's Daniel Gómez pointed out that "the brand has some principles, e.g., beach, premium, imported brand, and there is a brand book, and one needs to adhere to these rules, but [we allow local businesses to] interpret them in the context of the local culture." Corona has just moved from using local marketing communications agencies to using such agencies with regional responsibility in order to support the creation of a distinct but consistent regional image. Importantly, marketing at Corona is still outsourced to the local distributors, and thus Gómez noted that one key element to local success "was choosing a distributor who knows how to market a premium brand in the local market."

Phase 2. Central Team as Advisor

The central team as an advisor takes a more active role in managing the firm's brands in a coordinated and synergistic manner across businesses and geographies. In this role, the central team not only participates in but also potentially leads the analysis to identify opportunities and threats in the different markets and in cross-market customer insights; the team also suggests strategic directions and marketing activities and helps to fine-tune strategic initiatives coming from the markets. Such a central advisor role tends to emerge in firms with greater international experience, and as the value of centralized support becomes more apparent to the markets, the role is often a transition from an initial facilitator role.

Asian Paints, which started down the road to internationalization quite some years ago, now has a central brand marketing group that plays just such an advisory role and supports its portfolio of brands that operate from the South Pacific in the east through Southeast and South Asia, the Middle East, and the Caribbean in the west. In its advisor role, the central brand marketing group, headed by Tom Thomas, ensures adherence to the brand planning processes that it has developed and disseminated across the organization, "so there is a common approach to the brand." As Thomas noted, "Without this process and adherence to it, regions would likely introduce any brand and in any manner." The central brand marketing team participates in strategic discussions with the regions to identify new opportunities, supports the development of new products to take advantage of opportunities or fill gaps in its portfolio across regions, agrees upon strategic priorities, and helps the regions develop their strategies. Thus, for instance, it identifies successful product brands in one region and helps introduce these across other regions, depending on identified consumer needs.

The central brand marketing team at Asian Paints also develops "platforms"—common building blocks—that can be and are leveraged across geographies. Thus, for instance, it developed a retail tinting system where the dealer is able to generate the exact shade an individual customer wants from the wide range of shades that Asian Paints offers—without having to carry an enormous range of pre-tinted shades in inventory—through a mixing process undertaken on the dealers' premises. This automatic and mechanized tinting system, branded as Colour World, is a completely standardized and branded retail platform that is common across all geographies and businesses around the world. All the marketing materials, shade ranges offered, and hardware are standardized. As Asian Paints' Thomas said, "It's getting done across all our stores; if you go to a thousand stores across our various markets, right from the Caribbean to South East Asia, they all look similar in terms of what customers will get from a store in terms of shades as well as marketing platforms."

Phase 3. Central Team as Strategic Driver

When playing a strategic driver role, the central team takes full ownership of the strategic management of brands across markets and businesses. The team is the body that is responsible for generating and acting on customer insights: this central brand marketing team decides on the strategic direction and the marketing strategy. The central team is also responsible for producing the marketing programs. The job of the local markets then is only to implement strategy, with some say over adaptation of marketing materials; the final sign-off still remains squarely with the central brand management team. This role requires strong marketing capabilities in the central brand marketing team, a good understanding of the local markets, and credibility and support within the organization. It also requires a sensitivity to the need to motivate local marketing staff, who otherwise might get demoralized by their lack of power, and it requires mechanisms to get buy-in from the local staff for the programs they are asked to implement. (We discuss some of these later in this chapter.) Thus, this is typically a role into which the brand marketing team evolves only after considerable experience, and several of the more mature EMNCs we interviewed had adopted this role.

Asia Pacific Breweries was one of the firms we talked to where the central brand marketing team had the role of strategic driver. According to Asia Pacific Breweries' Neo, the markets are clustered into regions, with each region being managed by a regional director. The regions report into Singapore, which is the headquarters of Asia Pacific Breweries. It is the central brand marketing team in Singapore that plots strategy in consultation with the operating companies and the ad agency. The central brand management team is the brand custodian and heads the brands globally. As Neo put it, "The local companies implement the stuff sent from Singapore. The thematic is sent from Singapore. The layout of the ads is provided by Singapore, be it print, TV, outdoor or in bar. Connection program handouts are sent from Singapore. Translation is done locally and some adaptation is permitted by the local companies; for example, advertisement headlines can be expanded. These can then be implemented by the local operating companies after sign-off from us. Packaging is handled entirely from Singapore and there is no debate about that."

LG Electronics, the largest player in our sample, has recently undergone a transformation, moving to a central brand setup to act as a strategic driver. Until early in the new millennium, LG Electronics' marketing efforts were uncoordinated. Each division (home appliances, digital displays, mobile phones, and so on) acted independently. In fact, these business units did not have a central marketing group. The marketing function initially resided with the geographies and functioned more as a sales department than a marketing department, selling products pushed by the manufacturing units.

Based on the realization of the shortcomings of this uncoordinated and product-focused model, LG Electronics embarked on a transformation that began with a broad education of the middle and senior management,

which emphasized the need for a customer-driven approach. LG Electronics created the position of CMO, which had a direct reporting relationship with the CEO; and the company assembled a team of around 50 people with strong marketing skills and market knowledge at the Seoul headquarters, drawn from both within LG Electronics and outside, to coordinate strategy across product divisions and geographies. Additionally, the product divisions were strengthened with their own central marketing strategy teams for interpreting the corporate brand and marketing strategy as developed with leadership from the CMO's office, adapting the brand and the strategy to their particular product space, e.g., home appliances, and pushing them to the geographies.

Coordination was achieved by the CMO's office through regular meetings between key people in the divisional marketing teams, key marketing people in the geographies, and the CMO and his team. These regular meetings were supplemented by an annual meeting of all marketing directors from around the world held in Seoul at the behest of the CMO. The ultimate authority for all marketing activity rests with the CMO, and plans discussed in regular meetings have to be approved by the CMO as being in sync with the corporate marketing and branding strategy, prior to implementation.

Thus, LG Electronics has moved rapidly in the course of the past five to seven years from a disparate bundle of marketing initiatives led by the markets to a coordinated effort led by the CMO's office, which plays a strategic driver role. The jury is still out on whether the move was successful. On the one hand, LG has become the premium appliances brand in the United States. For example, in washing machines, it commanded the highest average selling price and was reported to have the highest level of customer satisfaction by J. D. Power.[4] On the other, the financial performance of LG Electronics overall has been less than what was hoped for, leading to then CEO Yong Nam being replaced by Koo Bon-joon, a member of the founding family, in September 2010.

Implementing a Central Brand Marketing Team

Building a successful central global or regional brand marketing team is difficult, as such a team—even in the facilitator role—signals greater centralization and thus creates resentment locally. Moreover, it can also lead to poorer flows of ideas from the market to the center and can slow down local decision making because of the need for sign-off from the central team. As Lenovo's Deepak

Advani noted, "When you have a model where you have to go to the central organization to get the work done—doesn't matter where the central organization is—that always adds complexities in your process. So that was our biggest challenge. Before, if someone in Brazil needed to get something done, they just picked up the phone, called their local agency, set up a meeting, and hashed it out and you're done. In the model we were moving towards, if you wanted to get something done, you had to write a brief and send it over to a team at the hub and they would work with the agency in Bangalore and come back with a draft for you, you review it, they will make changes and they will come back and you're done."

Given the increased costs in terms of both slowed decision time and effort that this role taken by the central brand team imposes on the firm as a whole, and the resentment it may cause in the local teams due to the loss of control, it is important to have a clear strategy for going ahead with the creation of a central brand management team. To get buy-in from local marketing units and successfully implement on the decision to create a central brand management team, our research documented a four-step process, shown in Figure 8-3. The process begins with the development of marketing *expertise* (step 1). Next the brand needs to be *envisioned* (step 2) and articulated clearly. Then to move forward, one needs to engage with stakeholders broadly so that they *embrace* (step 3) the implementation of a central brand marketing team and, finally, take steps to *establish* (step 4) the team firmly within the fabric and culture of the organization by showing its value.

Build Expertise

In describing their evolution from multilocal brand management to the central brand marketing team roles, Titan CEO Bhaskar Bhat notes, "Initially they [local companies] knew about the brand and the whole ethos of Titan, but they were independent, they were funding their own advertising, creating their own advertising, selecting their own product, pricing them independently, and

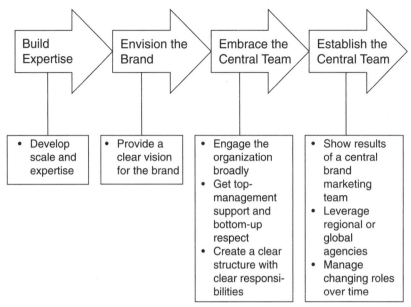

FIGURE 8-3 Road Map to a Successful Central Marketing Team

so on. Only in 2007 did we decide that now, having had enough experience about market evaluation and distribution etc., we could integrate it all."

Titan has now created a division for watches (and another for jewelry) that spans both the domestic and international business. Since, according to Bhat, "India had all the strength in terms of design, advertising, retailing, etc.," it made sense to centralize marketing in India, and it is now centrally managed from the Bangalore headquarters. The centralization worked because the international markets benefited from being able to leverage "the assets that India had already developed—and of course India also needed the experience that we gathered overseas, particularly from a brand point of view." It is important to highlight that the creation of a central brand management team helps both domestic and international business through more effective knowledge transfer.

Envision

The central brand marketing team needs to provide a clear vision of the brand by articulating what the brand stands for across the various markets and setting clear guidelines on all aspects of the brand and its usage. It then needs to communicate this vision throughout the organization, create buy-in, and ensure the vision is remembered and followed.

Brand Book. Several of the firms implementing a central brand marketing team, such as Apollo Tyres, Aramex, Mahindra & Mahindra, Marico, and Ranbaxy, began by articulating what the brand stands for and developing guidelines for the use of the brand through the creation of a "brand book." Thus, Marico has a brand manual for its Parachute brand, which articulates what the brand stands for and which defines the dos and don'ts regarding the marketing of the brand. Ranbaxy noted that its brand book specifies the rules about how the brand is to be used and represented in its communications. As Dani said, "It is a checking process. No sign goes on a building unless it is aligned with the book. Nobody is allowed to make any changes."

Likewise, Aramex's Ghandour noted that "we have a brand book. So, everywhere, that's the image. And we have an office that focuses on that here in Jordan." The Aramex brand book goes to great lengths in spelling out the brand elements so that "we look the same from the car, to the office, to the pouch." Interestingly, while Aramex has a brand book and a team focusing on the brand at its headquarters in Jordan, other than the physical look and feel of the brand, no other brand marketing element is managed centrally. Thus, such brand books are only a first step and need to be followed up with effective internal communication about what the brand stands for, so that personnel understand the spirit of the brand over and beyond the letter of the law regarding the brand as contained in the brand books. Moreover, processes need to be in place to weed out any deviations from the stated brand norms.

Processes and Communication. Brand books are a first step, but in and of themselves, they are not sufficient. Their content needs to be actively communicated to and internalized by the local market executives. To achieve this, at Asia Pacific Breweries, Neo noted, "You can email of course, you can send brand books, you can send catalogues, nothing I think still beats sitting across the table and saying 'right here it is.' " Asia Pacific Breweries sees huge value not only in interpersonally communicating the brand and its values but in bringing people over to Singapore. Neo commented that "nothing beats coming to the roots of the brand itself, which for Tiger Beer is here in Singapore. They go down to select breweries, they go to where Tiger Beer lives, and they begin to really immerse in the brand and that makes them sell it a lot better." By meeting a lot of people who are the carriers of the brand essence, meeting the advertising agency, and so on, local marketers visiting Singapore develop an understanding of what the Tiger Beer brand stands for.

In this same spirit, at Vitra there is a regular monthly meeting at the management level. This helps Vitra to not only communicate its brand values throughout the organization but routinely emphasize those values across a broad swath of employees, as well as identify and weed out any activities that are inconsistent with the brand. Importantly, by making this a cross-functional and organization-wide effort, it engages the entire organization behind the brand through the process of "internal branding."

Embrace

Once the brand vision has been articulated, it is important that the brand team be able to generate an organization-wide strong and favorable response in support of the proposed brand identity and brand strategy. To do this, the global brand team needs to engage the organization broadly, get support from top management and the rank and file, and create a brand culture as well as an understanding of the role each organization member plays in living that culture.

Engage the Organization Broadly

Most non-marketing executives and even some marketing executives believe that brands are about advertising and communications and thus should be dealt with by just the marketing department. This is a myopic view and limits the organization's capability to deliver on its promise to the target consumer. Thus, engaging with personnel throughout the organization, building an understanding of the role of branding among them, helping them understand the importance of brands for the health of the business, creating an understanding of what the organization's brands stand for, helping personnel internalize the implications of this for their actions and behaviors, and creating buy-in are crucial tasks for the central brand marketing team if it is going to be able to put brand strategy at center stage. This requires both an appropriate organizational structure and appropriate processes, which are discussed below.

Such internal branding efforts are especially important for service and B2B businesses, in which the customer's multiple interactions with company employees are the determining elements of their experience of the brand. At the Indian (Taj) Hotels Group, Ajay Misra noted the importance of "communicating and delivering a consistent brand experience across all hotels." That this is a "people challenge" is clearly recognized, and Misra noted that because people from different cultures have different service standards, acculturation of employees to the Taj value system to deliver the brand promise in overseas markets is crucial for the Taj Hotels.

Not surprisingly, Taj Hotels has invested in internal brand building among its employees, particularly in the key source markets of the United States and the United Kingdom. Brand standards for service have now been defined across all hotels and rolled out to ensure consistency in service delivery. The look and feel of the brand has also become consistent across all hotels in India and overseas as a part of the branding exercise. In recognition of the role of people in brand delivery, a human resource talent pool of global managers has been created who can move from India to overseas hotels and carry with them the values and ethos of the Taj brand, the so-called Taj-ness. Local employees in overseas markets are given acculturation programs to understand the Taj value system, the brand's vision, and its mission and to internalize Taj-ness to ensure service delivery that lives the Taj brand.

To engage the entire organization in building the corporate MTS (telecom network) brand, MTS created a high-level central body, a brand council, to signal the importance of the brand and give brand strategy and the central brand marketing team legitimacy. MTS's brand council is chaired by the CEO. Furthermore, as noted by Cynthia Gordon, the CMO of MTS, "The brand council brings together all the VPs. So every VP, for both the business units as well as the corporate centre teams such as HR, is there on the brand council. It's important that the brand is really the leader of the entire business and one of the mistakes we were making a couple of years ago was thinking of the brand as communications, that is, the brand and advertising are the same thing. I think we now really understand that the brand is about this entire company."

To gain acceptance and credibility, beyond such formal structures such as MTS's brand council (which provides a formal seal of approval by a broad group of top management), it is also important for the brand marketing council to engage broadly with individuals within the organization at an interpersonal level. Thus, Lenovo's Advani talked about spending a lot of time with a broad group of people in the various markets to make sure they understood what the firm was trying to do with the brand and the central brand management team. Lenovo went as far as bringing some of the key sales leaders in each of the geographies to Bangalore, where the central brand marketing team was located, so that they had "a chance to meet the people, to feel the energy, and get a chance to really build the relationship. That personalizes it . . . makes it very different."

Get Top-Management Support—and Bottom-Up Respect

Getting CEO support is crucial in successfully implementing a central brand marketing team, particularly if the team is to play a more hands-on role such as an advisor or strategic driver role. As already noted, these roles necessitate a transfer of power from local markets to the center, and they are thus deeply resented. Describing the difficulties faced with implementing a central brand marketing team to play a strategic driver role at Lenovo, ex-CMO Advani recalled, "It was difficult, you had to overcome political challenges, both on the Lenovo side as well as the agency side, because there are a lot of people in many countries around the world who wanted nothing more than to see this thing fail." Advani attributes the ultimate success of the creation and operation of the central brand marketing team to the support of the CEO and the board. He noted, "At the end of day it was very successful and one of the big reasons it was successful is because of the strong support of the CEO, the chairman, and the board."

The story at LG Electronics is no different. The CMO's office faced strong resentment, and but for the strong support of CEO Yong Nam, the central brand marketing team would have had no chance to achieve its goals. Today to further legitimize the CMO's team and role, LG Electronics, as already noted, has appointed recently retired and highly respected LG veteran and North American CEO Michael Ahn to the role of special advisor to the CMO, lending both gravitas and credibility to the office.

Create a Clear Structure with a Clear Delineation of Roles and Responsibilities

Beyond getting the organization on board, it is important to have a clear structure to define roles and relationships. The most common structure—at least in the beginning stages—was a regional grouping of countries, based on both proximity and similarities in consumer behavior, with marketing personnel within each country and region. Thus, for instance, for Asian Paints, South Asia was a region because within this cluster of geographically adjacent countries, the building styles, paint application styles, paint buying mores, and paint color preferences were similar. As well, the climate and distribution systems were similar, which collectively provided a clear rationale for creating this regional grouping.

Given such a regional structure, with countries responsible for business individually within each region, the country marketing team typically reported to the country business head and the regional marketing team, while the regional marketing team reported to the regional business head and the central brand marketing team at the center. As noted earlier, while the central brand marketing team, in most cases, was located at headquarters, this need not be the case, and Lenovo opted to locate its central brand marketing team in Bangalore, India. We discuss the rationale for this in detail in the next section.

In most of the firms with a regional structure, there is an expensive replication of resources at the country and regional levels for most functions, including marketing. Therefore, many EMNCs eventually move to a matrix structure, partially or completely, as at Tata Tea. At Tata Tea, the portfolio of brands is divided into two groups: regional and global. The consumer-focused regional organization has autonomous control over the regional brands. As Tata Tea's Percy Siganporia noted, "These regions will develop everything, and are a consumer focused organization, creating the route to market, developing consumer insight or business propositions. But, even for them, the supply chain and support services were global, to provide the leverage of global capability." Their global brands, e.g., Tetley, have a global positioning with local execution. The strategy for these global brands is formulated by the central brand marketing team, with the execution undertaken by the regions according to the global template created by the central brand marketing team.

LG Electronics too is currently in the process of moving to a global strategy complemented by a local autonomy-in-execution model. In this model, the global strategy is set by the CMO's office in consultation with the manufacturing companies (i.e., home appliance, digital displays, air conditioning, and mobile phones) and markets. The global strategy is next interpreted by each company's central brand marketing team and passed on to the markets that are responsible for strategy execution. Moreover, LG Electronics has also embarked on an initiative to more clearly articulate the roles and responsibilities for the central brand marketing team as well as the local in-market teams.[5] Such a global matrix model provides depth in capability while eliminating duplication of resources, enabling the firm to maximize impact while optimizing cost efficiency.

Establish

To get the importance and respect that a central team needs to lead the organization's marketing efforts across geographies, it needs to establish its leadership role clearly in the minds of the marketing people in the local markets. To do so, it is important to show real results and do so early.

Show Results

Given the antipathy that often greets the creation of a central brand marketing team due to the actual and perceived loss of power in the markets, it is imperative to show the results from a central organization—and to show them fast. It is also important to leverage the strengths of marketing partners such as research agencies, advertising research agenices, and the like. Several of our interviewees talked about the initial buzz within the organization when the central brand marketing team was put in place, which was primarily negative, raising the question of how and what this one more new initiative was going to deliver. Therefore, explaining what the economic deliverables may be, delivering on them, and communicating and celebrating the success throughout the organization become important steps. MTS's CMO Gordon noted, "You can turn it into an economic argument and it's one of the strongest arguments. We were very much suffering because of inconsistency in our advertising. With the media, we had to spend 30–40% more GRPs to reach the same level of awareness as our competitors. With consistency, that situation changed and you've put a value on consistency and the importance of brand identity. People really understand that. The other thing that has helped is the quality because if you step into Ukraine, Uzbekistan, or Belarus, it's quite difficult to create high quality of advertising. The use of better-crafted materials is a very strong argument."

Lenovo's Advani also attributed the success of creating the firm's central brand marketing team to the visible benefits that accrued from such centralization. Advani pointed to three benefits: cost savings on developing advertising and other marketing materials by eliminating duplication, the superior quality of advertising and marketing materials due to more focused resources, and the availability of more funds for local activation. To create costs savings that were significant while at the same time having impactful materials, and to achieve this beyond just that achieved by eliminating duplication, Lenovo took the interesting step of housing its central brand marketing group, which played a strategic driver role, in Bangalore, India—not in China, the company's original home country, and not in the United States, the home of the ThinkPad brand that Lenovo had acquired.

This is an interesting twist, as most TMNCs house central brand management in their home market. Lenovo housed its central brand management team in India to take advantage of both cost and capability; India has low-cost but world-class quality advertising production capability, for example, as documented by the fact that the movie *Slumdog Millionaire* was produced for a paltry US$15 million and that significant work on the film, in terms of editing, sound mixing, and so on, was done in India. Notably, the film won Oscars for these categories, among the eight Oscars it bagged in 2009, attesting to the high quality of such capability. Interestingly, such a move also reduces some of the internal criticisms by creating champions in the market or markets where the centralized function is located. It makes the logic and global spirit of the organization transparent, getting the markets on board more easily.

The move was successful. As Advani observed, "At the end of the day we got significant savings and we also improved the quality of the deliverables. People were reinventing the wheel; it was annoying because we are selling the same product everywhere, for the most part to small businesses. A lot of the stuff that we were doing for businesses was product centric: we weren't selling a shampoo, and so the messaging wasn't very different from country to country. A lot of it was like 'here's ThinkPad, with the water proof keyboard.' Given these needs, it's a real shame to take money away from your in-market spend and spend it towards creating redundant assets." When the local units saw the benefits of greater resources for marketing spending through the creation of standardized ads, they gained respect for the centralized brand management structure.

Leverage Regional or Global Partners

When embarking on this journey of creating a centralized brand management structure, the path is difficult not only because there is internal resistance but because the organization does not have the requisite knowledge and experience in developing and managing a global brand management function. One way to overcome some of this inexperience and the knowledge gap is by appointing and partnering with marketing services providers such as advertising agencies and market research firms that are already global in their organization. Thus, Lenovo appointed Ogilvy & Mather as its global agency. Since Ogilvy & Mather is set up to operate as a global agency, it could help Lenovo with the transition to this more global centralized model of management, sharing its experience and expertise that it acquired in the process of having gone through the transition itself and having worked with other globally organized businesses.

Manage Changing Roles over Time

As a firm expands internationally, the lack of central brand management has potentially costly consequences, as we noted earlier. Thus, it is not surprising that firms try to move to a more centralized model of brand management. Arçelik's Hasan Subaşi was vehement about the importance of moving toward some form of central brand marketing. He said, "In my opinion if you are managing a brand, this needs to have a central component. Let's say we gave the brand to a couple of people in Romania, so that they manage the Beko brand, its positioning, pricing etc.—it would become impossible for us to control the business. Dealership, transportation, or warehouses could be outsourced to local firms, you can delegate that; but you cannot delegate brand management. Strategy making is central, from Arçelik's headquarters in Sütlüce. In specific periods of the year, our country and region managers come together, discuss, conduct SWOT analyses, benchmark what the competitors are doing, examine what the threats are, etc. According to this data, a strategy is developed and turned into a directive to be shared with everyone. But the last word is the CEO's—the CEO and his staff make the final decisions. In branding issues, it is not possible—nor right—to decentralize."

The role played by central brand marketing evolves through the three roles we have identified. Indeed, some of the firms we talked to clearly see an evolving pattern into the future. For example, in reaching critical mass in new geographies, one of the firms we talked to noted that its plan is to cluster geographically proximate country markets under new regional entities. At the same time, it hopes to see the central group headquarters play a more significant role, the role of advisor. The executive responsible for internationalization hoped "that it will lead to a healthy mix of centralized and decentralized decision making."

In the longer term, as business grows, it plans to have in place a regional brand manager reporting to the corporate brand management team at headquarters to more actively and consistently manage its brands across geographies. Thus, the long-term vision is to have the central brand marketing team playing the strategic driver role. This is clear from this executive's comment: "We're in the process of harmonizing. Before we get there though, we first have to establish our presence and get scale. As we do that, we will be gravitating towards a system having some regional brand responsibility, but with overall brand responsibility at headquarters. The local teams would run the activations and executions thereof."

We next turn to the challenge of managing global talent.

Managing Talent in a Global Context

Relying on Local Talent

Importantly, the EMNCs that we talked to believed in leveraging local talent, as it is far less expensive than the expatriate talent that TMNCs tend to rely on. Moreover, they believed that local employees were not less talented—rather, they lacked the skill-building exposure that expatriate managers had, which was easily remedied. As Aramex's Ghandour noted, "Bring in the talent [local], get it exposed, get it trained, send it out, send it global, send it to good offices, send it to education programs across the world. That investment will return back to you many fold." The reliance on local talent is not only a matter of understanding the quality of these people and believing in them, but also an imperative if EMNCs are to maintain one of their core strengths, cost competitiveness, as expat talent costs at least double if not four to five times more than equally competent local talent. (See Chapter 2 on the imperative for EMNCs to increase their cost competitiveness over TMNCs.)

Recruiting Local Talent

EMNCs often find it difficult to recruit top local talent, however. Aramex's Ghandour noted, "In the initial 10 to 15 years we had a difficult time recruiting talent, because talent wants to go to a [TMNC] brand and wants to learn and wants to be able to achieve its own ambitions." Of course, once the EMNC brand is established, this problem disappears. Indeed, local companies with a credible ambition often find top talented local people who wish to remain in the region, as leading and ambitious EMNCs can offer more exciting opportunities and a career path to the top within the region, something that is not possible with a TMNC headquartered in a completely different part of the world. Thus, Ghandour recounted that "once our brand was established and once we established ourselves as the company for the region that is going global, that is going places, that is the first company on NASDAQ, we were a magnet for talent."

Retaining Local Talent

While this was not universally true, the level of employee loyalty in several of the firms we talked to, e.g., LG Electronics, Mahindra & Mahindra, and Aramex, was very high. Ghandour explained, "We invest heavily in them so that they stay with us. That's why you will find a lot of our country managers and senior managers of the company have been with us for ten, fifteen, twenty years even. The biggest challenge for us in terms of talent was in the past three or four years as the Gulf was booming; we had crazy companies coming in and offering outrageous salaries. We were concerned; we didn't lose many people but there was a heck of a lot of talk about, you know, my neighbour is getting ten times my current salary." In such situations, rather than by competing on salaries, EMNCs try to retain talented employees by creating a better working environment that is more entrepreneurial, a learning environment with opportunities for professional and personal growth through work opportunities as well as investments in employee training. These initiatives were utilized successfully by Aramex, Mahindra & Mahindra, and others.

Managing Local Talent Globally

Having said that, one of the key shortcomings that we noted with many of the EMNCs we talked to was their reliance on staff from headquarters to manage the subsidiaries. Career opportunities for personnel from the companies acquired in local markets remained local. There was no real thinking, in all but a small minority of companies such as LG Electronics, Tata Tea, Natura, and Ranbaxy, to bring in top talent from local markets to headquarters or recruit top talent globally as needed. Marico's Subramaniam noted, "Given our stage in evolution, we haven't done that. We have situations where people from the India operations of Marico move to these geographies. We have situations where acquired talent continues to run the local operations. In the case of South Africa, we brought the team of managers to India, we had a detailed induction process where they spent a lot of time understanding the company, going through everything. Some of them even visited the businesses in other geographies to get a better perspective. So we've been doing stuff like this. But if you ask me if there's an employee from South Africa working in the Indian business I would say no, it's a bit too early for that. As we globalize hopefully we'll get there someday."

To become a true global player with global capabilities, it is important to be able to induct top talent from the markets one is in and provide these people with growth opportunities to the very top, as leading TMNCs do. Thus, Priti Rajora, Wipro's GM for Talent Acquisition, noted that the single biggest challenge that Wipro faced going forward was transforming itself from being an Indian company to a global one where global talent from its far-flung operations could be woven into the company culture and given an opportunity to rise to the highest levels of the organization.

Maintaining and Diffusing the Organization's Culture

As EMNCs expand and hire local talent from around the world, a key challenge they grapple with is how to maintain their corporate culture and values in the context of the changing face of their employee base. We found two ways in which this issue was tackled: through a recruiting strategy and through internal communications. Thus, Aramex's Ghandour noted, "We never hire from competitors because we think we have a unique culture and we don't want to have to break the habits from competitors. We like to recruit young college grads or with two or three years' experience in other businesses and we mould them into our corporate culture. You have to purposefully make sure you're always communicating it across your network because people need to understand what the corporate culture is, so that they identify with this company."

Marico's Subramaniam also commented on the importance of managing the corporate culture as the organization expanded, which was primarily through acquisitions. "Let's talk about the cultural part as we expand. Marico has a certain set of values we believe in and as we expand and acquire new companies, it's very important that we integrate them into Marico so that they have a similar set of values." Interestingly, with Marico, as with the brand, and so too with its corporate culture, it tries to retain the core cultural values by interpreting local practices in the context of Marico's cultural values and modifying them accordingly. Thus, Subramaniam noted, "In Egypt, one of the acquisitions that we made was a purely family-run operation. In the past the owner would go on the shop floor and if he found somebody doing a good job, he would immediately reward him with cash. That's not a practice that we follow. We changed it to a card system, with performance incentives linked to it. With this, we are able to maintain our core values, but we interpret them in the local context."

Summary and Key Takeaways

The firms we talked to had acquired many of the skills and capabilities that are important for building brands internationally. However, this was not the case across the board, and several clear shortcomings emerged that EMNCs, with a few exceptions, need to improve on. These shortcomings provide an opportunity to TMNCs to exploit, as they compete with these emerging EMNC challengers. The two areas of weakness are (1) emerging-market firms by and large were still in the early stages of evolving toward centrally managed brands, and (2) they lacked local market knowledge and experience.

While most EMNCs we talked to had moved to a regionalized structure with a central brand marketing team, except for a few firms like Asia Pacific Breweries, LG Electronics, Natura, and Tata Tea, they did not manage brands regionally in the true spirit of integrated brand management across geographies. Thus, for instance, Mahindra & Mahindra's auto division CEO Shah told us, "We have certain standards which are common, which definitely need to be maintained by all geographies. These are how the corporate identity is to be handled, the brochures, how showrooms are to be done up, what kind of dealer has to be there, what kind of sales force, etc. However, in terms of brand positioning across geographies it is not really standard or consistent." Similarly, at Dabur, there is an effort to have consistency, but in reality, the brands could be quite different across markets. For instance, in Nigeria, Dabur has six varieties of Dabur Herbal Toothpaste, while in India, Dabur markets its herbal toothpastes under distinct brand names such as Babool and Meswak.

Part of the reason for the lack of stronger central control is the relative recency of their expansion across markets, which means that EMNCs suffer a severe disadvantage compared with TMNCs in terms of local knowledge. Acknowledging the lack of local knowledge, Marico's Subramaniam said, "Being an Indian-based company trying to expand, information is always a scarce commodity, when it comes to new geographies and doing business there. So one of the key challenges we have faced is we don't have immediate access to readymade databases and information based on past experiences as compared to say Unilever. It is something we have to construct as we go along." Even a large firm like LG Electronics did not understand the U.S. market as recently as a decade ago. It did not recognize that consumers in the United States typically get a choice on which side of a refrigerator the door opens. LG's product did not offer this flexibility and bombed in the U.S. market. LG also did not understand the fit, feel, and finish requirements in the United States, which departed significantly from those in Korea, which also contributed to its failure.[6]

Importantly, EMNCs are taking aggressive steps to deal with this lack of knowledge. The rapidly growing and successful EMNCs, such as LG Electronics, Tata Motors, Tata Steel, Natura, and HTC, are recruiting global talent. They are poaching talented senior managers to bring in the knowledge and to help them put in the systems and processes to become globally competitive in this domain. They are also acquiring entire companies with the same goal, as we discussed in Chapter 4. Thus, by acquiring Tetley, Tata Tea has been able to turn itself from a domestic Indian

- Do you have a clear brand vision; that is, has the brand identity been clearly articulated, documented, and communicated?
- Do you have a central brand marketing team to develop a cohesive international strategy and coordinate with the in-market sales and marketing teams to implement strategy?
- Is the central brand marketing team knowledgeable, experienced, credible, and respected enough to successfully play the desired role?
- Does the central brand marketing team have the support of the organization broadly to develop a common international brand strategy and coordinate implementation with the markets?
- Does the central brand marketing team have top-management support?
- Are the roles and responsibilities of the central brand marketing team and the members of the sales and marketing teams in the markets clearly defined?
- Are the ways the roles and responsibilities of the central and in-market teams articulated and the way their reporting relationships are set up reasonable; that is, do they allow for smooth and market-responsive functioning of the teams without duplication or conflict?
- Are you leveraging regional or global marketing services suppliers like ad and research agencies effectively to help you think globally and execute locally?
- Do you have a clear plan for maintaining a common shared vision of the brand throughout the organization over time, that is, for maintaining the culture that supports the brand vision?
- Do you have a clear long-term plan for the role of the central brand marketing team?

FIGURE 8-4 How Well Are You Managing Your International Brand Marketing? An Audit

tea company, leveraging its tea gardens, to a global beverage company. Figure 8-4 provides a checklist to help you audit the way you manage your brand internationally, so that you can move it to the next level.

The relative immaturity of the management capabilities, structures, and processes of EMNCs provides an opportunity to TMNCs to leverage their global capability and local knowledge to better meet the needs of consumer segments everywhere. To go there, however, TMNCs need to more seriously consider more local opportunities; and given where today's growth is coming from, this means considering emerging-market opportunities much more seriously. Some TMNCs have begun to do so and are tapping into people who have local knowledge, according to Pepsi's Indra Nooyi. She said, "Markets are shifting more and more towards Asia as the growth is happening in this part of the world. So these executives are in great demand. That's the reason why a lot more Asians are now becoming visible in global corporations."[7] Consistent with this, we see the recent appointments of Rakesh Kapoor to global CEO of Reckitt-Benckiser and Harsh Manwani to COO of Unilever (Unilever earlier had Vindi Banga as the global president of its foods, home, and personal care divisions). Manwani's appointment comes at a time when Unilever hopes to drive growth from emerging markets, with the goal to raise share of business from these markets, which currently stands at 53 percent, to over 70 percent.[8]

To truly take advantage of the less sophisticated management systems and processes of EMNCs, TMNCs also need to lower their costs. Here, there is much to learn from the EMNCs. The belief in using local talent and investing behind them, rather than paying huge expatriate salaries, is one lesson. Many firms are indeed tapping into this. As one senior executive from Whirlpool said, the company is today scaling back the use of expat packages and is offering local packages to fill its needs in China and India. Whirlpool managers are faced with accepting a local package to move to these geographies, or the positions are being filled by locally recruited talent, which Whirlpool finds to be as capable as their American counterparts.

TMNCs also need to consider all the elements of their value chain dispassionately and move all the elements that are executable at lower-cost locales into such locations. The assumption that only routine work such as call centers can be located in emerging markets is a limiting one. Firms such as Lenovo and Wipro are executing world-class marketing from India. Indeed, some TMNCs have understood this. Glaxo Smith Kline, GE, and others have already moved some of their R&D to India (see Chapter 2).[9] But a lot more could potentially be done by many more TMNCs in moving more business functions and processes to lower-cost locations, if they are to compete more effectively with these EMNCs. The framework offered by Jessie Paul in her recent book, *No Money Marketing*, might help in generating possibilities.[10]

9

Key Takeaways

A quick and casual reading might suggest that the cases and strategies we have described in this book are irrelevant to most businesses, since they deal with companies you probably haven't heard about, building their businesses and brands in countries you don't care about. But we think this would be a grave misreading of the lessons that can be learned from the analysis in this book. We believe the lessons from our cases have major implications not only for other EMNCs, and the TMNCs they are competing against, but for challenger businesses everywhere—everyone who is going up against stronger, better-resourced incumbent market leaders (which means almost every business).

We begin this concluding chapter with a summary of the four strategy types that we started this book with, and we offer some thoughts on which ones are more likely to be sustainable for these EMNCs in the long term. We then present the key lessons for all challenger businesses, including the EMNCs we studied. We next discuss the lessons for TMNCs. Finally, at the end of this chapter, we take a look at some broader "macro" issues that may shape the severity and rapidity of this EMNC threat to incumbent TMNCs.

The Four Strategies—Summary
and Sustainability Assessment

Naturally, each of the four strategies in our opening typology has various strengths and weaknesses. While some rely more on the initial strengths of EMNCs, others demand more mindful competency building done with greater effort. While each of these may be a good fit for a particular EMNC, we do believe the four strategies are not equally sustainable—and thus a wise choice—for the long term. We make this case below.

The Cost Leader Strategy

As we showed in Chapters 1 and 2, the Cost Leader strategy is a natural and well-established strategy for emerging-market firms to execute. This strategy enables EMNCs to exploit the less expensive human resources in emerging markets—often an order of magnitude cheaper than in developed countries—to develop large-scale businesses that encompass developed markets. Especially noteworthy is our observation that the firms following the Cost Leader strategy are now exploiting this cost advantage in ways that go beyond low-cost manufacturing: they are extending the low-cost mantra across the value chain. Thus, in Chapter 2, we saw how EMNCs have acquired the capability of frugal design and R&D; effective, low-cost supply chain and logistics capabilities; and effective and more cost-efficient distribution and marketing. They are doing so by not just relying on the lower cost of labor, but by developing creative, new operational and business models that combine their starting low-cost labor advantage with costly capital outlays and by converting costly capital outlays to variable costs. This makes their business more easily scalable, with larger scale in turn creating further cost economies. EMNCs are thus combining the country-specific asset of low-cost labor with new firm-specific capabilities to create novel business processes and models. These new business models give these EMNCs a more sustainable competitive advantage against other EMNCs as well as against the TMNCs that have begun to move parts of their value chain to emerging markets to benefit from the same low costs that the EMNCs have enjoyed.

However, is such an augmented Cost Leader strategy a viable one for the long term? Even this more sophisticated cost-focused EMNC strategy is eventually easy for TMNCs to copy. Consider the IT industry in India. It has grown dramatically for the last two decades using the global delivery model pioneered by a group of firms led by Infosys, TCS, and Wipro. The model combines the country-specific asset of low-cost skilled labor with firm-specific process capabilities, to create a competitive advantage. This advantage, however, is being slowly but surely eroded. Key global competitors, including IBM and Accenture, have set up their own large offices in India to take advantage of the lower-cost skilled labor in that country to cater to their global clients, and they are building their own version of the global delivery model. Similarly, other TMNCs too have begun to source more of their global R&D, design, and other operations from lower-cost emerging-market locations (as we describe further below). Cost Leader strategies by EMNCs may thus not be viable for the long term.

The Knowledge Leverager Strategy

Knowledge Leveragers, in addition to low-cost capabilities, also need to have mastery over a geographically extendable capability such as a technology or skill; have deep knowledge and insight into the customers in their home market; possess a product portfolio that speaks to the home-market customers well; and have the capability to identify new markets and segments where they can win with these assets, as we discussed in Chapter 2.

The Knowledge Leverager strategy is more defensible against the TMNCs than a Cost Leader strategy, as it relies more heavily on firm-specific capabilities, honed over decades in markets and segments that have typically been shunned by TMNCs. However, this is changing rapidly, as the last decade has seen an accelerating and broad rush into emerging markets by TMNCs in search of growth. Given the TMNCs' discovery of emerging markets and growing investments there, it is not clear how long the home-knowledge advantage can be sustained by EMNCs in these markets.

The Niche Customizer Strategy

For most TMNCs, the name of the game is selling huge volumes and wringing out economies of scale through global standardization. As a result, they do not cater to lower-volume, idiosyncratic local needs. This creates an opening for entrepreneurial EMNCs with good insight into customer needs to win by outlocalizing large TMNC competitors. Often, but not always, these opportunities are in other "peripheral" emerging markets in which consumer and channel needs are different from those in the developed-market "economic center."

To profitably tap in to this lower-volume and localized strategy, EMNCs need to have a business model that fits. They need to have the customer insight-generation capability to identify local needs, the design and technical capabilities to create customized versions of products, and the ability to manufacture small volumes at high quality and at a profit. EMNCs can therefore obtain an advantage over TMNCs by judiciously investing in cutting-edge technology to attain high and consistent quality, while leveraging their low-cost but skilled local labor to make the manufacturing changeovers that small volumes entail.

The Niche Customizer strategy thus requires more advanced capabilities than were needed to execute on either the Cost Leader or the Knowledge Leverager strategy. However, a key ingredient underlying success with this strategy is cheap local labor to offset the small volumes, and as we have seen recently in China, with its seemingly inexhaustible pool of labor, labor costs do rise, particularly costs for skilled labor (see Chapter 2). Further, the number and size of segments that can be attacked using such a strategy may also be limited. As a result, this strategy too may become problematic unless one can leverage one's capabilities and scale up to a Global Brand Builder strategy, the fourth strategy in our strategy matrix.

The Global Brand Builder Strategy

The Global Brand Builder strategy is, on the one hand, the most ambitious and difficult strategy for EMNCs, but the most promising and exciting opportunity, on the other. It requires the successful penetration of developed markets, typically against strong local TMNC competition, by grabbing consumers' imagination. This strategy too has many elements that can lead to failure, some of which we discuss below, but in our judgment it is the one that seems to contain the best odds of long-term success for EMNCs that understand and execute it well. To leap to this fourth strategy, there are two clear pathways for EMNCs: through organic growth or through acquisitions.

To become a Global Brand Builder through organic growth, EMNCs need to have one or more disruptive, scalable, and sustainable insight-leveraging innovations, because such innovations capture attention and create buzz, communicating benefits and creating desirability among consumers, as well as easing access to distribution channels. EMNC players like LG and HTC have clearly succeeded in making this transition; some others, like Arçelik and Haier, are arguably still on their way. Clearly, the steps needed to gather insights and build innovation capabilities are much easier to describe (see Chapter 2) than to implement. As is made clear by our example of LG's patented steam-washing technology used in washing machines in the United States at first, and then around the world, EMNCs following an innovation path to global brand building need to develop and deploy patented and disruptive technologies to ensure that the innovation investments are likely to be disruptive, scalable, and sustainable.[1]

Indeed, the importance of coming up with innovations that meet all three criteria—being disruptive, scalable, and sustainable—is underlined by looking at two examples from our research. One could argue that Haier, the Chinese player in the same appliance space as LG, has stalled in its efforts to grow in the United States and to garner premium prices because of its inability to come up with one or more scalable, disruptive, and sustainable innovations. Its "no tail" television (see Chapter 2), while disruptive and sustainable, was not truly scalable, as it did not address an important problem that a broad group of consumers wanted a solution for. Similarly, Titan's foray into Europe failed, quite possibly due to its inability to offer something sufficiently novel and disruptive to gain the attention of either consumers or the channels in Europe, forcing it to withdraw from that market.

A second strategy for transitioning to becoming a Global Brand Builder is through acquisitions. Companies as diverse as Arçelik, Lenovo, and Tata Tea have successfully used acquisitions to transition into successful Global Brand Builders. Such acquisitions can provide them with established brands, a broader product portfolio, distribution channels, global brand building know-how, and the like. However, such acquisitions are also risky. As discussed in Chapter 3, successful acquirers must possess deep pockets, a good process for choosing a suitable target, the ability to close the deal, and the skills to integrate the acquisitions into their existing portfolio of businesses. Each of these steps is important, and a misstep in any one can lead to failure. For instance, Tata Tea failed to acquire Tetley in 1995 because of its failure to have funds lined up prior to bidding for Tetley, and it was lucky to have a second opportunity to acquire it in 2000, when it was able to do so successfully and with great subsequent reward.[2] The lack of a good process for choosing the acquisition target got in the way for firms like Evyap, LG Electronics, and TCL. Evyap's acquisition of the Elida Gibbs brand failed because Evyap did not understand that it was a poor choice of target, as the brand's equity had withered in the years since it had been withdrawn from the market. Likewise, at least from the point of view of the value of the acquired brand, the acquisition of Zenith by LG Electronics was a failure, as LG

Electronics failed to gauge that Zenith was not perceived as a premium brand in the United States and would be unable to help it reach up from the low-price end, where it played with the Goldstar brand, into the premium segment. TCL misjudged the direction of technology and bought Thompson for its rear-projection TV technology, just as the market shifted to today's flat-panel LCD and plasma screen TVs. Thus, becoming a Global Brand Builder via acquisitions too has many potential pitfalls.

Three Broad Lessons for Challenger Businesses and Aspiring EMNCs

Going beyond these four strategies, our research offers three broad lessons for challenger businesses everywhere, including aspiring EMNCs. Each broad lesson leads to four specific activities that challenger businesses need to undertake if they are to join the ranks of the EMNCs in our sample—such as HTC, LG Electronics, MTS, Arçelik, Natura, Mahindra & Mahindra, Tata Motors, and Tata Tea—which are now Global Brand Builders or are on the threshold of becoming so. We present these lessons below for all challenger businesses (including other EMNCs), and they are summarized in Figure 9-1.

Don't Overreach

For any challenger business (including aspiring EMNCs), with fewer resources and a weaker market position than that of the incumbent leaders that it is challenging, we believe our first major learning is: don't overreach. This shows up in, and has major implications for, four areas of business strategy.

The first is taking careful stock of the situation at hand and not acting impulsively. Challenger businesses usually have more limited resources than the successful incumbent leaders they have to fight, and one would therefore think that challengers would make their resource deployment decisions deliberately and carefully. It

Don't Overreach	Don't Stay Still	Take a Long View
Deepen and leverage initial capabilities	Invest in innovation	Develop a long-term mindset
Focus, focus, focus on customers, customer needs, etc., as those at home	Execute on innovation cycles visibly faster than the category norm	Achieve the core quality of the offer first
Remain under the radar of TMNCs and avoid head-to-head competition	Innovate beyond products to create novel customer experiences	Invest systematically behind the activities in the brand pyramid
Avoid overreaching in terms of customer acquisition	Move carefully but systematically, using a test-and-learn strategy	Create, embed, and transition to a central brand marketing team

FIGURE 9-1 Lessons for Challenger Businesses and Aspiring EMNCs

is commonplace, however, to see EMNCs and other challenger businesses entering or expanding into new markets opportunistically and in haste, without assessing either the attractiveness of the opportunity or the firm's ability to take advantage of it. For example, Natura entered Chile, its first market outside Brazil, in 1983, not because a strategic analysis indicated that it was the logical first market to enter outside of Brazil, but because a local distributor from Chile approached Natura.[3] The outcome was weak results, mostly attributable to the fact that the distributor was a poor fit. Savola's entry into Jordan was not underpinned by a proper strategic assessment of the opportunity, and Jordan turned out to be too small a market to defray the significant costs Savola incurred in entering the market. Each of these poor decisions could have been avoided had the firms undertaken a proper strategic assessment before acting.

Failing to properly assess a firm's competencies and resources to decide if it is up to the mark for the particular expansion challenge being considered is another reason for failure. Consider Natura again. At the time of entry into Argentina in 1994, growth in Brazil was so high that there were no internal resources to devote to Argentina. This led to the sales structure in Argentina being different from the structure in Brazil, which led to both high sales representative turnover and low sales volumes. Titan's failure in Europe was also due to lack of resources and competencies. Titan failed to analyze and appreciate the financial resources it would need to crack the European market, particularly in the face of the competitive attack it faced, which too it did not anticipate.

In contrast, successful EMNCs seem to gain by first consolidating, deepening, and leveraging the areas in which they possess initial strengths. Those lower in location-based cost structures seem to gain even more potency (1) by reducing their cost structures even further through radical reinvention of their business models, converting fixed costs into variable (Bharti Airtel in India and Africa); (2) by reconfiguring the manufacturing mix of efficient-but-expensive capital and cheap labor (BYD); and (3) by implementing radical and frugal redesign of products (Tata Nano) and of marketing expenses (Lenovo and Wipro). What we found very interesting and important, as we noted in the previous section, was that these firms were combining country-specific cost leadership benefits that accrued to all local firms (as well as TMNCs located or relocating there) with firm-specific capabilities, to create sustainable competitive advantages.

On the technology front, we found the same focus on deepening mastery. Firms deepened their technology skills, but typically in narrow product markets that these companies already knew a lot about (HTC, Marico, Godrej). With these deepened technological mastery and firm-specific cost leadership capabilities, these firms had the platforms that they could leverage to leap to more sophisticated strategies—such as the Niche Customizer and Knowledge Leverager strategies—in similar markets that are easy to understand, exploit, and manage. Going first into proximal and similar markets also helps a low-resource challenger to cost-efficiently harvest spillover awareness, similar-needs customers, and already existing supply chains and HR and management practices and organizations. Choosing segments similar to those served at home also creates a cohesive consumer base that, on the one hand, helps to transfer knowledge, skills, and capabilities from home to the international markets, while, on the other, helps to transfer the knowledge acquired from the new markets back home.

The second area where this determination to "not overreach" is manifest is the imperative to always *focus, focus, focus*—on the R&D expertise these successful EMNCs invest in (such as HTC or Natura), the geographic or product markets they extend to, even the number of product lines or brands invested in. Thus, Mahindra Tractors focuses on tractors with under 100-HP engines, Mahindra & Mahindra and Tata Motors on rugged and durable vehicles for value-seeking markets, Ulker on new food products for hot-weather African countries, Marico on pre– and post–hair wash needs in Asian and African markets, etc. Indeed, failure to focus is costly, as it turned out for Asian Paints. During 2009 and 2010, it withdrew from China, Thailand, Malaysia, and Hong Kong, having to sell its loss-making units there because the company was stretched too thin.

A third way to avoid overreaching the resources and capabilities of challenger businesses is to avoid head-on confrontation with the giants in the business. To do so, EMNCs need to strive to be first to identify small but growing segments or categories while they are still below the radar of TMNCs, as LG did with its choice of the small but growing segment of front-loading washing machines when it entered the United States.[4] To avoid direct competition with TMNCs, many of our EMNCs also focused on products and markets that offered reduced functionality but greater value and that were typically of less interest to TMNCs, which competed with full-featured products. This not only gave them a natural advantage but also helped them sidestep TMNCs, which typically tended to compete on the basis of more advanced features and emotional connections with their target consumers.

The fourth such area in which we see an avoidance of overreach is in customer acquisition strategies. For under-resourced challengers to keep customer acquisition costs low, it is likely to be more cost efficient to seek new business by increasing the share of existing customers and markets than to move into newer ones. It makes more financial sense for an under-resourced challenger business to sell more product lines to an existing trade partner than to seek out a new one, and it makes more sense to try to add or stretch products and brands at more price tiers in an existing geography than it does to expand into a new one. Growth and expansion are necessary for a branded business to move forward, but it is wiser and less risky to do so step by careful step than to bite off more than one can reasonably handle (as LG and Haier seem to have done, while Titan did not in Europe in the 1990s).

If it becomes imperative to go after new customers, it is crucial to go after only a small number of new customers, especially those who are more technically knowledgeable, who are more willing to switch, and who value functional and life-cycle cost benefits (such as B2B, small business, and/or trade customers; for example, Lenovo and Temsa). It is also sounder to seek out markets and segments that are growing (or likely to grow) rapidly, so as to gain new-to-category users than to wage expensive steal-share battles. And it is wiser to identify those markets, segments, and products where marketing costs are likely to be lower and the consumers' or trade customers' willingness to try is higher (such as value-seeking end customers or hungrier-to-grow trade partners).

Don't Stay Still

Complementary to the set of business imperatives described above is this next one: to avoid getting stuck in a commodity trap, those challenger businesses that seek viable long-term futures need to have the stretch goals of building their competencies to launch themselves into a higher-margin orbit. After leveraging and deepening existing competencies and assets, challenger businesses need to strategically and deliberately ramp up their abilities in quality, technology, innovation, design, and even marketing and branding. Such "ramping up" can begin stealthily via OEM and private label production and can be executed through organic means (such as by HTC) or through the selective acquisition of needed skills and assets (such as done by Tata Global Beverages).

But unless there is a clear strategic intent to become branded players with innovative products—as did HTC, Mahindra & Mahindra, and Arçelik—challenger companies will fail to trigger the virtuous cycle of superior products, higher margins, and higher R&D-fueled innovation that is needed to truly challenge established market leaders. In building these more advanced capabilities, we again see four key learnings.

The first competency-building learning for challenger businesses and aspiring EMNCs is that they need to unambiguously invest heavily in innovation, but to conserve and target these investments in only those areas where the innovation creates demonstrable value for end consumers and where it is likely to create new growth segments or take advantage of emergent trends. Like Apple, which underspends on R&D relative to its competitors and yet leads in innovation, smart challenger businesses need to use insight to come out with innovation that creates game-changing, disruptive new products and value-adds, such as superior customer interfaces and experiences. These investments need to create new sub-categories, as did LG with its front-loader washing machines, where the challenger's new products can scale up and dominate.

The second competency-building learning is that challenger firms and aspiring EMNCs everywhere need to innovate at a visibly faster rate than the industry standard. Thus, LG broke into the U.S. market successfully, establishing itself as the premium large-appliance brand in the United States within 5 years of launch, by introducing innovations in categories like washing machines and refrigerators every 2 years, rather than the 5- to 10-year cycles that were the norm in the category. HTC has sprung to prominence from being an ODM supplier of smartphones to being a premium global brand within 7 years from the time it launched its first own-brand smartphone in 2004. It did so by launching between 15 and 20 new smartphones each year, often introducing the latest technologies to the market. Its rate of innovation is significantly higher in the focused smartphone space than even that of the category creator and market-share leader Nokia. The result is that it has become the largest-selling smartphone brand in the United States during the third quarter of 2011 and has entered the list of Interbrand's top 100 brands as well.[5] Natura saw its sales jump by approximately 30 percent when it shortened its new-initiative cycle from 30 to 21 days. By breaking the traditional category cycles, companies can garner media attention, as the innovations naturally provide interesting content for news-hungry media. The innovations also garner attention from retailers and salespeople who are constantly on the lookout for talking points to interest and draw in more customers. EMNCs can leverage their lower-cost but highly skilled talent pool to achieve these faster innovation rates without driving up costs through the roof, as John Wang of HTC told us.

The third learning in this competency-building context is that innovations need to go beyond product innovation and focus on the total consumer experience. Firms like LG Electronics, HTC, and Mahindra & Mahindra are aggressively building and leveraging their service capabilities to compete. As an example, LG Electronics has become the number one player in the Indian market in almost every category that it participates in, including refrigerators, air conditioners, and televisions. It did this not just on the strength of its products but also through the service it offers. LG first built a network of over 100 branch and sales offices around the country, five times as many as those of its competitors. This created both the actual ability and the perception of proximity and thus a superior ability to meet service needs among retailers and end customers.[6] This was a huge competitive advantage in the more remote and smaller towns and their outlying villages, where the majority of Indians still live. LG then backed this up with a service delivery network that could rapidly answer customers when they called for service, rapidly send someone to diagnose the problem, and rapidly and reliably resolve the customer's problem. The initial target for the network was 3-3-3; that is, answer customers' phone calls within 3 rings, send a technician within 3 hours, and resolve the problem within 3 days. Today, LG is striving to reach

95 percent compliance with a 1-1-1 service level, a service level hitherto unheard of in India.

To deliver a total customer experience, competency building needs to include superior and innovative marketing and brand-building competencies as well. Despite their relatively more limited resources, challenger businesses and aspiring EMNCs too need to build brands that have adequate awareness, perceptions of high quality and leadership, and compelling brand associations. As Chapter 4 made clear, such brand building must begin with clearly high-quality products and services. Chapters 5 and 6 then laid out the shoestring-budget techniques to build high awareness and quality perceptions, including the harnessing of credible and cheap third-party endorsements and coverage by media and other opinion leaders, the leveraging of the budgets and reputations of trade partners and associations to gain multiplier effects for their own small budgets, etc. Such brand building too must be focused and targeted on a limited number of brands and geographies and trade partners.

The fourth key learning is that while firms are building competencies and moving forward, the innovations and forward steps they are taking should not be so aggressive that they are "betting the farm." The successful firms in our sample, particularly those that were pursuing the most advanced strategy, the Global Brand Builder strategy, all appeared to be following what we would call a *test-and-learn* approach. These firms innovated, acquired competencies, and moved forward, each time taking small steps, learning from what they did and moving ahead using the newly acquired resources, skills, and capabilities. Thus, Tata Tea started as a marketer of bulk tea in India, primarily selling tea from its own gardens at the Kolkata tea auctions—and in doing so it acquired the skill of growing and auctioning tea. It then moved into exporting bulk tea to the CIS countries and elsewhere, developing a knowledge of international markets and international trade. In the mid-1980s, Tata Tea entered the branded tea market at home and grew to become a strong number two player after Hindustan Unilever, the domestic arm of global giant Unilever. Along the way, it learned the skills of generating consumer insights and building brands to take advantage of those insights, all the while competing against the global giant on its doorstep. Then, in March 2000, it acquired Tetley to jump on to the world stage of branded tea, thereby acquiring knowledge of global consumers, global distribution access, and skills in global brand building. It also acquired knowledge of tea bags and tea packaging that was more advanced than what it had possessed prior to the acquisition. Tata Tea brought Tetley to India, its home market, and to other South Asian markets, developing a good understanding of managing a brand globally before expanding into new markets with the Tetley brand, such as China. It has since made a series of smaller acquisitions to enter herbal infusions and also strengthened its sourcing and branding capabilities. Today it has sold its tea gardens and entered into the beverage business, experimenting broadly with ready-to-drink beverages in diverse markets around the world, in the process renaming itself Tata Global Beverages.

Take a Long View

We believe that another key learning for all challenger brands and aspiring EMNCs is the importance of taking a long-term view, if one is to build a successful global branded business. There are four points that are noteworthy in this regard.

First, building brands needs a long-term perspective. However, since many challenger businesses and aspiring EMNCs either are family owned, with significant portions of the family wealth tied to the business, or come from a trading background where they are used to quick payback periods, they often seek quick outcomes from reasonably modest budget outlays. But such outlays and time horizons are simply not adequate if one is to try and build a large branded business. To do so successfully requires taking at least a three- to five-year horizon for payback, compared with the one to two years these firms are used to. Thus, to successfully build significant branded businesses, these challenger companies first need to go through the difficult transition to a longer-term mind-set. This takes vision and guts. Some challenger firms, for instance Savola Foods of Saudi Arabia, are currently making this transition, investing in the transformation by bringing in people with brand-ing experience at the leading brand-building TMNCs of the world (e.g., Coca-Cola, P&G, and Unilever) and giving them positions of power within the organization. It is training the middle man-agement, those responsible for execution, with a view to chang-ing their mindset and also providing the tools necessary to design and execute brand-building programs. Such changes take time, but efforts followed diligently yield fruit, as they are beginning to at Savola Foods today.

Second, challenger businesses and aspiring EMNCs need to resist the desire to jump into brand building through clever adver-tising campaigns often associated with brand building before they are ready. We believe the journey of building a global branded business begins first with getting the *core quality* of the offer right. This takes time and patience, and even long periods of low-mar-gin status as unbranded suppliers to OEMs or large retailers, but we believe that the time is not ripe for significant marketing invest-ments until that core quality has been established. Chapter 4 makes this point very clear.

Third, as we have pointed out in the branding pyramid pre-sented in Chapter 4, and elaborated on in Chapters 5, 6, and 7, brand building is a systematic, step-by-step process that needs to unfold in the proper sequence over time. Thus once the core quality has been established, challenger businesses and aspiring EMNCS must be willing to make the large and slow-payout investments in all the other elements of building a strong brand, beginning with building brand awareness.

Fourth, challenger businesses and aspiring EMNCs need to build the brand marketing team, set out a clear set of processes to connect the central brand marketing team to the various markets, properly articulate the roles and responsibilities of the central team and the in-market teams, and embed the central team within the organization. As experience accumulates (as spelled out in Chapter 8), the processes, roles, and responsibilities of brand management evolve, and firms need to manage this evolution effectively. Go too fast, and without getting the key players on board, and the whole concept of brand management may fall into disrepute, as it did at one of the consumer appliance and electronics firms we talked to. The backlash was strong enough to cause a downturn in performance, which culminated in the ouster of the CEO.

Having offered some lessons for challenger firms and aspiring EMNCs, we turn now to implications and lessons for the TMNCs that are being increasingly threatened by the EMNCs described in this book.

Lessons for TMNCs

Our research offers lessons for TMNCs, and we have referred to these lessons at the end of each of the chapters. Here we consolidate and highlight the most important lessons for TMNCs to heed, if they hope to remain competitive against the rising tide of the new EMNCs. The emergent threat is not idle speculation on our part; GE's Jeffrey Immelt also sees the same threat. As we pointed out in our opening chapter, he recently noted that "GE has tremendous respect for traditional rivals like Siemens, Philips, and Rolls-Royce. But it knows how to compete with them; they will never destroy GE. *However, the emerging giants very well could*" (p. 5, emphasis added).[7] The key lessons for TMNCs are summarized in Figure 9-2.

Exploiting TMNC Strengths and EMNC Weaknesses

Exploiting their distinctive strengths is an obvious way for TMNCs to compete against the rising tide of EMNCs. We see four clear lessons of this type from our research.

First, we believe that TMNCs can reinforce their brand superiority by (1) stressing and enhancing their "leadership aura" and

Exploiting TMNC Strengths and EMNC Weaknesses	Learning from EMNCs
Strengthen the superior brand and marketing capabilities and harness the power of vastly higher budgets to deploy "shock-and-awe" campaigns	Cut costs relentlessly and across all levels of the value chain, outsourcing or relocating all value chain elements to where they can be done at a world-class level but lowest cost
Deploy a brand architecture strategy that leverages the superior brands of TMNCs to compete against the outlocalizing product strategy of EMNCs	Focus more on emerging markets. They are fast growing and in some cases are already the largest markets in the world. They are the future of business growth
Exploit superior customer and market knowledge to generate superior insights and bring superior products, services, and experiences to market	Leverage frugal innovation capabilities of emerging markets
Leverage organization structure and processes to deploy global marketing initiatives and transfer products, insights, and learnings speedily across markets	Develop a light touch in acquiring and integrating new businesses

FIGURE 9-2 Lessons for TMNCs

(2) creating brands that consumers *love*, not merely like, by building and bolstering the higher-level aspirational and identification associations that TMNC brands often possess.[8] On both these fronts, global brands from the developed world often begin with huge advantages over brands that have their origins in developing countries (our EMNCs). Yet these initial advantages are susceptible to erosion: a Nokia and Blackberry (RIM) can give way to an HTC. To bolster their leadership perceptions, TMNCs should invest even more in creating and communicating their unique dominance and mastery over key technologies and competencies to build the kind of market-winning confidence and trust that smaller-scale EMNCs will find very difficult to match. And on the association-building front, TMNCs arguably have more "cultural capital" assets they can leverage than EMNCs, since so much of global consumer culture today flows from the economic center to the economic periphery. These assets should be milked for all they are worth. To do so, TMNCs can harness their much-larger

budgets for shock-and-awe campaigns that EMNC and other challenger businesses could never hope to match.

Second, TMNCs need to leverage their powerful brands more effectively. That is, rather than thinking about a global versus a local dichotomy, TMNCs need to think about a brand architecture strategy (see Chapter 7) to compete more effectively against the "outlocalize" product strategies of EMNCs. To better fight EMNCs following such a strategy, or simply to better satisfy local market needs, TMNCs might benefit from a more strategic use of sub-branding and endorsement-branding strategies, which both prominently use a globally known parent brand, but also allow for (and signal) local-market responsiveness through the specific sub-brand or endorsed brand sold in that local market. Thus, brand architecture, not just brand associations, needs to become an important tool in the global-branding playbooks of brands from TMNCs.

Third, EMNCs have only recently entered global markets, and they have only a limited knowledge of these markets. TMNCs need to exploit their superior knowledge of local customers around the world to generate superior consumer insights and bring to market product, service, and customer experiences that the less knowledgeable EMNCs and other challenger businesses and brands simply cannot.

Fourth, EMNCs have weaknesses in global organization structure and processes, as we noted in Chapter 8, which can be exploited. The superior organization structures and processes for managing global businesses and brands that TMNCs typically possess need to be strengthened and leveraged more effectively in two ways. One is to use these superior assets to develop and deploy marketing initiatives globally. This has the advantage, on the one hand, of lowering the costs of developing marketing initiatives significantly by eliminating duplication of effort and, on the other, of raising the quality of these marketing initiatives, as top talent at the global level becomes responsible for the development of the initiatives. The lower cost of development of these marketing initiatives further increases the effectiveness of the already formidable budgets that TMNCs possess.

A related way for TMNCs to leverage the superior structures and processes that they possess is to more effectively and speedily transfer products, insights, and learnings across markets. For example, the recently developed low-cost portable medical diagnostic devices developed by GE have already been rapidly transferred and deployed in numerous markets across the world where GE is present and where it believes these devices will have a significant market.[9] Likewise, Unilever has taken its low-cost detergent initially developed to compete with Nirma in India to other emerging markets, where as a first mover in this space, it has created a strong and defensible position.

Learning from the EMNCs' Successful Strategies

Given the success of some of the EMNCs that we have talked about, against all the odds that were stacked against them, there are clearly some key lessons to be learned by TMNCs from these EMNC strategies. Four such lessons are summarized in Figure 9-2 above.

A key capability underlying all four of the EMNC strategies in our strategy matrix involves leveraging the low-cost advantages they possess. Clearly, since several of the new EMNCs are now able to erode the competitiveness of the TMNCs (e.g., HTC in smartphones, LG in appliances, and Lenovo in computers), it is important that TMNCs learn from the EMNCs' relentless focus on costs across all levels of the value chain and their clever cost-cutting solutions.

TMNCs thus need to look at every element of their own value chains and dispassionately cut costs everywhere. One particularly important way is for TMNCs to move all their activities that are executable in lower-cost locales, but with world-class quality, into lower-cost locations. The assumption that only routine work such as call centers can be located in emerging markets is a limiting one. Even activities that require significant skilled and high-knowledge content should be moved. Some TMNCs have clearly understood this. Glaxo Smith Kline, GE, and some others have already moved some of their R&D to India (see Chapter 2 and also see below on the movement of R&D to emerging markets).[10] But a lot more could potentially be done by many more TMNCs in moving more high-knowledge, high-skill business functions and processes to lower-cost locations. For instance, Lenovo has moved its entire marketing function to India because India offers a world-class marketing services support infrastructure at a fraction of the developed-world cost. More TMNCs need to take such dramatic steps if they are to compete more effectively with the new EMNC challengers.

We warn you though that such TMNC moves will be tough. To date, the movement of TMNC business processes to emerging markets has mostly been for repetitive blue-collar jobs. What we are suggesting extends this idea to the job in the office next to you. This makes it more difficult and painful to execute. To help you in making these difficult decisions, the framework offered by Jessie Paul in her recent book, *No Money Marketing*, for outsourcing marketing functions can be applied more broadly to business processes at large.

To use this framework, break each element of the value chain into its core set of activities. These can then be plotted on a matrix where one dimension is the labor intensity of the activity and the other its cultural specificity (see Figure 9-3). Activities that are not culturally specific, i.e., do not require an understanding of local culture, can be relocated or outsourced to the lowest-cost, high-quality location, particularly if they are labor intensive. Not only do such moves reduce cost, but to the extent that such activities are outsourced, they can be run with much stricter control in terms of the deliverable outcomes and can also be scaled up and down more flexibly as needed.

A different approach to managing costs more carefully, and one that is not a mutually exclusive either-or option, is to teach one's own managers and partners how to do business in a lean manner. This could be done by developing pro forma plans assuming that

		Labor Intensity	
		Low	High
Cultural Specificity	Low		
	High		

FIGURE 9-3 Business Process Geographic Configuration Matrix
Source: Jesse Paul, *No Money Marketing,* New Delhi: Tata McGraw-Hill, 2009.

budgets are slashed, e.g., by 50 percent, or by using zero-base budgeting and planning methods. Organizational theorists have long pointed out that large, successful organizations often develop tremendous slack, or wasteful practices; learning how EMNCs do things can help TMNCs to identify and uproot these.

Second, TMNCs need to focus even more attention on emerging markets for their own growth. These markets are arguably the markets of the future. China today is already the largest market for many goods and services (e.g., cars and smartphones). Importantly, major players in these categories are often EMNCs—for instance, ZTE, the Chinese smartphone marketer, is a key player in China as a supplier of low-cost smartphones.[11] TMNCs thus need to focus more on emerging markets; and instead of bringing products to those markets that are designed and developed for the developed markets, TMNCs need to spend the necessary resources to understand emerging-market consumers and, based on those insights, develop products that are more suited for them.

Some TMNCS have already understood this. Unilever has recently announced its desire to grow its emerging-market business from an already healthy 52 percent of revenues to over 70 percent. It has, through bitter experience, learned the need to develop emerging-market solutions and today has a portfolio of brands that speak to consumers in these markets, which Unilever leverages across emerging markets all the way from Latin America to Asia. Others, such as P&G, a relative latecomer to emerging markets, are trying hard to learn about these markets. P&G has recently struck an agreement with India's CSIR government laboratories for joint R&D efforts to leverage the local knowledge—and of course lower-cost talent—of CSIR's scientists.

Third, if EMNCs are taking the world by storm and bringing to market innovations developed in their home markets, it is only logical for TMNCs to consider moving significant parts of their R&D to emerging-market locations and take advantage of the frugal R&D capabilities that we described in Chapter 2. This has several advantages. First, this can lead to lower costs of R&D: the cost reductions through such a move can be very significant. Thus, for example, GE has developed an ultraportable ECG in India that sold in the local market for less than $1,000. That innovation, with minor modifications, is also today being sold in the United States for less than $3,000. The development cost of this new line of low-cost and ultraportable machines in India was a fraction of what it would have cost to develop in the United States. Indeed, the sales prices reflect these low development costs. Aside from lowering cost, by moving R&D to these locations, TMNCs can also put a larger pool of talent to work on these projects. GE has done this, bringing the ultraportable ECG to market far faster than it would have been able to, had the development work been done in the United States.

Locating R&D in emerging markets could be beneficial from a third perspective: by making emerging markets serve as lead markets. This has not been done much in the past, but with the larger emerging markets now coming of age and in some cases becoming the highest-growth markets, it makes sense for TMNCs to develop new global products in these markets. Thus, for cars, smartphones, and other products where China is the largest market, or for certain medical conditions including not just malaria and tuberculosis but also diabetes, India is a logical lead market. It is also a logical lead market for generic pharmaceuticals, due to its accumulated expertise in this area, just as Turkey (with its long history in tile making, dating back to the fifteenth century for Iznik tiles) might serve as a lead market for ceramics. Thus, TMNCs should factor in local expertise and local demand in choosing where to locate R&D, which might also lead them to consider emerging markets more actively.

A final important lesson for TMNCs comes from an interesting observation from our data (as well as recent data from large-scale studies) showing that the success rate of acquisitions by EMNCs is higher than that reported in studies of acquisitions by TMNCs. This surprising finding provides cause for reflection. One key difference between EMNCs and TMNCs, when it comes to acquisitions, is the light-touch approach preferred by the majority of our EMNC acquirers we discussed in Chapter 3. Since the amounts spent on acquisitions are far higher by TMNCs than by EMNCs, taking a light-touch approach to acquisitions could be another learning for TMNCs to take away from our successful new EMNCs. The light-touch approach also has the potential additional benefit of making such acquirers the "acquirers of choice" by the to-be-acquired firm, thus also influencing the ability to make the acquisition in the first place.

Broader Constraints on EMNC Success

Finally, we turn our attention to a few broader policy-related macro factors that may shape the degree to which the EMNC challenge we document could become an even larger tidal wave in the immediate future. Hundreds of EMNCs we have not talked about are waiting in the wings to join the ones we did talk about. How successful are they likely to be, and what types of broader challenges remain for such EMNCs?

Negative Country-of-Origin Image

As was pointed out several times in the earlier chapters, especially Chapter 6, a major problem that EMNCs face is the generally negative country-of-origin image that consumers in many developed markets have of the EMNCs' home countries. Thus, many consumers in North America and Western Europe—indeed, even many consumers in developing countries like India—believe that goods made in China are simply not of high quality and will break down quickly. Some survey data to this effect were presented in Chapter 6. If these beliefs do not change, they will continue to limit the growth and expansion potential of our EMNCs.

Naturally, the slow building up of quality reputations and of their brand imagery by specific EMNCs will likely be the only sure way in which such negative country-of-origin imagery will become more positive over time. It seems hard to believe now, but Japanese products that today are presumed to be of very high quality, especially in product categories such as automobiles and consumer electronics, were actually not perceived in such positive ways when they were initially launched in North America. "Pre-war Japanese products had a worldwide reputation for poor quality. To most people, the label 'Made in Japan' meant a cheap and poorly made product," write Phil Kotler and colleagues Liam Fahey and Somkid Jatusripitak in their analysis of Japanese global marketing strategy.[12] Over many decades, through the delivery of superior-quality products targeted at carefully chosen segments where there was a market gap—and through a subsequent broadening out of market offerings—Japanese products developed the highly positive country-of-origin reputations they have today.

Similarly, South Korean companies Samsung and LG have clearly turned around any negative country-of-origin baggage they began with (Hyundai Motor Company is arguably doing so a little more slowly), and HTC from Taiwan has not suffered as much from a negative home country image. In all these past cases, it would seem that the obviously high quality of these brands' products—combined with the strong brand-specific associations they have invested in building up through their branding campaigns—has reduced any negative impact that their initial country-of-origin imagery might have created. It seems logical that when overseas consumers have a strong and salient EMNC brand-specific image to tap into, and when they can see from media editorial coverage and consumer magazine ratings that these brand-specific products clearly possess high quality, that they then place less weight on the country of origin of that EMNC when forming brand evaluations. Put another way, it is the EMNCs that fail to build strong individual brands (using the techniques described in Chapters 4, 5, and 7), and fail to establish high-quality and leadership reputations (using our Chapter 6 techniques), that will continue to be hurt by any negative country-of-origin imagery they are saddled with.

It is true that the challenge for EMNCs in building their own strong, positive brands is not trivial. Consumers who have strongly held negative country-of-origin stereotypes will resist changing their opinions about EMNC brands from such countries. There has been considerable academic research into the nature of negative, stereotypical country-of-origin imagery and the difficulty of changing the stereotypes.[13] This research has found, for instance, that negative home country stereotypes play less of a role when consumers are making a brand choice in more carefully considered, thoughtful ways or when they see multiple, diverse pieces of evidence about EMNC brands that provide stereotype-busting quality evidence. (Thus, HTC's many standards-changing new products every year might be helping it quite a bit in a category where consumers evaluate features carefully; in contrast, China's negative reputation as a country of origin might take a long time to change simply because there are so many China-made goods that consumers buy today that do not provide enough evidence of high quality to change their negative impressions.) It is fair to say that research has not yet found any surefire ways for EMNCs to quickly and persuasively turn around any negative country-of-origin imagery in consumers' heads, and so it is likely to be a slow and long slog for most EMNCs on this front.

That being said, there may be a small role for governments and cooperative industry associations in smoothing the way by attempting to neutralize and make more positive the imagery of their countries through what have been called "nation-branding" campaigns.¹⁴ Several countries have attempted to change the brand imagery that they evoke, through ad campaigns, country logos, and the like, including Taiwan. In the early 1990s, the Taiwanese government sponsored a program focused on promoting the quality of Taiwanese products and manufacturing. Slogans such as "It's Very Well Made in Taiwan" were aimed at consumers as well as MNCs seeking product suppliers. During the late 1990s and early 2000s, Taiwan began branding itself more as a modern innovator than just a high-quality manufacturer. For many years, Turkey has had a "Turquality" brand-building program, which supports global brand-building efforts by Turkish companies overseas. Services such as the Anholt-GfK Roper Nation Brands Index provide quarterly data on country imagery, which obviously affects not just the EMNCs from those countries but also in-bound tourism and investments and immigration into those countries. It is not clear, however, how much these communication campaigns themselves have an impact, because the stronger influence by far on consumer perceptions is what consumers experience themselves through direct contact with a country's products and people, third-party media coverage of that country, and that country's perceived policies and actions.

Sufficient-Impact R&D

While the cases we have described of some individual EMNCs using innovative approaches to product development and brand building are impressive and inspiring, critical questions need to be asked about whether these are rare exceptions or are indicative of deeper, sustainable, system-level transformations. Just because an HTC from Taiwan or a Natura from Brazil or a Tata Motors from India shows it has the ability to seek out and leverage innovation in its business and marketing efforts, can we really conclude that they are the front end of a wave to come, in which EMNCs as a group cleverly marshal their lower-cost technical human talent to create more cost-efficient processes and more consumer-satisfying products? Is the scale of the R&D efforts of these companies and these countries sufficiently large and will the efforts have a large enough impact to really create new champion MNCs that win on the basis of their innovation?

The evidence on these questions is mixed. There are certainly some emerging-market countries where significant system-level improvements have been made in the ability to innovate. In South Korea, the leading *chaebols* (such as Samsung, LG, and Hyundai) clearly have very powerful corporate R&D capabilities, and the country now has several world-class national institutes and laboratories (such as KIST and ETRI). Taiwan too has national research laboratories such as its Industrial Technology Research Institute (that helped create the Taiwan Semiconductor Manufacturing Corporation) and very successful government-created "science parks" with entrepreneurial cultures. Israel has a very strong high-technology industry, strong industry-academic collaboration, and arguably the largest per capita venture capital availability. And the Chinese government has very aggressively sought to upgrade the quality of its top research universities as part of an explicit, national long-term plan to massively increase the country's ability to innovate and gain technological leadership in targeted areas (such as electric cars and solar energy).[15] There are also noticeable differences across sectors: while the overall innovation system in India, for example, is still very poor, industries like pharmaceuticals and software have demonstrated a strong ability to come up with process innovations.[16]

Overall, however, the sense among many experts[17] is that the task of raising a country's ability to innovate is a very complex and multifaceted one, including:

- Increasing the incentive to innovate, for example, through intellectual property law changes, restrictions on easy and low-cost technology imports, salary incentives to high-publishing academics, etc.
- Supporting the ability to innovate by creating high-quality universities and national research labs that actively partner with industry, encouraging low-cost financing including angel

and venture investment funds, giving breaks to corporate owners that understand why innovation matters and what it takes, etc.

- Creating an enabling environment, including a social, cultural, and political environment that celebrates risk taking and eschews hierarchy and bureaucratic meddling.

When such a broad systems perspective is taken, it does appear that emerging-market countries—and the companies that come from them—might still have a very long distance to go, all the stories about Indian *jugaad* (informal, low-cost, guerrilla-type improvisational innovation) notwithstanding. This is reflected in the patent records of the United States and Europe, an imperfect but still very useful indicator of innovation. With very few exceptions (such as Korea's Samsung Electronics), the lists of top patent winners are still dominated by the TMNCs (such as IBM, Microsoft, Intel, and HP—and Canon, Matsushita, Toshiba, Fujitsu, and Sony). Thus, while it is all very well for a few EMNCs to display noteworthy product and process innovation, it does seem that emerging-country policy makers, not just individual EMNCs, still have a long list of things to do before this trickle becomes a flood. (They need to learn from the strategies followed by Japan's Ministry of International Trade and Industry in the 1950s through 1970s.)[18] And as mentioned in Chapter 2, our individual EMNCs need to be very careful to spend their limited R&D budgets in just the right places—focusing on critical capabilities aligned with overall strategy and customer-impacting priorities.[19]

So Just How Serious Is This EMNC Threat to TMNCs?

The two discussion sections immediately above suggest that the EMNC challenge is going to take significant time before the trickle turns into a flood: it might be many years before overseas consumers adjust their country-of-origin stereotypes adequately and before the R&D in those companies and countries begins to reach sufficient impact levels. Additionally, many of our EMNCs are making inroads in narrow and low-end slices of the market rather than launching across-the-board, frontal assaults. Does this mean that TMNCs should not take the EMNC threat seriously right now because EMNCs have only limited potential to threaten their large global businesses?

We think not, because these current low-end and narrow-slice attacks have the very real potential to quickly cascade into much broader attacks. An Arçelik or an LG or a Haier that gains its toehold with a small set of appliances can soon become a much broader durables-product threat; a smartphone or GPS competitor like HTC or Mitac could certainly decide soon to extend into tablets and laptops. If proof is needed that such threat broadening is possible, one has only to look at the strategies that Japanese companies employed in the United States in the 1950s through 1970s.[20] Companies like Toyota entered with economy-priced (but reliable and high quality), small sub-$2,000 Corona and Corolla cars, up to 20 percent cheaper than the domestic Pinto and Vega; Sony initially entered the United States with small, cheap, battery-operated transistor-based TV sets; and Honda began by introducing small, cheap, lightweight motorcycles selling for $250, compared with $1,000 to $1,500 for Harley-Davidsons. Over time, however, these companies brought disruptive R&D-based innovations into their categories and broadened their product offerings, moving upward and outward to successively bigger and bigger chunks of their markets. Sony innovated into large-scale solid-state TVs (and much else), Honda stretched its bikes from 250 cc all the way up to 1,000 cc, and Toyota stretched its product line to 82 models by the mid-1970s. In 1970 Toyota had a 2 percent sliver of the U.S. automobile market; by 2006 this had risen to 13 percent (and General Motors had fallen from its 40 percent 1970 share to 26 percent). As Kotler and colleagues document in their 1985 book, the Japanese began by just "injuring the corners" of their much-larger U.S. competitors' businesses by initially following a "flanking" and "niching" strategy; over the next two decades, these turned into highly successful broad-scale frontal attacks. Thus, TMNCs that ignore this new wave of EMNCs do so at great peril.

Appendix:
Company Descriptions

Apollo Tyres (India)
Interview with Avik Chattopadhyay, Head of Corporate
Marketing
Apollo Tyres, an Indian company with 2010 revenues of US$1.99
billion, 41 percent of which comprised sales outside India. Markets and manufactures tires under the Dunlop, Apollo, and Regal
brand names.

Aramex (Jordan)
Interview with Fadi Ghandour, Founder and CEO
Aramex, a global provider of logistics and transportation solutions
headquartered in Amman, employs more than 9,000 people in over
310 locations across 240 countries, providing worldwide presence
via a strong alliance network.

Arçelik (Turkey)
Interview with Hasan Subaşi, Member of the Board of Directors
Arçelik, headquartered in Istanbul, with 2010 revenues of
US$4.60 billion, 51 percent of which come from sales outside
Turkey, manufactures and markets consumer durables, electronics,
and kitchen furniture under the Arçelik, Beko, Blomberg, Elektra
Bregenz, Leisure, Flavel, and Arctic brand names.

Asia Pacific Breweries (Singapore)
Interview with Edmond Neo, Director of Group Commercial
Asia Pacific Breweries, listed on the Singapore Exchange, with revenues of US$2.5 billion in 2010,[1] oversees a portfolio of over 40 beer brands and variants, including Tiger Beer (sold in 60 countries worldwide), Anchor, and ABC Stout.

Asian Paints (India)
**Interview with Tom Thomas, General Manager
of International Business**
Asian Paints, an Indian company with a 2011 turnover of US$1.5 billion, has 24 paint manufacturing facilities around the world servicing over 65 countries with the Berger, Apco Coatings, SCIB Paints, and Taubmans brands.

Bajaj Auto (India)
Interview with Rakesh Sharma, CEO of International Business
Bajaj Auto, a manufacturer and marketer of two- and three-wheeled vehicles, is headquartered in India. The company is the fifth largest two-wheeler maker in the world, with a distribution network in 50 countries and with 2011 revenues of approximately US$3.75 billion.

Chigo Group (China)
**Interview with Peter Liao, General Manager
of Overseas Marketing Division**
Chigo Group, headquartered in Foshan (Guangdong), and with 2011 revenues of US$1.01 billion, manufactures and markets residential and commercial air conditioners under the Chigo and Hyundai brands. Approximately 38 percent of its sales come from outside China.[2]

Dabur (India)
Interview with Sunil Duggal, Managing Director
Dabur, headquartered in New Delhi, with 2010 revenues of US$920.6 million,[3] manufactures and markets food and dairy products via its subsidiaries in Egypt, Pakistan, the United Arab Emirates, and Bangladesh and has manufacturing facilities in eight countries.

Dilmah (Sri Lanka)
Interviews with Merrill J. Fernando, Founder and CEO, and Dilhan Fernando, Director of Marketing
Dilmah, with 2011 revenues of US$250 million, is a global brand of Sri Lankan tea available to consumers in 92 countries. Dilmah is known for its quality, and it has revitalized a category in decline through innovation, quality, and freshness.

Evyap (Turkey)
Interviews with Mehmed Evyap, CEO and Board Member; Mustafa Arin, Marketing and R&D Director and Board Member; and Serdar Sarigül, General Manager of International Sales
Evyap, headquartered in Istanbul, generates 60 percent of its revenues of US$600 million (2010) from international markets, producing and marketing soap, personal-care products, hygiene products, and detergents under the Duru, Arko, Evy, Gibbs, Fax, Activex, and Sanino brands.

Godrej (India)
Interview with Hoshedar K. Press, Vice Chairman
Godrej Consumer Products Limited (GCPL), with revenues of US$809 million in 2010, produces and markets soaps, toiletries, hair-care, household-care, and fabric-care products under its Keyline, Rapidol/Kinky Ambi Pure, Brylcreem, Good Knight, Hit, and Jet brands in Europe, Australia, Canada, Africa, and the Middle East.

Grupo Britt N.V. (Costa Rica)
Interview with Pablo Vargas, CEO
Grupo Britt, with 2010 revenues of US$70.7million,[4] sells coffee and chocolates under the Britt name and through 92 Britt branded airport stores in the United States, Antigua, Barbuda, Curaçao, Chile, Dominican Republic, Peru, St. Thomas, and Mexico.

Grupo Modelo (Mexico)
Interview with Daniel Gómez, Director, Europe, Asia, and Latin America
Grupo Modelo, with worldwide revenues of US$6.9 billion in 2010, has a portfolio of beer brands, including the flagship Corona brand, which is available in over 170 countries and is the top-selling imported beer in the United States.

Haier (China)
Interview with Michael Jemal, CEO of Haier America
Haier Group, a Chinese company with 2010 revenues of US$20.7 billion,[5] manufactures and markets white goods and consumer electronics under the Haier brand in over 100 countries, reaching a market share of 6.3 percent globally in 2009.

HTC (Taiwan)
Interview with John Wang, Chief Marketing Officer
HTC, headquartered in Taiwan, with 2010 revenues of US$9.57 billion—of which 49.9 percent come from sales from North America, 31.5 percent from Europe, 13.8 percent from Asia, and 4.8 percent from other continents—sells smartphones under the HTC brand.

Indian Hotels Company (Taj Group) Limited (India)
Interview with Ajoy Misra, Senior Vice President of Sales & Marketing

Indian Hotels Company Limited, headquartered in Mumbai and with 2010 revenues of US$647.4 million, of which 26 percent come from sales outside India, acquired the Ritz Carlton Hotel in Boston, Campton Place in San Francisco, and Asia Pacific Hotels Limited in 2007.[6]

Infosys Limited (India)
Interview with Srinivas Uppaluri, CMO

Infosys Limited, headquartered in Bangalore, is a technology services company with a market capitalization of over US$30 billion in 2011[7] and with offices in 33 countries.

Jim Thompson (Thailand)
Interview with Eric Booth, Marketing Director

Jim Thompson traces its roots to Thai silk. It markets a range of clothes, household furnishings, and fabrics through a chain of Jim Thompson branded stores in Thailand and abroad. It has also ventured into restaurants internationally under the Jim Thompson brand.

Lenovo (China)
Interviews with Deepak Advani, ex-Chief Marketing Officer, and Reid Walker, Vice President of Global Communications and Sponsorships

Lenovo, listed on the Hong Kong Stock Exchange with 2011 revenues of US$21.59 billion,[8] out of which 57 percent was from outside China, manufactures and markets notebooks, desktops, workstations, and monitors under the ThinkPad, IdeaPad, ThinkCentre, Lenovo, ThinkVision, and ThinkServer brands.

LG Electronics (South Korea)
Interviews with Michael Ahn, President and CEO North
America; Chang Min Ma, Vice President of Mobile
Communications; Eunju Park, General Manager, Strategic Brand
Management Group, Digital Appliances; Shin B Moon, CEO
India; and others.
LG Electronics, established in 1958 in South Korea, with 2010 rev-
enues of US$48.2 billion, has 98 subsidiaries, 27 liaison offices,
48 R&D centers, and 6 design centers around the world manufac-
turing and marketing mobile communications, digital appliances,
home entertainment products, and air-conditioning and energy
solutions.[9]

Mahindra Group (India)
Interviews with Arun Nanda, Executive Director of the
Mahindra Group (from 1992 to 2010) and founder, Director,
and Chairman of Mahindra Holidays & Resorts India; Gautam
Nagwekar, Chief Executive of Mahindra Tractors; Pravin
Shah, Chief Executive of International Operations; and Rajesh
Jejurikar, Chief Executive of the Automotive Division
Mahindra Group, headquartered in Mumbai, has 2011 revenues
of US$6 billion and a presence on five continents. Its automotive
and tractor divisions account for approximately half the group's
revenues[10]

Marico (India)
Interview with Vijay S. Subramaniam, Head of the International
Business Group
Marico produces and markets hair-care, skin-care, and healthy
food products, generating a turnover of US$600 million in 2010,
under its Parachute, Saffola, Sweekar, Hair & Care, Nihar, Shanti,
Mediker, Revive, Manjal, Kaya, Sundari, Aromatic, Camelia, Fian-
cee, and HairCode brands in SAARC countries, the Middle East,
Egypt, South Africa, and the United States.[11]

Mavi (Turkey)
Interview with Ersin Akarlilar, CEO

Mavi, headquartered in Istanbul, manufactures and markets jeans and apparel under the Mavi brand name, generating 2010 revenues of US$174.8 million, 40 percent of which come from sales outside Turkey, mainly from Western Europe and North America.[12]

Midea (China)
Interview with Zhang Leling, General Manager of the International Marketing Group, Refrigerators

Midea Holdings, headquartered in China, with 2010 revenues over US$17.2 billion, of which 30 percent come from the rest of the world, produces and markets air conditioners, refrigerators, and washing machines sold under the Midea brand in over 60 countries.[13]

Mitac (Taiwan)
Interview with Chris Wu, Director of the Global Technical Support Division

Mitac, produces enterprise computing and wireless communication products such as handheld GPS devices, with overseas assembly centers located in the United States, United Kingdom, Germany, Belgium, and Japan. It markets GPS devices under the Mio and Magellan brand names.

Mobile TeleSystems OJSC (MTS) (Russia)
Interview with Cynthia Gordon, CMO

Mobile TeleSystems OJSC (MTS), the largest mobile phone operator in Russia and the CIS, with revenues of US$11.2 billion in 2010, provides mobile communications in Russia, Ukraine, Uzbekistan, Turkmenistan, Armenia, Belarus, and India.

Natura Cosméticos S.A. (Brazil)
Interview with Mauricio Bellora, COO, Natura International

Natura Cosméticos, with revenues of US$3.2 billion in 2010, develops, produces, distributes, and sells cosmetics, fragrances, and hygiene and health products under the Natura brand name in Brazil, Argentina, Chile, Peru, Venezuela, Costa Rica, Colombia, Uruguay, Mexico, France, Spain, Portugal, and the Netherlands.

Pollo Campero (Guatemala)
Interview with Roberto Denigiri, President of Pollo Campero USA

Pollo Campero, founded in Guatemala, operates a portfolio of businesses, ranging from flour milling and meat processing to lumber, construction, and hydroelectric power. Pollo Campero had revenues of over US$400 million[14] in 2011, garnered through its chain of 340 fast-food restaurants spanning 13 countries across the Americas, Europe, the Middle East, and Asia.

Ranbaxy Laboratories (India)
Interview with Sanjeev Dani, Senior Vice President

Ranbaxy Laboratories (Ranbaxy), an Indian pharmaceutical company, with manufacturing operations in 9 countries, ground presence in 49 countries, and product availability in over 125 countries, had revenues of US$1.37 billion in 2010.[15]

Savola Foods (Saudi Arabia)
Interview with Tarik Hadi, CMO

Savola Foods is part of Saudi Arabia's Savola Group, which had revenues of US$5.62 billion in 2010.[16] The Savola Group has interests in businesses that include edible oils and fats, sugar, retail, real estate, packaging materials (plastics), dairy, and fast food. Savola Foods is in the edible oils and sugar businesses and expanded its reach into Egypt, Morocco, China, Afghanistan, Sudan, Kazakhstan, Iran, and Turkey.

Tata Global Beverages (India)
Interview with Percy Siganporia, Managing Director
Headquartered in Kolkata, Tata Global Beverages, with an annual turnover of US$1.3 billion in 2010, has a portfolio of global and regional brands including Tata Tea, Tetley, Good Earth, Eight O'Clock Coffee, Jemča, and Vitax, enabling the company to generate over 65 percent of its revenue from markets outside India.

Tata Motors (India)
Interview with Ravi Kant, Managing Director
Tata Motors, headquartered in Mumbai, with 2011 revenues of US$27.46 billion,[17] of which 18.4 percent come from sales outside India, owns 100 percent equity in Daewoo Trucks, a 21 percent stake in Hispano Carrocera SA, and 100 percent equity in Jaguar and Land Rover. Outside India, the company has manufacturing facilities in Argentina, South Africa, and Thailand.

Temsa (Turkey)
Interview with Mehmet Buldurgan, CEO
Temsa, headquartered in Istanbul, generating 20 percent of its net sales of US$619 million in 2010 from sales outside Turkey, manufactures and markets buses and coaches under the Temsa brand name mainly in Europe, the Middle East, and North Africa.

Titan Industries (India)
Interview with Bhaskar Bhat, Managing Director
Headquartered in Hosur, Titan produces and markets watches under its Titan brand and jewelry under its Tanishq brand, generating revenues of US$1.46 billion in 2010, out of which 3.4 percent were from sales outside India.

Turkish Airlines (THY) (Turkey)
Interview with Temel Kotil, CEO, Member of the Board and of the Executive Committee
Turkish Airlines (TA), the official flag carrier airline of Turkey, joined the Star Alliance network in 2008 and generated US$5.6 billion in revenues in 2010, carrying 29 million passengers to 187 airports.

Ulker (Turkey)
Interview with Cafer Findikoğlu, CEO (Ülker Bisküvi, Fresh Cake Gida, İdeal Gida, Atlas Gida)
Ulker Biscuit, headquartered in Istanbul, with 2010 revenues of US$1.12 billion, 18 percent of which come from sales outside Turkey, manufactures and sells chocolate and biscuits under the Ulker, Godiva, and over 50 other brand names, exporting its products to more than 110 countries.

Vara Food and Drink Company (Thailand)
Interview with Tedsak Kiatsukasem, Director and Co-Owner
Vara Food and Drink Company, with revenues of US$45 million in 2011, is a purveyor of branded traditional Thai foods and beverages. Its products and brands are available in over 50 countries, including the United States, the European Union, Australia, and New Zealand.

Vitra (Turkey)
Interview with Hüsamettin Onanç, President of the Eczacibaçi Building Products Group
Vitra, headquartered in Istanbul, manufactures and markets tiles and ceramic sanitary bathroom and kitchenware under the Vitra, Burgbad, Engers, and Villeroy & Boch brands, generating 2010 revenues of US$750 million, 65 percent of which come from sales outside Turkey.

Wipro (India)
Interviews with Jessie Paul, CMO, and Priti Rajora, General Manager of Talent Acquisition
Wipro, an Indian IT services company, provides a comprehensive range of enterprise solutions, primarily to Fortune 1000 and Global 500 companies, generating revenues of US$6.97 billion in 2011.

Notes

Introduction and Overview

1 Tim Culpan, "HTC Market Value Passes Nokia as Smartphones 'Change Mindsets,'" April 7, 2011, accessed July 13, 2011, http://www.bloomberg.com/news/2011-04-07/htc-surpasses-nokia-s-market-value-as-smartphones-drive-profit.html.

2 Data are from Euromonitor International, which ranked Haier first in its Global Major Appliances Brands 2009 ranking by brand shares (by global brand name), with a retail volume market share of 5.1 percent. Euromonitor International's rankings also place Haier's refrigeration appliances and Haier's home laundry appliances first by global brand name, with 10.4 percent and 8.4 percent retail volume market share, respectively.

3 Nirmalya Kumar, *India's Global Powerhouses*, Boston: Harvard Business Press, 2009, p. 10. Why Is Accenture's Market Cap Less Than Infosys'?," June 13, 2007, accessed October 11, 2011, http://seekingalpha.com/article/38200-why-is-accenture-s-market-cap-less-than-infosys; "Accenture: Why This Revenue Leader Is Not the Leader by Market Value," October 6, 2009, accessed October 11, 2011, http://seekingalpha.com/article/164984-accenture-why-this-revenue-leader-is-not-the-leader-by-market-value.

4 World Economic Outlook Database–June 2011, International Monetary Fund, accessed January 31, 2012, http://www.imf.org/external/pubs/ft/weo/2011/01/weodata/index.aspx.

5 "Emerging Giants," *BusinessWeek*, July 31, 2006.

6 Jayant Sinha, "Global Champions from Emerging Markets," *McKinsey Quarterly*, vol. 2, 2005, pp. 27–35; Boston Consulting Group, *The*

New Global Challengers, Boston: Boston Consulting Group, May 2006.

7 Jeffrey R. Immelt, Vijay Govindrajan, and Chris Trimble, "How GE Is Disrupting Itself," *Harvard Business Review*, October 2009, pp. 3–11.

8 See Kumar, *India's Global Powerhouses*; Anil K. Gupta and Haiyan Wang, *Getting China and India Right: Strategies for Leveraging the World's Fastest Growing Economies for Global Advantage*, Hoboken, NJ: John Wiley & Sons, 2009; and Ravi Ramamurti and Jitendra V. Singh, "Emerging Multinationals in Emerging Markets," Cambridge: Cambridge University Press, 2009. See also Ming Zeng and Peter Williamson, *Dragons at Your Door*, Boston: Harvard Business School Press, 2007; Lourdes Casanova, *Global Latinas*, London: Palgrave Macmillan, 2009; and Antoine van Agtmael, *The Emerging Market Century*, New York: Free Press, 2007.

9 While some sources (e.g., Nielsen) see global brands as those that have some specified minimum percentage of their total sales coming from each of several different geographies, we define them here as brands marketed in a generally similar manner across multiple countries, employing central coordination of their marketing strategies and tactics (following the definition suggested by Steenkamp, Batra, and Alden in the *Journal of International Business Studies*, 2003, 34, 53-65). Thus some brands we are calling global may be called regional brands by others.

10 "Fortune Global 500," *Fortune*, July 25, 2011, p. 1F-7.

11 These statistics are taken from Kumar, *India's Global Powerhouses*, p. 209.

12 Assif Shameen, "Getting to Know Hankook," *Barron's*, July 25, 2011, p. M7.

13 Michael Porter, *Competitive Advantages of Nations*, New York: Free Press, 1990; Pankaj Ghemawat, *Redefining Global Strategy: Crossing Borders in a World Where Differences Still Matter*, Boston: Harvard Business School Press, 2007.

14 Modelo (producers of Corona Beer of Mexico), Asia Pacific Breweries (producers of Tiger Beer of Singapore), and Natura of Brazil are arguably exploiting overseas a different kind of home-country advantage, what some might call "cultural arbitrage," as they leverage the myths, legends, and imagery associated with their home markets or home regions to carve a niche for themselves.

15 Talk by Bob Fregolle, chief customer officer, Procter & Gamble, at the Ross School of Business, University of Michigan, November 15, 2010.

16 Business strategies like these have been recognized by strategy writers under the term *adaptation*, which at the same time also takes advantage of lower-cost "R&D arbitrage."

17 "Nestle Plans a Research Center to Focus on Indian Foods," *New York Times*, September 22, 2010.

18 Barry Jaruzelski and Kevin Dehoff, "The Global Innovation 1000: How the Top Innovators Keep Winning," *Strategy+Business*, vol. 61, Winter 2010, Exhibit 12.

19 Natura, February 23, 2011, accessed October 12, 2011, http://natura.infoinvest.com.br/enu/3628/CD_ENG_4T10.pdf.

20 Amitava Chattopadhyay, Betania Tanure, and Nina Paavola, "Natura: Expanding beyond Latin America," INSEAD Case Study # 09/2011-5365, 2006.

21 Jaruzelski and Dehoff, "The Global Innovation 1000," Exhibit 9.

22 Rolfe Winkler, "Moto Must Weigh Greater Scale," *Wall Street Journal*, April 8, 2011, p. C8.

23 Naazneen Karmali, "Mahindra's Secret Global SUV," 2011, accessed September 22, 2011, www.forbes.com/2011/0509/global-2000-11-asia-anand-mahindra-autos.

24 See Ramamurti and Singh, "Emerging Multinationals in Emerging Markets," p. 31 for Wells and p. 58 for Rugman.

Chapter 1

1 Svend Hollensen, *Global Marketing: A Decision-Oriented Approach*, 5th ed., Harlow, UK: Prentice Hall, 2010; Johny K. Johansson, *Global Marketing: Foreign Entry, Local Marketing and Global Management*, 5th ed., Burr Ridge, IL: McGraw-Hill Irwin, 2009.

2 Esteban R. Brenes, Amitava Chattopadhyay, and Daniel Montoya C., "Pollo Campero," INSEAD-INCAE Case Study, pre-release version, 2011.

3 Esteban R. Brenes, Amitava Chattopadhyay, and Daniel Montoya C., "Grupo Britt NV: Building the Britt Brand Business in the United States," INCAE Business School and INSEAD Case Study (# 30616), Alajuela, Costa Rica, 2011.

4 "Diminishing Returns," *The Economist*, June 21, 2011, www.economist.com/node/18988758/print.

5 "Corporate India Finds Greener Pastures—in Africa," *Bloomberg BusinessWeek*, November 8, 2010, pp. 61–62; Will Connors, "Nigeria Gives Huawei a Place to Prove Itself," *Wall Street Journal*, September 12, 2011; "Ottoman Dreaming," *The Economist*, March 27, 2010, p. 57.

6 Arzoo Dina, "Godrej-Darling: Crossing New Frontiers," *Business India*, June 26, 2011, p. 99.

7 Southern Italy has a per capita GDP that is approximately 55 percent that of the more developed parts of the country, i.e., northern and central Italy. http://en.wikipedia.org/wiki/List_of_Italian_regions_by_GDP_per_capita#Southern_Italy.

8 Bruce Einhorn, "Good Times for Cheap Cell Phones," *BusinessWeek*, May 11, 2009, p. 28.

9 Peter Wonacott, "China Investing in Rust-Belt Companies," *Wall Street Journal*, 2009, accessed March 3, 2010, www.wanxiang.com; Craig Simons, "Generic Giants," *Newsweek*, July 27, 2009, pp. 30–33.

10 Paulo Prada, "Plane Speaking," *Wall Street Journal*, March 29, 2010, p. R8.

11 Peter J. Williamson and Ming Zeng, "Value for Money Strategies for Recessionary Times," *Harvard Business Review*, March 2009, pp. 2–9.

12 Amitava Chattopadhyay, Eunju Park, and Nina Paavola, "LG in India: Reinventing the Brand," INSEAD Case Study (#10/2008-5558), 2008.

13 Einhorn, "Good Times for Cheap Cell Phones."

14 Chattopadhyay, Park, and Paavola, "LG in India."

15 Amitava Chattopadhyay, Betania Tanure, and Nina Paavola, "Natura: Expanding beyond Latin America," INSEAD Case Study (#09/2011-5365), 2011.

16 John A. Quelch and Nathalie Laidler, "Bajaj Auto Ltd.," Harvard Business School Case Study # 9-953-097, 1996.

17 Peter J. Williamson and Ming Zeng, "Value for Money Strategies for Recessionary Times," *Harvard Business Review*, March 2009, pp. 2–9.

18 Kineta Hung, Flora Fang Gu, and David K. Tse, "Improving Media Decisions in China: A Targetability and Cost-Benefit Analysis, *Journal*

of Advertising, vol. 34, no. 1, 2005, pp. 49–63; "Television Basics in a New Decade," accessed July 12, 2011, www.mediacenteronline.com; "Vehicle Advertising: Driving Customers to Your Business," accessed July 12, 2011, http://www.articlesbase.com/small-business-articles/vehicle-advertising-drivingcustomers-to-your-business-4193224. html#ixzz1RsWkPkM2.

19 Carla Power, "India's Leading Export: CEOs," *Time*, accessed August3, 2011, www.time.com/time/magazine/article/0,9171,2084441,00.html.

20 Amitava Chattopadhyay, Eunju Park, and Joseph Lajos, "LG Electronics Inc: Making Waves in the North American Market for Washing Machines," INSEAD Case Study (#11/2007-5463), 2010.

21 Chattopadhyay, Park, and Paavola, "LG in India."

22 Philip Kotler, Liam Fahey, and Somkid Jatusripitak, *The New Competition*, Upper Saddle River, NJ: Prentice-Hall, 1985.

Chapter 2

1 "KPMG's India Automotive Study: Domestic Growth and Global Aspirations," accessed July 15, 2011, http://www.kpmg.com/Global/en/WhatWeDo/Industries/Automotive/Documents/India-Automotive-Study-2007.pdf.

2 Nebahat Tokatli and Omar Kizilgun, "Upgrading in the Global Clothing Industry: Mavi Jeans and the Transformations of a Turkish Firm from Full Package to Brand-Name Manufacturing and Retailing," *Economic Geography*, vol. 80, no. 3, 2004, pp. 221–240.

3 Alex Taylor III, "Tata Takes on the World," *Fortune*, May 2, 2011, p. 90.

4 Peter J. Williamson and Ming Zeng, "Value for Money Strategies for Recessionary Times," *Harvard Business Review*, March 2009, pp. 2–9.

5 "A Snip at the Price," *The Economist*, May 30, 2009, p. 68.

6 Norihiko Shirouzu, "After Stumble, BYD Retools Strategy," *Wall Street Journal*, January 12, 2011, p. B6.

7 Personal correspondence with Mr. Nakul Gupta, assistant general manager, Car Product Group, Tata Motors; Paul W. Farris, N. Raghu Kishore, Amy Lemley, and Rajkumar Venkatesan, "The Tata Nano: The People's Car," Darden Case UVA-M-0768, Darden Business Publishing, 2009, p. 6; Taylor, "Tata Takes on the World," p. 92.

8   Reena Jana, "From India, the Latest Management Fad," *Bloomberg BusinessWeek,* December 14, 2009, p. 57.

9   C. K. Prahalad and M. S. Krishnan, "Bharti Airtel (B)," Globalens Case 1-428-864, Ann Arbor, MI: Ross School of Business, William Davidson Institute, 2009.

10 Dhanya A. Thoppil, "Bharti Airtel and IBM Strike Deal in Africa," *Wall Street Journal,* September 18, 2010, p. B5.

11 Haier, accessed September 21, 2011, http://www.haierme.com/Details.aspx?id=135.

12 Jessie Paul, *No Money Marketing,* New Delhi: Tata McGraw-Hill, 2009.

13 Amitava Chattopadhyay, Eunju Park, and Nina Paavola, "LG in India: Reinventing the Brand," INSEAD Case Study (#10/2008-5558), 2008.

14 These examples are taken from Kannan Ramaswamy, "LG Electronics: Global Strategy in Emerging Markets," Ref. No. TB0073, Thunderbird School of Global Management, 2007.

15 Quoted in J. Quelch and C. Knoop, "Lenovo: Building a Global Brand," HBS Case No. 9-507-014, Boston: Harvard Business School Publishing, 2006, p. 1.

16 H. E. Wei, "Lenovo Seeks to Become the Apple of World's Eye," *China Daily,* June 20, 2011, p. 13.

17 "Lenovo Takes Product Demo to New Heights," *Advertising Age,* July 13, 2011, web edition.

18 Rolfe Winkler, "Lenovo Group Computes as Value Play," *Wall Street Journal,* February 14, 2011, p. C8.

19 Aries Poon, "PC Giant Acer Faces Rising Tablet Challenge," *Wall Street Journal,* June 3, 2011, p. B5.

20 Lorraine Luk, "HTC Invests in Two Mobile Software Companies," *Wall Street Journal,* February 8, 2011, web edition.

21 Ethan Smith, "HTC to Acquire Majority of Beats, Maker of Dr. Dre Headphones," *Wall Street Journal,* August 11, 2011, web edition.

22 "HTC to Buy U.S. Graphics Firm," *Wall Street Journal,* July 7, 2011, p. B7.

23 J. Quelch and A. Harrington, "Samsung Electronics Company: Global Marketing Operations," HBS Case No. 9-504-051, Boston: Harvard Business School Publishing, 2004.

24 Susan Decker, "IBM, Samsung Lead 31% Record Jump in New US Patents in 2010," *Bloomberg,* January 10, 2011, accessed July 13,

2011, http://www.bloomberg.com/news/print/2011-01-10/ibm-samsung-lead-31-record-jump-in-new-u-s-patents-in-2010.html.

25 John Quelch, "Bajaj Auto," HBS Case No. 9-593-097, Boston: Harvard Business School Publishing, 1996.

26 Ali Farhoomand, "Haier: How to Turn a Chinese Household Name into a Global Brand," Ref. 07/347C, Asia Case Research Centre, University of Hong Kong, 2007, p. 8.

27 Jeannie J. Yi and Shawn X. Ye, *The Haier Way*, Dumont, NJ: Homa & Sekey Books, pp. 58–59.

28 Barry Jaruzelski and Kevin Dehoff, "The Global Innovation 1000: How the Top Innovators Keep Winning," *Strategy+Business*, no. 61, Winter 2010.

29 Yi and Ye, *The Haier Way*, p. 58.

30 W. Darren Dahl, Amitava Chattopadhyay, and Gerald J. Gorn, "The Role of Imagery in New Product Design," *Journal of Marketing Research*, vol. 46, February 1999, pp. 46–55.

31 Geoff Colvin, "Motorola's Uphill Battle," *Fortune*, June 22, 2011, accessed January 31, 2012.

32 All these statistics are taken from the Bain & Company article by Jaruzelski and Dehoff cited above, as well as from Martin Peers, "RIM: Less Research = More Motion," *Wall Street Journal*, March 30, 2011, p. C16.

33 Jennifer Valentino-DeVries, "Apple Wins More Patents," *Wall Street Journal*, January 12, 2011, p. B5.

34 Amitava Chattopadhyay and Swati Srivastava, "Ranbaxy Laboratories Limited: At the Crossroads," INSEAD Case Study (#5112), 2003, p. 8.

35 Amitava Chattopadhyay, Joseph Lajos, and Eun-Ju Park, "LG Electronics Inc: Making Waves in the North American Market for Washing Machines," INSEAD Case Study (#09/2007-5463), 2007.

36 Heather Timmons, "Nestle Plans a Research Center to Focus on Indian Foods," *New York Times*, September 22, 2010, Business section.

37 David B. Yoffie and Renee Kim, "HTC Corp. in 2009," HBS Case No. 7-094-66, Boston: Harvard Business School Publishing, 2009, p. 8.

38 Yi and Ye, *The Haier Way*, p. 95.

39 Amitava Chattopadhyay and Ayesha Kohli, "WIPRO: Building a Global B2B Brand," INSEAD Case Study (#06/2009-5615), 2009.

40 For an excellent review of some of these insight-generating research techniques, see Keith Goffin, Fred Lemke, and Ursula Koners, *Identifying Hidden Needs: Creating Breakthrough Products*, London: Palgrave Macmillan, 2010.

41 John E. Forsyth, Nicolo Galante, and Todd Guild, "Capitalizing on Customer Insights," *McKinsey Quarterly*, 2006, pp. 43–53.

42 Chattopadhyay, Park, and Paavola, "LG in India: Reinventing the Brand."

43 Amitava Chattopadhyay, Eunju Park, and Joseph Lajos, "LG Electronics Inc: Breaking the Ice in the North American Market for Refrigerators," INSEAD Case Study (#11/2007-5488), 2007.

44 Tarun Khanna, Ingrid Vargas, and Krishna G. Palepu, "Haier: Taking a Chinese Company Global," HBS Case No. 7-064-01, Boston: Harvard Business School Publishing, 2005, p. 15.

45 Ali Farhoomand, "Haier: How to Turn a Chinese Household Name into a Global Brand," Ref. 07/347C, Asia Case Research Centre, University of Hong Kong, 2007, p. 8.

46 Jasjit Singh, "GE Healthcare (A): Innovating for Emerging Markets," INSEAD Case Study (#09/2011-5776), 2011; and Jasjit Singh, "GE Healthcare (B): A CSR Dilemma," INSEAD Case Study (#03/2011-5776), 2011.

Chapter 3

1 Sathyajit Gubbi, Preet S. Aulakh, Sougata Ray, M. B Sarkar, and Raveendra Chittoor, "Do International Acquisitions by Emerging Economy Firms Create Value? The Case of Indian Firms," *Journal of International Business Studies,* vol. 41, 2010, pp. 397–419.

2 Bulent Aybar and Ficici Aysun, "Cross-Border Acquisitions and Firm Value: An Analysis of Emerging-Market Multinationals," *Journal of International Business Studies*, vol. 40, 2009, pp. 1317–1338.

3 Gubbi et al., "Do International Acquisitions by Emerging Economy Firms Create Value?"

4 Anusha Chari, Wenjie Chen, and Kathryn M. E. Dominguez, "Foreign Ownership and Firm Performance: Emerging-Market Acquisitions in the United States," *NBER Working Paper Series*, Working Paper #14786, National Bureau of Economic Research, 2009, http:www.nber.org/papers/w14786.

5 Prashant Kale and Harbir Singh, "Building Firm Capabilities through Learning: The Role of the Alliance Learning Process in Alliance Capability and Firm-Level Alliances Success," *Strategic Management Journal*, vol. 28, 2007, pp. 981–1000.

6 Maurizio Zollo and Harbir Singh, "Deliberate Learning in Corporate Acquisitions," *Strategic Management Journal*, vol. 25, 2004, pp. 1233–1256.

7 Amitava Chattopadhyay and Ulrike Lege, "Tata Tea Limited: How to Go Global?," *International Journal of Marketing Education*, vol. 1, no. 1, 2005, pp. 93–112.

8 Ibid.

9 Prashant Kale, "The Global Indian Firms: Growth and Value Creation through Overseas Acquisitions," *Indian Journal of Industrial Relations*, vol. 45, 2009, pp. 41–53.

10 Gubbi et al., "Do International Acquisitions by Emerging Economy Firms Create Value?"

11 Mehul Srivastava, "Tata: Still Reeling from Its Jaguar–Land Rover Buy," *BusinessWeek*, August 11, 2009, accessed May 25, 2011, http://www.businessweek.com/globalbiz/content/aug2009/gb20090811_307608.htm.

12 Chattopadhyay and Lege, "Tata Tea Limited: How to Go Global?"

13 Drew Johnson, "Mahindra Decides Not to Bid on Jaguar and Land Rover," September 14, accessed May 26, 2011, http://www.leftlanenews.com/mahindra-decides-not-to-bid-on-jaguar-land-rover.html.

14 Amitava Chattopadhyay and Nina Paavola, "Hyundai Card/Hyundai Capital and GE Money: Re-branding Decisions in a Successful Joint Venture," INSEAD Case Study (#01/2009-5557), 2009.

15 Freek Vermeulen, "Toads and Acquisitions—Where Does CEO Hubris Come From?," *Forbes*, July 2011.

16 Prashant Kale, Harbir Singh, and Anand Raman, "Don't Integrate Your Acquisitions: Partner with Them," *Harvard Business Review*, vol. 87, no. 12, 2009, pp. 109–120.

17 "Being Eaten by the Dragon," *The Economist*, November 13, 2010, pp. 81–83.

18 "China Food Firm Nears Major Deal," *Wall Street Journal*, August 16, 2011, p. B3.

Chapter 4

1 Michael Ahn, retired president and CEO of LG Electronics North America, "LG Brand Strategy Overview," presentation at the Global Brand Management Conference, Koc University, Istanbul, June 21–22, 2010.

2 J. Quelch and A. Harrington, "Samsung Electronics Company: Global Marketing Operations," HBS No. 9-504-051, Boston: Harvard Business School Publishing, 2004.

3 Tomi Ahonen, "Bloodbath Update: Smartphone Market at June 30, 2011," July 5, 2011, accessed July 14, 2011, http://www.brightsideofnews.com/news/2011/7/5/bloodbath-update-smartphone-market-at-june-302c-2011.aspx.

4 Amitava Chattopadhyay, Eunju Park, and Joseph Lajos, "LG Electronics Inc: Making Waves in the North American Market for Washing Machines," INSEAD Case Study (#12/2009-5463), 2010.

5 The material in this section (including Figure 4-1) is taken from Rajeev Batra, *Building Strong Brands for Fun and Profit*, unpublished manuscript.

6 A terrific history of the brand building of Coca-Cola can be found in Mark Pendergrast, *For God, Country and Coca-Cola*, 2nd ed., New York: Basic Books, 2000.

7 See, for example, David Aaker, *Building Strong Brands*, New York, Free Press, 1996; Kevin L. Keller, *Strategic Brand Management*, 3rd ed., Upper Saddle River, NJ: Pearson Prentice Hall, 2008; Jean-Noel Kapferer, *New Strategic Brand Management*, Philadelphia: Kogan Page, 2008.

8 See Keller, *Strategic Brand Management*, p. 395, for a description of this BAV finding.

9 Our pyramid framework above is not identical to, but is reasonably similar to, those proposed by others, such as Keller, *Strategic Brand Management*.

10 Kevin Roberts, "*Lovemarks: The Future Beyond beyond Brands*," New York: Powerhouse Books, 2005.

11 Ahn, "LG Brand Strategy Overview."

12 "LG Electronics and Global Shop BBH Split," *Advertising Age*, 2011, accessed August 19, 2011, http://adage.com/print/229302.

13 Rajeev Batra, Aaron Ahuvia, and Richard P. Bagozzi, "Brand Love," *Journal of Marketing*, March 2012, vol. 76, pp. 1–16.

14 Jan-Benedict Steenkamp, Rajeev Batra, and Dana Alden, "How Perceived Brand Globalness Creates Brand Value," *Journal of International Business Studies*, vol. 34, 2003, pp. 53–65.

15 Dana Alden, Jan-Benedict Steenkamp, and Rajeev Batra, "Brand Positioning through Advertising in Asia, North America and Europe: The Role of Global Consumer Culture," *Journal of Marketing*, January 1999, vol. 63, pp. 75–87.

Chapter 5

1 Amitava Chattopadhyay and Ayesha Kohli, "WIPRO: Building a Global B2B Brand," INSEAD Case Study (#06/2009-5606), 2009, Exhibit 1.

2 Normandy Madden, "Will Geely's Volvo Deal Give China a Shot at Being a Global Automaker?," *Advertising Age Global News*, March 30 2010, accessed March 31, 2010, http://adage.com/globalnews/article?article_id=143056.

3 Chattopadhyay and Kohli, "WIPRO: Building a Global B2B Brand."

4 Esteban R. Brenes, Amitava Chattopadhyay, and Daniel Montoya C., "Grupo Britt NV: Builiding the Britt Brand Business in the United States," INCAE Business School and INSEAD Case Study (# 30616), Alajuela: Costa Rica, 2011.

5 Amitava Chattopadhyay, "Building a Global B2B Brand," Wipro Book of Case Studies, vol. 1, Wipro Council for Industry Research, Wipro Technologies, 2009, pp. 33–40.

6 Amitava Chattopadhyay, Eunju Park, and Joseph Lajos, "LG Electronics Inc: Making Waves in the North American Market for Washing Machines," INSEAD Case Study (#11/2007-5463), 2007.

7 J. Quelch and A. Harrington, "Samsung Electronics Company: Global Marketing Operations," HBS No. 9-504-051, Boston: Harvard Business School Publishing, 2004.

8 "Lenovo Partners with Google TV to Increase Brand Awareness," *ANA Advertiser*, February 2009, p. 19.

9 Jessie Paul, "Globalization of Marketing," presentation, May 7, 2008.

10 Rajeev Batra, John G. Myers, and David A. Aaker, *Advertising Management*, 5th ed., Upper Saddle River, NJ: Prentice-Hall, 1996, p. 557.

11 Sarit Moldovan, Jacob Goldenberg, and Amitava Chattopadhyay, "The Different Roles of Product Originality and Usefulness in Generating Word-of-Mouth," *International Journal of Research in Marketing*, vol. 28, no. 2, 2011, pp. 109–119.

12 "The World Is Flat," accessed July 25, 2011, http://en.wikipedia.org/wiki/The_World_Is_Flat.

13 Thomas L. Friedman, *The World Is Flat: A Brief History of the Twenty-First Century*, New York: Farrar, Straus and Giroux, 2005.

14 Chattopadhyay, Park, and Lajos, "LG Electronics Inc."

15 HQ BCR (Brand Competitiveness Research) Study, '05-'09 United States. Presented by Michael Ahn at the Global Branding Conference, Koc University, Istanbul, June 21–22, 2010.

16 Quelch and Harrington, "Samsung Electronics Company."

17 "How to Win the World Cup!," Integration Marketing Communications, September 2006, accessed January 31, 2012, http://www.integration-imc.com/pdf/World%20Cup%20Presentation.pdf.

18 Amitava Chattopadhyay, Eunju Park, and Nina Paavola, "LG Electronics: Revamping the Brand in India," INSEAD Case Study (#10/2008-5558), 2008.

Chapter 6

1 Diane Buss, "Chinese, Indian Brands Face Obstacles in Mimicking Hyundai-Kia Success," Brandchannel, 2011, http:// www.Brandchannel.com, August 29, 2011.

2 Debanjan Mitra and Peter N. Golder, "Customer Perceptions of Product Quality: A Longitudinal Study," Working Paper 05-120, Boston: Marketing Science Institute, 2005.

3 John R. Hauser and Don Clausing, "The House of Quality," *Harvard Business Review*, vol. 66, no. 3, May–June 1988, pp. 63–73.

4 Ali Farhoomand, "Haier: How to Turn a Chinese Household Name into a Global Brand," Ref. 07/347C, Asia Case Research Centre, University of Hong Kong, 2007, p. 3.

5 Amitava Chattopadhyay, Eunju Park, and Nina Paavola, "LG Electronics: Revamping the Brand in India," INSEAD Case Study (#10/2008-5558), 2008.

6   Rajeev Batra and Youjae Yi, "Brand-Building Challenges in Overseas Markets for Korean Companies," in Rajeev Batra (ed.), *Marketing Issues in Transitional Economies*, Boston: Kluwer Academic Publishers, 1991, pp. 243–277.

7   Farhoomand, "Haier: How to Turn a Chinese Household Name into a Global Brand."

8   Emanuel Rosen, *The Anatomy of Buzz Revisited*, New York: Doubleday, 2009.

9   Amitava Chattopadhyay and Ayesha Kohli, "Wipro: Building a Global B2B Brand," INSEAD Case Study (#06/2009-5606), 2009.

10   J. Quelch and A. Harrington, "Samsung Electronics Company: Global Marketing Operations," HBS No. 9-504-051, Boston: Harvard Business School Publishing, 2004.

11   Assif Shameen, "Getting to Know Hankook," *Barron's*, July 25, 2011, p. M7.

12   Quelch and Harrington, "Samsung Electronics Company: Global Marketing Operations."

13   Amitava Chattopadhyay, Eunju Park, and Joseph Lajos, "LG Electronics Inc.: Making Waves in the North American Market for Washing Machines," INSEAD Case Study (#12/2009-5463), 2009.

14   Quelch and Harrington, "Samsung Electronics Company: Global Marketing Operations."

15   Nebahat Tokatli and Omar Kizilgun, "Upgrading in the Global Clothing Industry: Mavi Jeans and the Transformations of a Turkish Firm from Full Package to Brand-Name Manufacturing and Retailing," *Economic Geography*, vol. 80, no. 3, 2004, pp. 221–240.

16   Tarun Khanna, Ingrid Vargas, and Krishnas G. Palepu, "Haier: Taking a Chinese Company Global," HBS No. 7-064-01, Boston: Harvard Business School Publishing, 2005.

17   J. Quelch and C. Knoop , "Lenovo: Building a Global Brand," HBS No. 9-507-014, Boston: Harvard Business School Publishing, 2006.

18   Amitava Chattopadhyay, Eunju Park, and Joseph Lajos, "LG Electronics, Inc.: Making Waves in the North American Market for Washing Machines," INSEAD Case Study (#11/2007-5463), 2010; Quelch and Harrington, "Samsung Electronics Company: Global Marketing Operations."

19   Nirmalya Kumar, *India's Global Powerhouses*, Boston: Harvard Business Press, 2009, p. 87.

20 Esteban R. Brenes, Amitava Chattopadhyay, and Daniel Montoya C., "Grupo Britt NV: Building the Britt Brand Business in the United States," INCAE Business School and INSEAD Case Study (# 30616), Alajuela: Costa Rica, 2011.

Chapter 7

1 The association-targeting framework in this section draws on the unpublished manuscript by Rajeev Batra, "Brand-Building for Fun and Profit," in addition to models previously published by David Aaker, Kevin Keller, and others.

2 Amitava Chattopadhyay, Betania Tanure, and Nina Paavola, "Natura: Expanding Beyond Latin America," INSEAD Case Study (#09/2011-5365), 2011.

3 Esteban R. Brenes, Amitava Chattopadhyay, and Daniel Montoya C., "Grupo Britt NV: Builiding the Britt Brand Business in the United States," INCAE Business School and INSEAD Case Study (# 30616), Alajuela: Costa Rica, 2011.

4 Rajeev Batra, Aaron Ahuvia, and Richard Bagozzi, "Brand Love," *Journal of Marketing*, 76, (March 2012), 1–16.

5 Deep insight into how these processes (labeled "meaning transfer") work has been provided by anthropologist-marketer Grant McCracken, *Culture and Consumption*, Bloomington: Indiana University Press, 1988.

6 Amitava Chattopadhyay and Ayesha Kohli, "Wipro: Building a Global B2B Brand," INSEAD Case Study (#06/2009-5606), 2009.

7 Of note are David Aaker and Erich Joachimsthaler, "The Brand Relationship Spectrum—the Key to the Brand Architecture Challenge," *California Management Review*, Fall 2000, and David Aaker, "Should You Take Your Brand to Where the Action Is?," *Harvard Business Review*, October–November 1997, pp. 135–143.

8 Rajeev Batra, V. Ramaswamy, J. B. Steenkamp, D. Alden, and S. Ramachander, "Effects of Brand Local/Non-local Origin on Consumer Attitudes in Developing Countries," *Journal of Consumer Psychology*, vol. 9, no. 2, April 2000, pp. 83–95, and Jan-Benedict Steenkamp, Rajeev Batra, and Dana Alden, "How Perceived Brand Globalness Creates Brand Value," *Journal of International Business Studies*, vol. 34, 2003, pp. 53–65.

9 David Aaker and Erich Joachimsthaler, "The Lure of Global Branding" *Harvard Business Review*, November–December, 1999.

10 Steenkamp, Batra, and Alden, "How Perceived Brand Globalness Creates Brand Value."

Chapter 8

1 Amitava Chattopadhyay, Eunju Park, and Joseph Lajos, "LG Electronics Inc: Making Waves in the North American Market for Washing Machines," INSEAD Case Study (#12/2009-5463), 2010.

2 Aysegul Ozsomer and Sevilay Sezen, "A Turkish Soap Company in Eastern Europe: Evyap," Koç University Case Study, January 1, 2011.

3 See David A. Aaker, *Silos,* Cambridge, MA: Harvard Business Press, 2010, for a discussion of how TMNCs manage brands across markets.

4 Amitava Chattopadhyay's personal conversations with Eunju Park, general manager of the Digital Appliance Marketing Strategy Group, LG Electronics.

5 Ibid.

6 Amitava Chattopadhyay, Eunju Park, and Joseph Lajos, "LG Electronics Inc.: Breaking the Ice in the North American Market for Refrigerators," INSEAD Case Study (#11/2007-5488), 2007.

7 Nandini Sen Gupta, "Asian Execs Are in Great Demand," *Times of India*, June 27, 2011, accessed September 1, 2011, http://articles .timesofindia.indiatimes.com/2011-06-27/india-business/29708721 _1_asians-harish-manwani-companies.

8 Chaitanya Kalbag, Suman Layak, and Anusha Subramanian, "Interview with Harish Manwani, Chairman HUL," *Business Today*, May 24, 2011, accessed September 1, 2011, http://businesstoday.intoday .in/story/interview-with-harish-manwani-chairman-hul/1/15763.html.

9 Jasjit Singh, "GE Healthcare(A): Innovating for Emerging Markets," INSEAD Case Study (#311-048-1), 2011.

10 Jessie Paul, *No Money Marketing*, New Delhi: Tata McGraw-Hill, 2010.

Chapter 9

1 Amitava Chattopadhyay, Eunju Park, and Joseph Lajos, "LG Electronics Inc: Making Waves in the North American Market for Washing Machines," INSEAD Case Study (#11/2007-5463), 2010.

2 Amitava Chattopadhyay and Ulrike Lege, "Tata Tea Limited: How to Go Global?," *International Journal of Marketing Education*, vol. 1, no. 1, 2005, pp. 93–112.

3 Amitava Chattopadhyay, Betania Tanure, and Nina Paavola, "Natura: Expanding Beyond Latin America," INSEAD Case Study (#09/2011-5365), 2006.

4 Chattopadhyay, Park, and Lajos, "LG Electronics Inc: Making Waves in the North American Market for Washing Machines."

5 Kunur Patel, "Once-Nameless HTC Tops U.S. Smartphone Market," November 28, 2011, accessed November 29, 2011, http://adage.com/article/special-report-americas-hottest-brands/america-s-hottest-brands-htc/231204/?utm_source=digital_email&utm_medium=newsletter&utm_campaign=adage; 2011 Ranking of the Top 100 Brands, accessed November 29, 2011, http://www.interbrand.com/en/best-global-brands/best-global-brands-2008/best-global-brands-2011.aspx.

6 Amitava Chattopadhyay, Eunju Park, and Nina Paavola, "LG in India: Reinventing the Brand," INSEAD Case Study (#10/2008-5558), 2008.

7 Jeffrey R. Immelt, Vijay Govindrajan, and Chris Trimble, "How GE Is Disrupting Itself," *Harvard Business Review*, October 2009, pp. 3–11.

8 Rajeev Batra, Aaron Ahuvia, and Richard Bagozzi, "Brand Love," *Journal of Marketing*, 76, (March 2012), 1–16.

9 Jasjit Singh, "GE Healthcare (A): Innovating for Emerging Markets," INSEAD Case Study (#09/2011-5776), 2011, and Jasjit Singh, "GE Healthcare (B): A CSR Dilemma," INSEAD Case Study (#03/2011-5776), 2011.

10 Singh, "GE Healthcare (A)."

11 Michael Kan, "China Overtakes U.S. in Smartphone Shipments," IDG News, November 24, 2011, accessed November 24, 2011, http://www.pcworld.com/article/244812/china_overtakes_us_in_smartphone_shipments_says_research_firm.html.

12 Philip Kotler, Liam Fahey, and Somkid Jatusripitak, *The New Competition*, Englewood Cliffs, NJ: Prentice-Hall, 1985, p. 4. Also see Johny Johansson and Ikujiro Nonaka, *Relentless: The Japanese Way of Marketing*, New York: HarperBusiness, 1996.

13 See, for instance, Peter W. J. Verlegh and Jan-Benedict E. M. Steen-kamp, "A Review and Metaanalysis of Country-of-Origin Research," *Journal of Economic Psychology*, vol. 20, 1999, pp. 521–546, and Zeynep Gurhan-Canli and Durairaj Maheswaran, "Determinants of Country-of-Origin Evaluations," *Journal of Consumer Research*, vol. 27, 2000, pp. 96–108.

14 For an introduction to this branding practice, see, for instance, Rajeev Batra, "Note on Nation Branding," GlobalLens Case Note 1-428-772, William Davidson Institute, 2009.

15 John Bussey, "U.S. Firms, China Are Locked in Major War over Technology," *Wall Street Journal*, February 2, 2011, p. B1.

16 Rishikesha T. Krishna, *From Jugaad to Systematic Innovation: The Challenge for India*, Bangalore: Utprereka Foundation, 2010.

17 See Krishna, *From Jugaad to Systematic Innovation*, as well as Adam Segal, *Advantage: How American Innovation Can Overcome the Asian Challenge*, New York: Norton, 2011.

18 Kotler, Fahey, and Jatusripitak, *The New Competition*, Chapter 2.

19 Barry Jaruzelski and Kevin Dehoff, "The Global Innovation 1000: How the Top Innovators Keep Winning," *Strategy + Business*, vol. 61, Winter 2010.

20 The examples that follow are taken from Kotler, Fahey, and Jatusripitak, *The New Competition*, Chapters 3–7.

Company Descriptions

1 *Asia Pacific Breweries Annual Report 2011*, accessed on September 4, 2011, http://www.apb.com.sg/annual-report.html.

2 *Chigo Group Annual Report 2010*, accessed on January 15, 2012, http://pg.jrj.com.cn/acc/HK_DISC/stock_time/2011/04/20/001192493-0.PDF.

3 "About Dabur: Dabur at-a-Glance," accessed September 4, 2011, http://www.dabur.com/About percent20Dabur-Dabur percent20At-a-Glance; operating revenue data pulled from the Orbis database on January 15, 2012.

4 Esteban R. Brenes, Amitava Chattopadhyay, and Daniel Montoya C., "Grupo Britt N.V.," INCAE Business School and INSEAD Case Study (# 30616), Alajuela: Costa Rica, 2011.

5 "Haier," *Wikipedia*, accessed January 15, 2012, http://en.wikipedia.org/wiki/Haier.

6 Operating revenue data pulled from the Orbis database on January 15, 2012.

7 Yahoo! Finance: Infosys Limited, accessed September 5, 2011, http://finance.yahoo.com/q?s=infy&ql=1.

8 "Lenovo," *Wikipedia*, accessed September 6, 2011, http://en.wikipedia.org/wiki/Lenovo.

9 "LG Electronics," *Wikipedia*, accessed August 15, 2011, http://en.wikipedia.org/wiki/LG_Electronics.

10 "M&M Named Lead Bidder for SsangYong," *Economic Times*, August 13, 2010, accessed September 6, 2011, http://articles.economictimes.indiatimes.com/2010-08-13/news/27588978_1_m-m-access-bolero-ssangyong.

11 "Marico," *Wikipedia*, accessed September 5, 2011, http://en.wikipedia.org/wiki/Marico.

12 Annual sales pulled from "Ruban D'Honneur Recipient, European Business Awards 2011," Case Study on Mavi, http://www.businessawardseurope.com/download/EBA_case_study_Mavi_final.pdf.

13 *Midea: To Shareholders*, accessed on September 6, 2011, http://global.midea.com.cn/midea/about/midea100424up.pdf.

14 Amitava Chattopadhyay and Esteban Brenes, "Pollo Campero," INCAE Business School and INSEAD Case Study, Alajuela: Costa Rica, 2011.

15 *Ranbaxy Annual Report 2010*, accessed September 6, 2011, http://www.ranbaxy.com/investorinformation/annual_pr2010.aspx.

16 Operating revenue information available at *Savola Group 2010 Annual Report*, accessed January 15, 2012, http://www.savola.com/savolae/pdf/Savola_Annual_Report_2010_E.pdf.

17 "Tata Motors," *Wikipedia*, accessed September 7, 2011, http://en.wikipedia.org/wiki/Tata_motors; "Arçelik A.S.," http://www.arcelikas.com/Pages.aspx?pageId=72; "Temsa: Focused on the Future," http://www.temsaglobal.com.tr/tr/ekler/faaliyet-raporu-2010.pdf.

Index

About the Authors

Rajeev Batra is the S.S. Kresge Professor of Marketing at the Ross School of Business, University of Michigan. He has published more than 50 articles in the areas of global branding, brand building and brand management, and advertising in journals such as the *Journal of Consumer Research, Journal of Marketing, Journal of Marketing Research, International Journal of Research in Marketing,* and others. Several of these articles have won awards for their extensive and long-term impact. He also has had research, consulting, or teaching relationships with companies such as Black & Decker, Citibank, General Electric, the Interpublic Group, Johnson & Johnson, Siemens Medical Systems, and Wipro. He holds a PhD from Stanford University and a PGDM (MBA) from the Indian Institute of Management, Ahmedabad. He resides with his family in Ann Arbor.

Amitava Chattopadhyay is the L'Oréal Chaired Professor of Marketing-Innovation and Creativity at INSEAD. He is an expert on branding and innovation, and has published extensively in journals such as the *Journal of Marketing, Journal of Marketing Research, Journal of Consumer Research,* and *Marketing Science.* For his research, he has received several awards, including the Robert Ferber Award. He is a Fellow of the Institute on Asian Consumer Insight. Amitava is an associate editor for the *Journal of Consumer Psychology* and an area editor for the *International*

Journal of Research in Marketing. He serves as a member of the board of the Association for Consumer Research.

Amitava consults for and has conducted customized workshops on branding and innovation for companies such as Bayer Healthcare, Citibank, Diageo, Fresenius Medical Care, HSBC, Hyundai Motor Company, LG Electronics, Pernod Ricard, Tata Sons, and Young & Rubicam. He also serves on the advisory boards of several organizations. Amitava holds a PhD from the University of Florida, a PGDM from the Indian Institute of Management, Ahmedabad, and a BSc (Honors) from Jadavpur University, India. He lives with his family in Singapore.

~

Aysegul Ozsomer is an associate professor of Marketing at Koç University, Istanbul, Turkey. Her more than 20 years of experience in research, consulting, and teaching in the United States and Turkey focuses on global marketing, global brand management, and market orientation. She is the author and coauthor of many marketing and branding-related articles that have appeared in publications such as the *Journal of Marketing, International Journal of Research in Marketing,* and *Journal of International Marketing.* Her papers received several awards, the latest of which is the American Marketing Association Gerald E. Hills Best Paper Award in 2011. Aysegul holds a PhD in marketing from Michigan State University and an MBA and BA from Bogazici University, Istanbul, Turkey. She lives with her family in Istanbul, from which many successful global brands are emerging and disrupting world markets.

~

For more information, visit www.emncstrategies.com.